Sarah Laverick is a marine biologist and writer. She has visited Antarctica five times as scientist and Deputy Voyage Leader on board the RSV *Aurora Australis* and RV *Tangaroa*, and worked at the Australian Antarctic Division for over a decade. *Through Ice and Fire* is her first book.

THROUGH
ICE & FIRE

THE ADVENTURES, SCIENCE AND PEOPLE
BEHIND AUSTRALIA'S FAMOUS ICEBREAKER
AURORA AUSTRALIS

SARAH
LAVERICK

MACMILLAN
Pan Macmillan Australia

First published 2019 in Macmillan by Pan Macmillan Australia Pty Ltd
1 Market Street, Sydney, New South Wales, Australia, 2000

A catalogue record for this
book is available from the
National Library of Australia

Typeset in 11/15 pt Sabon by Midland Typesetters, Australia
Printed by McPherson's Printing Group

The author and the publisher have made every effort to contact copyright holders
for material used in this book. Any person or organisation that may have been
overlooked should contact the publisher.

Aboriginal and Torres Strait Islander people should be aware that this book
may contain images or names of people now deceased.

For all those touched by the *Aurora Australis*:
your stories are hers – as hers are yours.

For four generations of Lavericks who've also loved this ship.

And most of all, for the *Aurora Australis*:
a true Antarctic heroine.

CONTENTS

Limited General Arrangement Plan of the *Aurora Australis*

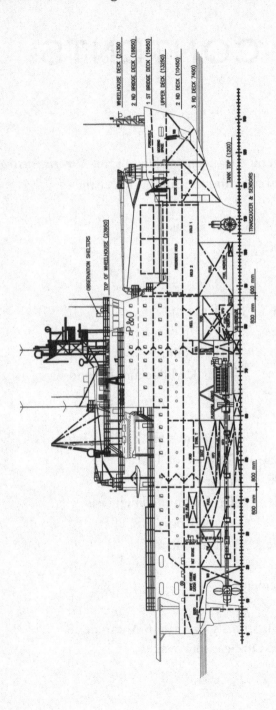

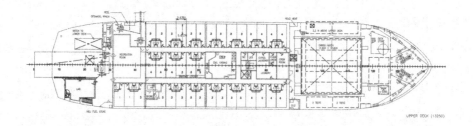

UPPER DECK (13250)

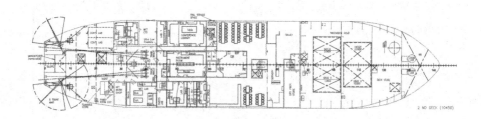

2 ND DECK (10450)

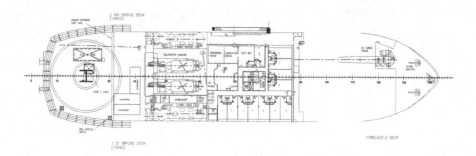

Courtesy of P&O Maritime Services, taken from full General Arrangement plan.

Antarctica and the Southern Ocean

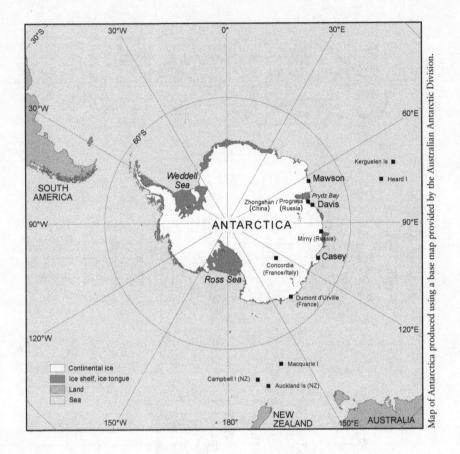

Map of Antarctica produced using a base map provided by the Australian Antarctic Division.

GLOSSARY

aft	At, in, or toward the stern.
athwartships	At right angles to the ship's keel.
Beaufort wind scale	The Beaufort wind scale relates wind speed to observed conditions at sea.
beset, besetment	(Of a ship) Trapped in ice.
bow	The front or forward part or end of a ship, boat, etc.
brash	Brash ice is an accumulation of floating ice made up of fragments not more than two metres across. It is the wreckage of other forms of ice. Brash is common between colliding floes or in regions where pressure ridges have collapsed.
cod-end	The closed end of a trawl net, where the fish are trapped.
complement	The full number of officers, crew and passengers on board a ship.
davit	A projecting piece of wood or iron (frequently one of a pair) on the side or stern of a vessel, fitted with a tackle, etc., for raising, lowering, or suspending a small boat, anchor, or other weight.
diesos	Expedition diesel mechanics, often in charge of station refuelling procedures.
draught	The depth of water a vessel needs to float it.
frazil	Fine spicules or plates of ice, suspended in water. Frazil ice formation represents the first stage of sea ice growth, and gives the water an oily appearance. In the open ocean the crystals may form, or be stirred to a depth of several metres by wave-induced turbulence.
gangway	A platform and ladder or stairway slung over the side of a ship.
grease ice	A later stage of freezing than frazil ice, when the crystals have coagulated to form a soupy layer on the surface. Grease ice reflects little light, giving the sea a matt appearance. Grease ice behaves in a viscous fluid-like manner, and does not form distinct ice floes.

haul-out	Behaviour associated with pinnipeds (seals) temporarily leaving the water. Hauling-out typically occurs between periods of foraging activity.
hove-to	(Also 'heaving-to'). When the ship slows right down in very rough conditions, maintaining just enough speed to keep a comfortable heading (generally into, or near-into, the wind and swell).
ice blink	A reflection of light off sea ice that is just beyond viewing range.
Inmarsat C	Communication via satellite, often used for emergencies at sea.
keel	In traditional wooden ship construction, the keel is simply the long, central wooden beam of a ship from which the rest of the ship is built, by adding ribs, etc. But for modern (steel) ship construction the 'keel' is simply the first module of the hull, and the ship develops from this single module.
launching ways	The sloping structures (ways) down which a ship slides at launch.
lead	An open channel through a field of ice.
mess	A place where service personnel, etc., eat together.
nilas ice	A thin elastic crust of ice, easily bending on waves and swell and under pressure, thrusting in a pattern of interlocking 'fingers' (finger rafting). Has a matt surface and is up to ten centimetres in thickness. May be subdivided into dark nilas (< five centimetres thick) and light nilas (> five centimetres thick).
Niskin bottle	A plastic cylinder with stoppers at each end, used to take water samples at a desired depth without the danger of mixing with water from other depths.
polynya	An area of open water surrounded by sea ice, as can occur in pack ice; of ecological significance when it recurs at the same time and place each year.
port, portside	The left-hand side of a ship or aircraft facing forward (opposed to *starboard*); larboard.
sastruga	A ridge, as in snow or sand, fashioned by the wind into a wave formation. Plural sastrugi.
starboard	The side of a ship to the right of a person looking toward the bow (opposed to *larboard* or *port*).
steerage	The practice or action of applying steering force to a vessel, either by helm or by tugboat.
stern	The hinder part of a ship or boat (often opposed to *stem*).
tween deck	The 'tweens' is the cargo hold accessed forward of the galley.
ways	See 'launching ways'. Alternatively: forward momentum of a ship through water.
weigh	To raise or lift (now chiefly in the phrase **weigh anchor**).

ABBREVIATIONS AND ACRONYMS

AA2	Workboat of the *Aurora Australis*
AAD	Australian Antarctic Division
AAE	Australasian Antarctic Expedition
ACC	Antarctic Circumpolar Current
AFMA	Australian Fisheries Management Authority
AIRBOX	Atmospheric Integrated Research facility for Boundaries and Oxidative Experiments
AMISOR	Amery Ice Shelf Ocean Research project
AMSA	Australian Maritime Safety Authority
ANARE	Australian National Antarctic Research Expeditions
APIS	Antarctic Pack Ice Seals program
ARM	Atmospheric Radiation Measurement mobile facility
ASETT	(Department of) Arts, Science, the Environment, Tourism and Territories
BANZARE	British, Australian, New Zealand Antarctic Research Expeditions
BIOMASS	Biological Investigations of Marine Antarctic Systems and Stocks
CAML	Census of Antarctic Marine Life
CCAMLR	Commission for the Conservation of Antarctic Marine Living Resources
CEAMARC	Collaborative East Antarctic Marine Census
CHINARE	Chinese National Antarctic Research Expedition
CPR	Continuous Plankton Recorder
CRC	Cooperative Research Centre
CSIRO	Commonwealth Scientific and Industrial Research Organisation
CTD unit	An instrument that measures Conductivity (a proxy for salinity, or saltiness), Temperature and Depth in the water column

DVL	Deputy Voyage Leader
FRC	Fast Rescue Craft
FTO	Field Training Officer
GA drawings	General Arrangement drawings
IASOS	Institute of Antarctic and Southern Ocean Studies (now IMAS – Institute of Marine and Antarctic Studies) at the University of Tasmania
IPY	International Polar Year 2007
IR	Integrated Rating; deck crew
JARE	Japanese Antarctic Research Expedition
JMSDF	Japanese Maritime Self-Defense Force
K-Axis	Kerguelen Axis, from the South Pole up the middle of the Indian Ocean
LARC	Lighter, Amphibious, Resupply, Cargo vehicle
MIDOC	Midwater Open and Closing net system
MIPEP	Macquarie Island Pest Eradication Project
MV	Merchant Vessel
RMT	Rectangular Midwater Trawl net
RSV	Research and Supply Vessel
RV	Research Vessel
SIPEX	Sea Ice Physics and Ecosystem eXperiment
SO–CPR	Southern Ocean Continuous Plankton Recorder
VL	Voyage Leader
WOCE	World Ocean Circulation Experiment, conducted from 1990 to 1997 (oceanographic sections WOCE-SR3 and WOCE-P11 ran between Tasmania and Antarctica). WOCE was followed by the CLIVAR (Climate and Ocean: Variability, Predictability and Change) project, and the SR3 and P11 sections also subsequently took this name. Confusingly, one of the *Aurora*'s early voyages in 1991/92 was named WOCE.

AUTHOR'S NOTE

The sources used in this book are wide and varied: much comes from interviews, but a great deal also comes from documents such as Voyage Leader reports, Captain's reports, the AAD's media archives, news reports, photographs, personal letters, Transport Bureau reports, scientific papers and audio files. To avoid interrupting the narrative with frequent citations, I have simply listed the sources for each chapter in a separate section at the end of the book. Documents in all cases have been faithfully reproduced, although typographical errors which do not admit interpretation have been corrected, and, where extra clarification was required, square brackets employed to aid comprehension. Occasionally names have been changed to protect people's privacy as requested. Any errors the book contains are my own.

Through Ice and Fire moves through the *Aurora*'s life more or less chronologically, but it is structured around the dramatic voyages in her history, condensing three decades of life into a handful of chapters. This book is written as a narrative, giving the *Aurora*'s story a personal perspective while being as historically and technically accurate as possible. As a result, I may have focused on particular voyages and/or individuals: in doing so,

I do not intend to downplay or trivialise the role or experiences of others. It is a touching truth that there are as many stories about the *Aurora Australis* as there were builders, crew and expeditioners; but sadly I cannot cover them all. While I have tried to encapsulate as much as of the *Aurora*'s life as I can, I have not described every voyage, every event or every finding over her thirty years – sparing you, dear reader, an element of monotony.

It is also important to note that many of the dramatic events described herein were the exception rather than the rule: much of the *Aurora*'s life has been an exercise in quiet, routine accomplishment, albeit set against some of the world's most breathtaking scenery.

PREFACE

The last time I ever sailed on the *Aurora Australis* was on Voyage 1 in 2017, a resupply voyage for Davis station – one of Australia's three permanent research stations in Antarctica. Being a marine biologist more used to the *Aurora*'s oceanic pursuits, it was the first time I had witnessed the exquisite logistical dance of an 'over ice' resupply. The first time I stepped off the *Aurora Australis* and planted my boots on the solid sea ice beside her, I looked up in awe at the radiant hull looming above me. I knew that construction of her replacement had recently commenced, and a lump grew in my throat as I thought about how this great ship had been my home and my workplace for months on end, how she had given me some of my greatest adventures and how she'd changed my life forever. The majestic orange icebreaker rested quietly beside me in the ice and (with approval and encouragement from the captain, Rob) I took off my glove and reached out to touch her bow in gratitude, on behalf of the thousands of people who I knew felt exactly the same.

She was warm.

The heat radiating from the tanks within her hull made the steel icebreaker feel alive beneath my palm. And as images of the *Aurora*'s life flashed through my mind, I realised that in a way, she was. Throughout her entire life, the *Aurora Australis* had thrived using the brains of her bridge and the beating heart of her engines, but it was the *Aurora*'s crew and expeditioners that were her lifeblood.

In the wild and desolate expanses of Antarctica there is a constant threat of danger – and a terrifyingly fine line between life and death. The legendary tales of tragedy and triumph experienced by heroic era explorers such as Shackleton, Mawson and Scott continue to inspire humankind to this day, and their faithful ships, the *Endurance*, *Aurora* and *Terra Nova* are vivid characters in their fateful voyages of discovery.

The RSV *Aurora Australis* has likewise secured her place in Antarctic history. Constructed at Carrington Slipways in Newcastle, New South Wales, and run by P&O Polar in Hobart, the *Aurora Australis* is Australia's first – and only – home-built and home-crewed icebreaker.

By the time she is due to be replaced in 2020, the *Aurora* will have operated in the unforgiving Antarctic wilderness for thirty years. And as that date approaches, it is time to take stock of her life and remarkable achievements.

The *Aurora Australis* is not just an icebreaker: to the thousands of expeditioners and crew that sailed on her she is a home, refuge, rescuer, messenger, lifeline, packhorse, laboratory, ferry and, overwhelmingly, an adventure. To those left at home she is a guardian to loved ones; shielding family and friends from the throes of the tempestuous Southern Ocean and the clutches of the unforgiving Antarctic sea ice. Over her years of Antarctic service, her expeditioners, her crew and the wider community have come to view the *Aurora* with true affection, even love.

Like any intrepid explorer, the *Aurora Australis* overcame considerable ordeals during her Antarctic exploits. She endured a problem-plagued construction, as well as repeated disasters including two devastating fires, a crippling besetment in ice and a blizzard-induced grounding in Antarctica. She bravely rescued stricken ships and souls from icy imprisonments, and heroically provided emergency care to those in need. In the face of howling blizzards and raging seas, the *Aurora* always triumphed over adversity; even when the odds seemed insurmountably stacked against her.

This resilience and tenacity, this ability to overcome hardship and go on to perform great deeds and unveil stunning scientific discoveries, make the *Aurora Australis* a compelling character in Australia's Antarctic story.

I was one of the lucky thousands who caught their first glimpse of Antarctica from the decks of the *Aurora Australis*, as a young marine biologist in 2003. Like every expeditioner who came before me I was instantly in wonder of the exquisite polar landscape she revealed. Every hulking iceberg, every ice-framed sunset, every awkward penguin was mercilessly stalked and photographed. I was hooked. But as much as I was enthusiastic about my spectacular surroundings, I found myself uncertain in my new social environment; the *Aurora*'s complement was an eclectic mix of scientists, tradies, deck crew, officers, engineers, chefs and, at times, the odd celebrity. But I quickly learned that each voyage formed its own close-knit 'family', a family born out of shared experience and total isolation. The bonds forged on board are strong, and can last a lifetime.

I admit I am no exception; I met my husband during my second voyage on board the *Aurora Australis*. While slightly embarrassing and completely cliché, this fact had wider ramifications in my own life than I knew at the time. Many months later I found out that my husband-to-be's grandfather, father and uncle built the *Aurora Australis*; they owned the shipyard where the *Aurora* was built and each of them personally had a hand in her construction. When Andrew and I eventually moved to the Hunter Valley in 2014, his family – knowing that I had sailed on the *Aurora* – regaled me with astounding stories of the problems they faced during the great ship's construction. This inspirational seed eventually grew into the overwhelming urge to tell the *Aurora*'s story.

By this time Andrew and I had our own children, and I realised our family was uniquely and inextricably linked to the iconic ship: the Lavericks had given life to the *Aurora*, and the *Aurora* had given life right back to the Lavericks.

As the outsider, I owed her, and I owed her big time. *Through Ice and Fire* is my attempt to repay some part of that massive debt, by bringing the *Aurora Australis*'s story out into the open and acknowledging her monumental role in the success of modern Australian Antarctic exploration.

I embarked on this journey in January 2015, when my children were three and one. I began simply, focusing on what had sparked this idea, by interviewing Andrew's family about the *Aurora*'s construction. Don and Maureen Laverick still had their shipyard workbook, dozens of scrapbooks containing hundreds of newspaper articles as well as video footage from their Carrington Slipways days; and they generously lent these to me. I carefully turned each yellowed page, rapt, and watched each piece of footage with relish, awed by seeing the ship that I'd come to know so well materialise in front of my eyes.

During my own voyages on the *Aurora* I'd heard countless yarns about the ship's many adventures and discoveries. Spurred on by these memories, I began stalking the Australian Antarctic Division (AAD)'s website, searching the historic shipping schedules and the AAD's systems for available records from the *Aurora*'s many voyages. Voyage Leader, or VL, reports, an invaluable source of information and opinion, rapidly began to pile up on my desk. I requested access to 'closed' design and tender files held by the National Archives of Australia (NAA), after which one incredibly helpful staff member even managed to locate more files that were not listed on their online system (having been moved up from Hobart and archived en masse). I travelled to Hobart several times on various reconnaissance trips, sleuthing through microfilms in the State Library of Tasmania's reading room, poring over thousands of images in the AAD's image library and meeting with persons of interest. Tess, the AAD librarian, sent me articles and files from the AAD library and archives, and crew members I met along the way sent me articles they'd collected over the years.

My desk became strewn with files and folders filled with evidence documenting the *Aurora*'s various adventures. The hardest part, I realised with some sadness as the files continued to mount, would be deciding what NOT to include in a single readable book about the great ship.

Over this period of about three and a half years I interviewed dozens of the *Aurora*'s voyage leaders, scientists, captains, crew, engineers and many others involved in various facets of the ship's history. One interview would often lead me to others that I had not yet considered; as a solo researcher I struggled under the weight of this mixed blessing. I spent countless nights painstakingly transcribing each account while my children slept soundly (for the most part) in their beds.

As I slowly committed the words of these now familiar voices to paper, I was constantly struck by the eagerness and pride with which every person spoke about the *Aurora Australis*. Their enthusiasm for this project and their willingness to share their memories of their experiences on board, even occasionally of traumatic events, was truly humbling.

I may have happened to write her story, but I can never claim the *Aurora Australis* as 'mine' above anyone else. The *Aurora Australis* really is beloved by thousands of people in Australia as well as around the world; and every one of them – myself included – has a unique bond with the iconic icebreaker.

This story belongs to all of us.

antarctic factor *Aust. and* NZ. *Also* **A *factor***

A (usu. humorous) term for the unpredictability of life in Antarctica, usually perceived to be greater than elsewhere and often attributed to the severe weather or extreme isolation.

The Antarctic Dictionary: A complete guide to Antarctic English, Bernadette Hince (CSIRO, 2000)

Introduction

A NEW ERA

The *Aurora Australis* and her crew had just begun a busy day delivering cargo at Mawson station. The bright orange ship nestled comfortably within the arms of Horseshoe Harbour, and the inhabitants of the colourful buildings dotting the rocky Antarctic hillside supervised the resupply operations with interest. The *Aurora*'s cranes danced over the ship, brightly punctuating the overcast sky as they feverishly lifted heavy pallets onto barges waiting patiently beside the icebreaker. The squat craft motored back and forth across the steel water to the snow-speckled granite shores of the station, where a shore crane eagerly took possession of the valuable bounty.

But a slight breeze that had begun to ripple the water at lunchtime soon intensified to a gale that sent wavelets and spray whipping across the harbour, bringing the hectic operations to a halt late in the afternoon. A blizzard was coming: the crew and expeditioners packed up their equipment and the cranes and barges were stowed for the day. Their efforts had already paid off: the ship and shore teams had managed to unload a large portion of the precious stores that would see Mawson station through the harsh, dark months of the approaching Antarctic winter of 2016. It had been a good day.

That evening, the *Aurora*'s complement lined up for their well-earned dinner in the ship's mess. The room slowly filled with buzzing chatter and the chink of cutlery on plates, and someone pointed out that snow was now swirling against the portholes. Unperturbed, the 68 people on board continued their evening's business; they'd already withstood a blizzard two days earlier and they all knew it was just a matter of time until it would ease off. They would simply get comfortable and wait it out.

But this was no ordinary blizzard.

By the next morning, the *Aurora* was mercilessly buffeted by vicious winds and driving snow, and the screaming gales showed no sign of moderating. The ship's massive mooring lines strained against the load, then stretched taut as the winds gusted at over 176 kilometres an hour. Then, incapable of taking any more, the hefty ropes and cables snapped; the resounding cracks and booms of the parting lines stifled by the immense white noise of the blizzard. The blizzard, now unimpeded, ruthlessly drove the *Aurora* toward the shore. Minutes later, the icebreaker shrieked and juddered in protest as her sturdy metal hull ground roughly against the uneven, dark rock of West Arm.

On station, the Mawson search-and-rescue alarm wailed throughout the corridors. The station's expeditioners gathered in the mess, then squinted anxiously against the whiteout while they were briefed on the unfolding crisis. For a fleeting moment the blizzard eased, revealing Australia's Antarctic flagship lying helplessly on the rocks at West Arm. A hazy photograph of the forlorn, snow-crusted ship was hastily taken and emailed to headquarters in Hobart.

The image went global. As news of the *Aurora*'s grounding spread, the world's media and the international Antarctic community held their collective breath while the ferocious storm continued to lash at the stricken ship. Was history repeating itself? Had the

The image of the grounded *Aurora Australis* taken from Mawson station during a break in the blizzard.

Aurora, just like her predecessor the *Nella Dan* 29 years earlier, met an untimely end on a desolate rocky shore at the far reaches of the Southern Ocean?

All over the world, they waited.

The *Aurora Australis*'s story begins three decades before that storm. She is the only icebreaker that has ever been built in Australia. She is also the first Australian-owned and -crewed icebreaker in the Australian Antarctic Program, which is run by the Australian Antarctic Division (AAD) on behalf of the Australian government. Previously, Australian National Antarctic Research Expeditions (ANARE), as it was then known, had chartered a series of European ice-strengthened ships to support Australia's operations in Antarctica, providing cargo and personnel for resupply operations to Australia's Antarctic bases and conducting limited marine science operations in Australian Antarctic Territory waters. Several of these ships, affectionately known as the 'Dans', were provided by the Danish J. Lauritzen line. The various Dans – the *Kista Dan*, *Magga Dan*, *Thala Dan* and *Nella Dan* – serviced ANARE programs for 34 years, from 1953 to 1987.

By the early 1980s the last of the Dan ships – the *Nella Dan* – was in her twenties and was starting to show her age. Like many ageing ships, she was thought of with great affection but also at times with frustration at her various – and by that age inevitable – limitations. In her history serving ANARE in Antarctica the *Nella* had been beset (a euphemism for being stuck in the Antarctic pack ice) numerous times. These sticky incidents included, among others, an eight-day besetment on her maiden voyage for ANARE in 1962, a 26-day besetment in 1967, and, later, a seven-week besetment in 1985 – from which she was eventually rescued by the giant Japanese icebreaker the *Shirase*, after rescue attempts by the German-built ANARE ship the *Icebird* had resulted in the *Icebird*'s own alarming besetment in the unforgiving ice.

The *Nella* had severe limitations for the sort of work that was being asked of her. She was not an icebreaker as we know them now: she had limited icebreaking capability and was, in essence, a cargo vessel unable to conduct much in the way of scientific operations at sea. In 1980, following a government review that indicated the need for ANARE to develop capability to conduct research in the Southern Ocean, the *Nella* underwent significant improvements to allow her to perform deep sea trawling and scientific acoustics. These improvements allowed Australia to participate in the international Biological Investigations of Marine Antarctic Systems and Stocks (BIOMASS) program: the largest coordinated marine biological experiment ever conducted in the world, involving fifteen ships from eleven countries. These improvements gave Australia exciting capacity for Antarctic marine science, which had not been conducted at this scale since Mawson's British, Australian, New Zealand Antarctic Research Expeditions (BANZARE) days of 1929–31. However, while the *Nella* now had substantially increased capability, she was only able to trawl nets at a research scale, not at the commercial scale. As interest in the fisheries of the Southern Ocean began to expand in the 1980s it became apparent that the ability to trawl commercial-sized nets and gear would be vital to conduct robust stock assessments for commercial fisheries.

The limitations of the capabilities of the existing shipping arrangements were becoming apparent. But the Australian government discussed the construction of a new icebreaker numerous times over the years before any commitment was made (some reports have these discussions beginning as early as 1953). In any event, the decision to acquire a new vessel to replace the *Nella Dan* was made in the early- to mid-eighties. In 1986 a project group was formed to determine the specifications ANARE required of its new icebreaker.

REPLACING THE *NELLA DAN*

David Lyons, head of the Projects and Policy Branch at the AAD, oversaw the Replacement Vessel Project. David recalls:

> The concept of the ship, which was developed at the AAD Executive level (in particular involving the Director and Deputy Director), was that it would be primarily a research vessel with a limited capacity to carry out resupply work; i.e. able to carry sufficient fuel, dry cargo and passengers to resupply and change over one station as part of a voyage which would be principally marine science and marine resource assessment work ... At this time, it was always intended to continue to charter a dedicated cargo–passenger vessel like the *Icebird* to carry out the majority of the resupply and passenger tasks, and to provide backup in the event of besetments, breakdowns, etc.

Over the next six months the project group, managed by Ivan Bear, held numerous working meetings with stakeholders such as scientists, technical personnel and operations managers. As David Lyons remembers:

> There were various iterations of this process to strike the compromises in the science fit-out to meet as much of the scientists' wish lists as possible, and the policy priorities around such things as scientific and resource data to support our role at CCAMLR.

The Commission for the Conservation of Antarctic Marine Living Resources (CCAMLR) was the international body established in the early 1980s to manage the fisheries in the Southern Ocean. Australia had been a leading light in the negotiations that led to the establishment of CCAMLR and, as a consequence, the Secretariat was situated in Hobart, but Australia needed the capacity to conduct research to contribute to CCAMLR's important work.

Whatever the final configuration of the new ANARE ship might be, she clearly needed to be a jack-of-all-trades. She would need to be an icebreaker, a trawler, oceanographic and biological laboratory, passenger vessel, fuel tanker and cargo-carrier. This one vessel would need all the facilities required of each of these normally separate ship types. She would also need capacity for helicopter operations, with hangars and capability for two helicopters. The ship would be on the cutting edge, and would significantly raise the bar of Australian Antarctic science and operations.

By July 1986 a set of major characteristics or 'wish list' had been put together, to be used to generate a conceptual design of a new icebreaker. Over the next year the planning process for the new icebreaker moved at a relatively sedate pace.

However everything changed dramatically on 3 December 1987, when a subantarctic storm dashed the beloved *Nella Dan* against the rocks of Macquarie Island and simultaneously tore a hole in the logistics of Australian Antarctic operations.

Initial hopes were that the *Nella Dan* might be repaired and saved, but first a dive team dispatched from Australia needed to travel to Macquarie Island to fully assess the damage to the *Nella*'s hull. By the middle of December the *Nella* was still stranded on the rocks, and the expeditioners at Macquarie Island had managed to manually salvage more than five tonnes of science equipment and personal belongings from the ship.

The *Lady Lorraine*, an oil rig tug and supply vessel, arrived at Macquarie Island with the dive team on 13 December. As dawn broke the next day divers inspected the hull and found, encouragingly, that the visible damage was not as bad as expected. As a safety precaution, the oil on board the *Nella* was transferred into the *Lady Lorraine*'s tanks, before the crews began to seal up the *Nella*'s holed compartments as best they could, filling them with compressed air and pumping water out of flooded spaces.

On 21 December, during high tide, the *Nella Dan* was towed off the rocks. At last, divers were able to properly examine the entire hull – and immediately discovered the damage was far more extensive than they had initially believed. Just before Christmas, the unhappy order came from the Danish owners to scuttle the *Nella Dan*.

The team at Macquarie Island immediately prepared to salvage everything they could from the *Nella* (while much of the ANARE equipment and cargo had already been retrieved, some personal belongings of crew and memorabilia remained). But within hours of the order to scuttle her, she listed dangerously, leaning an alarming twelve degrees to her starboard side. The salvage master urgently ordered all personnel to abandon ship. It was far too dangerous to do anything but get the *Nella* out of Buckles Bay while they were still able. With the remaining memorabilia and personal valuables packed and ready for evacuation, but regretfully still on board, the *Nella Dan* was towed out to sea to be scuttled.

But the *Nella Dan* refused to submit. Expectations had been that she would sink quickly after being towed offshore of Macquarie Island, yet the 'Antarctic factor' (or A factor) delivered an uncharacteristically still night, after which the *Nella* stubbornly remained afloat. Captain Arne Sorensen later declared that 'she had a mind of her own,' and she certainly appeared to be acting of her own accord. Seeing as she was still afloat, the salvage team seized the opportunity to rescue the abandoned items on board. But just as the team were primed to attempt the recovery, the *Nella* defiantly burst into flames. It was Christmas Eve, 1987.

After a number of hours the fire burnt itself out. Remarkably, the *Nella* still endured – even a fire could not dispatch her. The smouldering pyre was finally laid to rest by the salvage team, who released the compressed air in her forward compartments. The *Nella*'s 'Viking funeral' signalled a sad end of an era for Australia's Antarctic program.

And the beginning of another.

There was no ship available within ANARE to take the *Nella*'s place. The Australian government scrambled and managed to secure access to the Canadian cargo ship, the *Lady Franklin*, but this was a short-term solution. During the next two years the AAD made use of the *Lady Franklin*, in addition to the cargo ship the *Icebird* and the small Norwegian vessel, the *Polar Queen*. Both the *Lady Franklin* and the *Polar Queen* were capable of cargo and personnel operations, but neither was equipped for marine science activities, though some limited science was conducted on board both.

After years of discussion and planning, in December 1987, as the *Nella* lay crippled on the rocks at Macquarie Island, the government moved with a sense of urgency. Senator Graham Richardson, Federal Minister for the Environment and the Arts, announced on 16 December that there would be a ten-season charter for a new vessel, which would be built for P&O Polar; a joint venture between P&O Australia Ltd and their recently acquired partner in the venture, Polar Schiffahrts-Consulting GmbH.* This ship would be an icebreaker with all the advanced capabilities that the design team had been working on over the years.

The very morning that the *Nella Dan* made her sad journey out to sea to be scuttled, P&O Australia announced that a Newcastle shipyard called Carrington Slipways would be building the new Australian icebreaker, which would be designed by the renowned shipbuilding company, Wärtsilä Marine. Brian Baillie, Managing Director of P&O Australia, noted poignantly:

> It is ironic that as we make this announcement we have also heard of the final demise of the *Nella Dan*, a ship which has served the Australian Antarctic effort for many years. Her departure brings to a close thirty years of cooperation between the owners, J. Lauritzen A/S of Denmark and the Antarctic Division. Our hope is that with our new vessel we shall be able to carry on the high tradition of service and performance they have established.

After the contract with P&O Polar was announced, the mood at Carrington Slipways was buoyant. Don Laverick, Managing Director of Carrington Slipways, had been convinced from the start that this project was a perfect fit for his shipyard. Like the AAD and P&O, Carrington had been preparing for this project for years. Determined to win the contract, Don had travelled to Copenhagen, Oslo, Helsinki, New York and London on fact-finding missions, visiting ship designers experienced in producing icebreakers and networking with potential tenderers for

---

* The tender process was publicly challenged by a number of the unsuccessful bidders, who complained in the press that the specifications of the tender had changed during the process without their knowledge. The Federal Police became involved but found no evidence of improper conduct (Bowden 1997). The tender process and chartering/contractual arrangement both came under scrutiny in reports by DASETT and the Auditor-General, neither of which found issue with the actions of those involved (Bowden 1997; Auditor-General, DASETT 1990).

the ship-to-be. Among his travels, Don visited the shipyard of famed Finnish shipbuilders, Wärtsilä Marine.

WÄRTSILÄ: FROM HUMBLE ORIGINS TO EUROPEAN JUGGERNAUT

Wärtsilä, established in 1834 in the small Finnish village of the same name, actually began its life as a sawmilling venture on the banks of the local rapids. Over the next century and a half, Wärtsilä endured financial strife and world wars then, thriving in postwar industrialisation, relocated to Helsinki and was for a time the biggest industrial company in Finland. By the 1980s Wärtsilä had built a formidable reputation as world leaders in the shipbuilding industry, particularly in the design and construction of vessels that operate in ice-covered waters. Wärtsilä had by then separated two of its major business units into Wärtsilä Marine (shipbuilding) and Wärtsilä Diesel (diesel engine building). At the time P&O Polar and the Australian government engaged Wärtsilä to design the new Australian Antarctic icebreaker, they reportedly had 33 new ships on their order books, had previously constructed fifty icebreakers and were considered experts at producing icebreaking ships.

Don was impressed with Wärtsilä's shipyard from the outset. His tour of the facilities had left him in no doubt of the high calibre of the company. They had all the Computer Aided Design (CAD) systems and technology one would expect from an established global shipyard. It was also unlike any shipyard he had ever visited: it was absolutely freezing.

Don shivered under his coat and pulled his collar up higher. He wished he'd thought to pack better shoes: these thin soles did nothing for the cold . . . or the ice, he noted, slipping unsteadily. The route across the frigid yard was a path cut through waist-deep snow. Don cautiously followed his guide, who turned, sensing his discomfort.

'It's a nice day today,' he smiled, making small talk.

Don was astonished. 'Mate, I can't feel my feet, my ears or my nose . . . and you say it's a nice day!'

'You should be here when it's minus thirty,' his new friend shrugged. 'That's cold. We let the welders go home when it gets down to minus twenty or so.'

'That's very generous of you.' Don's Australian sarcasm was apparently lost on his Finnish host.

'Yeah, you just can't get the steel hot enough to weld it below that.'

Don couldn't help but smile. They bred a tough crew up here.

Carrington Slipways were themselves an experienced Australian shipbuilding company. Don's father John 'Jack' Laverick had founded the company with his two sons in 1957, initially building timber cable-operated vehicular ferries at a rented shipyard in Carrington, Newcastle. The yard was less than ideal. It was cramped, with a homebuilt wharf made of second-hand timber and a hand-operated slipway. But in this small yard Carrington successfully produced more than sixty vessels and earned themselves a wide reputation as leading Australian shipbuilders. By the time Jack handed the company over to his two sons, Don and John, the business had outgrown the yard at Carrington and in 1972 they moved up the Hunter River to their sixteen-hectare purpose-built yard at Tomago. A few years after the move, Don's sons Bruce and Alan also joined the family business.

The ships produced at Tomago were numerous and diverse. In fifteen years during the mineral and oil boom of the 1970s and 1980s, Carrington built 55 tugs and 26 oil rig–supply ships. Carrington Slipways were now building huge steel ships such as the *HMAS Tobruk*, an amphibious navy vessel 127 metres long, eighteen metres wide and displacing some 5800 tonnes of water when afloat. They built nine of the iconic Sydney Harbour

(Left to right) Bruce, Don and Alan Laverick on holiday in the early 1960s.

catamaran-hulled ferries, as well as two large single-hulled Manly ferries – the famous *Narrabeen* and her sister ship the *Collaroy*. From their foundation to the time of constructing the *Aurora Australis* in 1988, Carrington Slipways had produced tugboats, fishing vessels, barges, dredges, bulk carriers, ferries, tourist vessels, cruise ships, Navy frigates and minehunters. The new icebreaker was to be the next feather in the cap; a 'status symbol and exciting challenge' for Carrington Slipways.

In actuality, it would test the shipyard to its limits.

Chapter One

THE BIRTH
OF A LEGEND

On 28 October 1988, a stately group of Navy officials, politicians, Hunter Valley businessmen and the extended family of Carrington Slipways gathered at the Tomago yard for the keel-laying ceremony of the new icebreaker. But among the pressed suits and crisp white uniforms of the distinguished guests, one person in particular held the spotlight. It was Brett Webb, a twelve-year-old boy from Jindabyne who had given the ship its name.

A national competition to name the icebreaker, open to young Australians from ten to seventeen years of age, had been launched in February 1988 by Prime Minister Bob Hawke. A flood of more than 2000 entries was received, 108 of which nominated the name *Aurora Australis*. Brett had been chosen as the winner due to the quality of his explanation for the name:

[The *Aurora Australis*] illuminates the sky, and hopefully the scientific knowledge gained from this ship will illuminate mankind's knowledge. The name will also remind us of an earlier *Aurora* sailed by Captain John King Davis, which played a vital role in Antarctic exploration.

Brett's prize was to be a trip to Antarctica aboard the new icebreaker with one of his parents, but sadly Brett never got to take the trip as he was reportedly asthmatic and unable to meet the medical criteria required for polar travel. However, on the day of the keel laying, Brett was undeniably the media darling. The *Newcastle Herald* chronicled the huge amount of attention the young man received, joking that Brett outshone all the official guests, with only the Federal Minister for the Environment, Senator Graham Richardson, managing to 'get into the act', posing for photographs with Brett. 'Boy who names ship steals politicians' thunder', the headline proudly boasted.

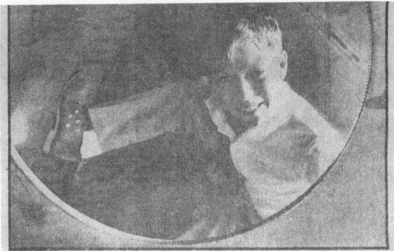

Brett Webb, of Jindabyne, who won a competition to name Australia's new research ship.

Boy who named ship steals politicians' thunder

Newcastle Herald, Saturday 29 October 1988.

A ship as novel and stupendous as the *Aurora Australis* understandably had an equally grand keel laying ceremony. This is an important event in the life of a ship: it marks the official beginning of construction, the first of four major parts of a ship's life – the others being launching, commissioning and decommissioning.

At the building berth, the *Aurora*'s huge rectangular keel was held aloft by two towering yellow gantry cranes, and adorned festively with bunting. The assembled crowd watched as Don and Senator Richardson performed the traditional coin ceremony to bless the ship and give it good fortune. Together they placed two newly minted fifty-cent coins on the timber footings directly underneath the suspended steel. They stepped back and Don nodded to his foreman. The keel was carefully lowered down to the footings before it eventually came to rest with a satisfying, muted clunk.

Don and Senator Richardson climbed the adjacent stairway and stood proudly atop the keel. The Senator gave a brief speech and unveiled a small plaque, thereby marking the official beginning of the *Aurora Australis*'s life. (Before the end of construction this plaque was installed for display on the bridge of the *Aurora*.) A staccato of photographic shutters filled the air as the ship was dedicated to the youth of Australia 'for whom this new ship will be a lasting symbol of national pride and achievement', and to the memory of those who sailed on the first *Aurora*: 'It carries with it a nation's pride in itself – in its past and its future'. It had been quite the journey to get to this point.

A year prior, Carrington Slipways had been poised for the announcement they had worked years toward achieving. When the announcement of the contract with P&O came on 23 December 1987, the starting gates soon opened. The yard was readied. The workforce swelled to over three hundred.

Building an icebreaker required materials not used before in Australia. Specialised high-tensile steel for the icebreaking hull was ordered from Finland. The steel was 25 millimetres thick and made to withstand Antarctic conditions. The remainder of the steel for the framework and superstructure was ordered from BHP in Australia, under a special 'rolling' for the shipyard.

This ship would be constructed like Carrington's other builds: with the hull upside down, in a method considered novel at that time. Building hulls upside down allowed the welders to work downhand instead of overhead, so stronger welds could be produced in less time, as welders had access to properly fill the angled joins between hull plates. This method also meant that less power was required during the welding process, which reduced the tendency for the steel plates to buckle from the heat.

By now the General Arrangement (GA) plans and specifications of the ship had been completed by Wärtsilä (these GA plans are akin to the basic design floorplans and elevations of a house design). The Aurora was to have a length overall of 94.8 metres and a breadth of just over twenty metres. Double-skin construction would protect her internally-housed fuel tanks from any hull ruptures, and her heavily reinforced hull had ribs closely framed to give her extra strength against the Antarctic sea ice. Being an icebreaker, she would not have the stabilising bulb that protrudes forward of the bow on most large seagoing ships; instead, her bow-rake angle would be approximately eighteen degrees, allowing her to ride up onto the ice and break it using her own weight. An ice knife would be fitted on her heavily reinforced stern to protect her rudder when manoeuvring astern.

She would have accommodation for up to 133 persons including crew, and the comfort of the accommodation would far surpass anything ANARE had seen to date. She would have a dedicated surgery, conference room, photographic darkroom, sauna, gym and bar. She would have numerous laboratories, including chemical, oceanographic and meteorological laboratories in addition to five multipurpose laboratories. She would have oceanographic sensors mounted in her hull and a central data logging system. And she would be able to trawl commercial-sized nets, conduct finer net sampling, and deploy scientific instrumentation to great depth. In short, she would revolutionise Australian Antarctic shipping.

A MIGHTY ICEBREAKER

The *Aurora* would be one of the most powerful ships ANARE had ever used, as well as being one of only a small handful of multi-functional icebreakers in the world. She would have two medium-speed diesel engines driving one controllable-pitch propeller. Maximum combined power in free-running conditions would be 7900 kW and in icebreaking conditions 10,000 kW. The ship would be capable of breaking 1.2 metres of first-year ice at a speed of 2 knots. She would have one bow thruster and two stern thrusters, enabling operations at 0 to 5 knots in up to Beaufort 6 conditions (described as having a 'strong breeze' with 22–27 knot winds and 3–4 metre waves). Cruising speed would be 13.0 knots, with a distance range of at least 24,000 nautical miles at cruising speed.

Despite the designs being drawn in Finland, around twenty draftsmen, engineers and designers were also working on the icebreaker in the drawing office located at the Tomago shipyard. The team were champing at the bit. Construction could not start until the detailed design drawings arrived from Finland (while the GA drawings are like floorplans and elevations of a house, the detailed design drawings are like an engineer's structural plans, of footings and walls and functional plans of drainage and plumbing, etc.). But these drawings would not arrive completed en masse from Wärtsilä. They were scheduled to arrive at various periods throughout the build; sent to Australia progressively as they were being produced by the office in Finland. The construction process was going to be very hand to mouth.

Carrington were going to use an 'Integrated Modular Technique' to build the icebreaker. This entailed building smaller prefabricated modules, completed independently and assembled together to form the ship. These modules – usually comprising about one thousand cubic metres or one hundred tonnes – were budgeted pieces of work that could be tasked to a crew or team in the shipyard to construct. The drawing office would issue work instructions and a work list (including materials) to the foreman, who would arrange for the appropriate crew to work on that module in the yard. In the manner of a production line, teams of tradies such as welders, electricians and plumbers could move progressively from module to module. Each module would have everything possible fitted before the unit was lifted by crane and incorporated into the ever-expanding superstructure.

Don was always puzzled as to why ships would be built any other way. The old, pre-World War II method of installing ships' systems after the hull was almost complete was for him – a born problem solver – a crazy thing to do.

'Why waste all that time and effort and create all that hassle and discomfort, when the fiddly systems could be put in place in the units on the ground then simply connected together once installed on the ship?' Don reasoned. It was a much speedier and more efficient method of ship construction.

Normally.

When the first detailed drawings arrived from Wärtsilä, the nervous excitement generated an electric atmosphere in the drawing office at Carrington. The team watched as the production control manager, Alan Laverick, opened the tube with the hollow *thunk* familiar to all of them. He reverently unfurled the drawings and spread them on the large table, then briefly examined and delegated each to the appropriate staff.

Each team member immediately bent over their charge and set to work. Firstly the drawings needed to be translated into the CAD system using a bank of state-of-the-art computers. Then the drawings were broken down into the modules for construction, in a process called work packaging.

It wasn't long before the drawing office noticed some troubling irregularities. This had started innocently enough – a few errors here and there that were easily fixed. But very quickly the errors mounted and the design team discovered the drawings were all over the place: hatches didn't align between neighbouring compartments, pipework didn't meet correctly or sizes differed between modules. These were not trivial errors.

Basic specification errors such as these would cause huge delays during production. The cost could become astronomical. With so many necessary alterations, version control of the plans at Carrington would also become a nightmare: keeping the various iterations of working plans current so that the final drawings categorically represented the finished product would be a task alone that could bring the drawing office to its knees.

The obvious question that troubled the Australian design team was: why? Why were the drawings so exceedingly inconsistent? The structure of the ship was sound – the GA drawings were complete and very good. But the quality of each of the detailed design drawings was shockingly different. Each system of the vessel, such as electrical, seawater piping, freshwater piping and fuel lines, were all trying to occupy the same space. For Alan, it seemed that each system had been designed in isolation with no crosschecking between plans. How could a single shipyard – especially one of Wärtsilä's calibre – not realise their own drawings were so inconsistent? His stomach lurched as the pieces fell together in his mind. Perhaps Wärtsilä had subcontracted the design drawings to an external company, or even possibly several external companies. This practice was not unheard of in the shipping industry.

WÄRTSILÄ – A LITTLE *TOO* POPULAR?

Wärtsilä had originally committed to providing both the GA drawings and the detailed design drawings used for construction of the new icebreaker. But it was well known that, due to recent corporate mergers and restructuring, Wärtsilä had inherited tenders from its newly merged partner, the shipbuilder Valmet, to build multiple ships for Soviet export. At about the same time, Wärtsilä had also independently won contracts to construct two major cruise ships and several cruise ferries. The high workload of the shipyard was seen at the time by P&O Polar and the Australian Government as commendable evidence of Wärtsilä's capability.

When Australia had announced Wärtsilä as the designer, there were 33 new ships on Wärtsilä's order books. Yet rather than being advantageous to Australia's icebreaker project, Wärtsilä Marine's busyness may well have become a liability.

Wärtsilä Marine's other ship orders were designed and constructed in Wärtsilä's own shipyards. Alan supposed that if manpower had become oversubscribed as their workload had increased, priorities for Wärtsilä's design office would logically, and understandably, go to their own builds.

Alan drew a deep breath before he voiced his suspicions to the team. It was time to call in the boss.

When Don marched into the design office he found Alan among a group hunched over the meeting table in deep discussion. Their expressions were grave as they looked up at him. This wasn't going to be good.

As Alan relayed the concerns and thoughts of the team, Don immediately recognised the danger. If the design team's suspicions were true, several sub-contracted companies would be working from the General Arrangement plan provided by Wärtsilä, with no information of how space was being used by any other system or subcontractor or any thought to system compatibility. It would send a chill down any shipbuilder's spine.

It was abundantly clear to Don that all construction plans would require checking and double-checking, making sure the drawings between design offices in Finland and Australia were compatible and that plans between modules were consistent. But Carrington's entire construction schedule had been based on the assumption of being able to work with Wärtsilä's drawings immediately. This process of rechecking everything would add a lot of expense to the project and potentially hold up production. However, it was the lesser of two evils: not checking at all was not an option.

Don called Bob Wyble, Chief Naval Architect working on the icebreaker, into his office. Don was frank, telling Bob of all his concerns – the interferences between systems, incomplete plans, cost overruns, delays; all of it. Bob was silent for a moment, thinking. There were few options. He'd been around shipbuilding long enough to know when it was time to take steps. By the end of the discussion it was agreed that they needed eyes on the ground in Helsinki.

Don's subsequent discussion with Wärtsilä was just as frank, if slightly terse. Don deeply respected the mighty shipbuilders; he recognised their expertise and personally liked working with the Wärtsilä staff he'd met over the last few years. But he knew what needed to be done. Don demanded, rather than requested, that his nominated staff be relocated to Wärtsilä's office in Helsinki and that they have the authority to check plans before they were sent to Australia. Wärtsilä conceded.

Before long, Bob and his wife moved their life temporarily across the globe, from the warm environs of the New South Wales coast to the less inviting Baltic coast of Finland. They would be there for however long it took, until the job was done. Two others travelled with him: Stan Harris and Ken Brownsmith, who respectively represented the electrical and outfitting sections of Carrington Slipways. It was hoped that their combined expertise would slow the stream of oversights coming out of Finland.

There was much to do in the meantime. While the new icebreaker was not the biggest ship that Carrington Slipways had ever built, she was certainly the heaviest. She was going to be so heavy that additional foundations had to be laid under the launching ways at Carrington Slipways to bear her weight. Laying the new foundations involved excavating massive trenches, metres deep, along the length of the building berth.

When construction of the *Aurora* was finally able to commence in mid-1988, it was the yard's turn to join in on the icebreaker action. In the massive shed that was the fabrication shop great flat sheets of steel were laser cut with pinpoint accuracy using sophisticated technology – which involved what looked like enlarged tickertape translating information from the computers to the cutting machines. Plasma cutters glided up and down the edges of the steel with a hydraulic hum, and the massive sheets then trundled across the shed floor via a system of elevated rollers. The sheets lay along the length of the shed while workmen crouched on top, sending showers of sparks and arcs of welding flares into the air. Frames and ribs punctuated the plates and a structure slowly began to materialise out of nothing but flat steel. It was not long before the keel module was

Workers stand atop one of the keel units during construction.

complete and the keel laying ceremony (at which young Brett stole the show) was held.

As the *Aurora*'s construction progressed through the early stages, it became clear even to Wärtsilä that the issues being experienced by Carrington Slipways were serious. Bob and his Australian colleagues were working successfully with the Wärtsilä team and, while they did catch many problems at the source, they did not, as hoped, stem the tide of problems flooding into the yard at Carrington. The problems were serious enough that two Wärtsilä staff were transferred to Carrington Slipways to assist with construction. This duo was based in the works office, working at the interface with the shipyard floor and the design office. When faced with the plans that the shipyard had to work with, they too were reportedly surprised and disappointed.

Difficulties with the plans were being encountered regularly enough at Carrington that they were thought commonplace. Despite the reciprocal staff arrangements, problems still occasionally slipped through both Wärtsilä's office and the design and works offices at Carrington, only to be discovered on the shipyard floor by flummoxed tradesmen. Yet the Carrington workers never sank into despondency; instead, the shipyard rallied. The discovery of each new problem resulted in a simple shrug of acknowledgment and then heads purposefully came together to find a solution. Despite the stress and time pressures, the literal and figurative family at Carrington were closer than ever and revelling in their can-do philosophy.

But Murphy's Law wasn't to be circumvented by such goodwill.

That summer, unseasonably heavy rain relentlessly teemed down on Newcastle, slowing construction of the hull modules to a painful trickle. The steel for the hull was treated with a highly specialised, extremely hard priming and painting system. It would protect the steel from corrosion and also withstand the cold and abrasion from the ice. The problem was, the anti-corrosive primer had to be prepared and applied under strict conditions – and humidity was not favourable. High humidity could affect the primer's bond to the steel; so even when it wasn't actually raining, the air humidity still prevented its application. To add insult to injury, if the steel was left exposed for any great length of time it required additional priming before painting. The ongoing deluge caused such substantial delays that Don and the managers decided the only way forward was to construct an additional shed to do the blasting and painting. This meant that the priming and painting process could be done twice as fast . . . when the conditions actually did allow.

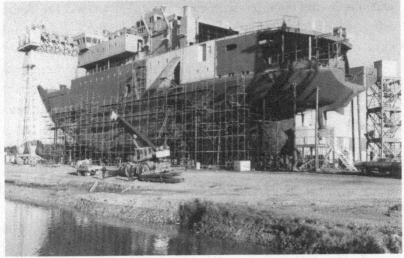

The *Aurora Australis* under construction at the building berth at Carrington Slipways.

By the end of summer, more and more modules were coming together on the building berth. Already, even in her patchy state – the steel was primed and painted with the edges of the modules left raw, so they could be easily welded together – the *Aurora*'s colour was unmistakable. She was painted 'International Orange', a colour used widely on polar ships and American coastguard vessels, but also instantly recognisable on one of the wonders of the modern world – the Golden Gate Bridge in San Francisco.

By March, two-thirds of the steel weight of the *Aurora* had been fabricated. Equipment was flooding in to the shipyard: 'The main storehouse is now a scene of crated generators, lubrication pumps, anchors and deck machinery, galley equipment, sonar, thrusters, workshop items and a garbage compactor', wrote Ivan Bear in his progress report in *ANARE News*.

It was a hectic time. Carrington's commitment to a specific handover day in December 1989 (extended slightly from the original due to the weather) was always of paramount importance. The design office was struggling to keep up – they had incoming plans to vet, load into CAD, and modify if issues were spotted; as well as updating working drawings and final plans; and managing version control on the shipyard floor whenever alterations were made in the drawing office.

As production control manager, Alan Laverick was in charge of the purchasing, planning and projects sections of the shipyard. 'It got to the ridiculous stage' he later remembered. '[Once a week] I would leave my office and just go for a walk around the shipyard and up through the ship, and I went to the same cabin three weeks in a row.'

The evolution of this particular cabin seemed to illustrate perfectly the problems occurring across the build. The first time Alan inspected the cabin, there was an air conditioning duct going straight across the space between the ceiling and the deck above. Fair enough. However, also emerging above each of the forward and aft walls were sizeable flanges for a pipe (a four-inch fire main, in fact) that needed to occupy the same space in the middle of the ceiling as the air duct. The offending piece of pipe lay pitifully on the floor of the cabin. 'Wonderful,' thought Alan, 'there's another one for the list.'

During his rounds the following week, Alan saw that the fire main had now been installed in position, but consequently the air conditioning duct had taken the pipe's place on the floor. On his third and final visit, the air conditioning duct and the pipe were both finally installed . . . with the addition of a large, ungainly

U-bend in the fire main to circumvent the duct. It wasn't pretty; but hell, it worked.

Alan later recalled 'The amount of work in that sort of stuff was horrendous. I think at one stage, the man-hours spent reworking just the pipe manufacture was up around 45 per cent, so we were spending 145 per cent of the man-hours budgeted just to make pipework. They had to go up and trial fit it, then come back and change it, and go back and try again . . . that sort of thing.'

Despite the persistent, recurring problems of design interferences and inconsistencies, over the next few months the construction of the ship made surprisingly good progress. The arterial pipework of the engine room was complete. The massive Wärtsilä V12 and V16 engines had fleetingly seen the light of day as they were installed, then the engine room was sealed over by the installation of the module above. Once the length of the hull was complete, the ship grew upward with terrific speed. Accommodation modules queued along the building berth, impatiently waiting for incorporation into the rapidly developing vessel.

Meanwhile, several other allied projects were also underway at the shipyard. They attracted much less fanfare than the new icebreaker, but were equally vital for the success of the project. The *Aurora* was such a novel build that she presented significant logistical issues for the shipyard in her launching and river transit. The two main problems involved her dimensions and her draught. Even before her construction had begun, Don knew these things would present significant problems for her launch and delivery.

Carrington Slipways used the side-launching method in their yards due to the limited launching area of the Hunter River. Most ships are built at right angles to the water and launched stern first, but this requires a large water area for the ship to enter and then float on its own merit. Side launching was pioneered in Holland, where narrow canals prevent launching stern first. This method requires more space on a building berth but less in the water. Ships at Carrington were built on launching footings, or 'blocks' that, during the ship's launch, would slide sideways down the launching ways along with the ship. But the *Aurora* had so much more width or 'beam' in comparison to her size than any other vessel Carrington had built that, in order for the shore side of her hull to clear the bank of the launching basin during the slide down, she would have to be built on blocks so high above the ground it presented significant safety risks and practical challenges. It was deemed unfeasible. Don and his Chief Mechanical Engineer Aldin Brunt had investigated various ship-launching techniques worldwide. The solution was found in the launching of Mississippi River barges using rocking mechanisms.

Rocking the *Aurora* just a few degrees to the outboard side would allow her inboard side to clear the launching-way bank. After the initial tilt she would then, it was hoped, slide down the remainder of the launching ways at an angle and plunge into the water as in any normal ship launch. It had never been done at Carrington Slipways or likely anywhere else in Australia.

In July 1989, just two short months before the *Aurora*'s launch was due, the new rocking mechanism was tested for the first time. After a few false starts it passed the test.

The second logistical problem was that, after her launch at Tomago, the *Aurora* would need to make her way down the Hunter River to Newcastle for completion and then sea trials; however, this seemingly simple requirement belied the complexity of the task. The Hunter River has a depth of five metres at high tide – and the draught of the *Aurora* was also five metres (without the weight of her mast and all the equipment that would be loaded in the final fit-out in Newcastle). Don hadn't let this minor detail interfere with his original bid for tender. As with any problem he faced, he was absolutely certain that with a little thought and ingenuity it would be overcome if they won the contract. Don knew they would just need to increase the buoyancy of the icebreaker to reduce her draught for the river transit. For Don, the solution was obvious; the method incidental.

In fact, the method had presented itself early in the build. Not long after the *Aurora*'s keel was laid, Carrington won a tender from Brambles to build several loading barges for roll-on roll-off vessels. This was a boon: by now Don had resolved that Carrington would need to build their own flotation tanks to raise the draught of the *Aurora*. With the costs mounting due to the design drawing problems, this was a depressing prospect. The Brambles contract was a win–win. Now, with the agreement of Brambles, the barges for that contract would be built to higher specification (with more watertight compartments) at Carrington's cost. The barges would be made in two sections each, creating four tanks total. After the *Aurora*'s launch, these would be welded to her sides to give her the extra buoyancy needed to clear the river bed safely.

The barges were now close to completion. Lugs were being welded to the hull of the *Aurora*; these would be used to bolt the barges to the ship after launch.

The countdown to launching day was well and truly on. The *Aurora*'s body was nearly complete, although her physique was still being honed. The forward cranes had been installed, but her mast and funnels had yet to be put in place and the rear of the accommodation block still needed painting. The davits for holding and launching lifeboats had been fitted, but were empty. All of this remaining cosmetic work was scheduled to be completed after launch. She may not have been match-fit, but she was ready to enter the tournament.

In the diplomatic words of Keith Lynch, General Manager of Carrington Slipways at the time, this build had 'provided the yard with a challenging project and an opportunity to demonstrate its diversity in shipbuilding'. In reality it had pushed Carrington to the limit: their team, ingenuity, fortitude and finances had all been tested. It had been hard. Damn hard. But the sense of achievement and pride felt by everyone involved was tangible.

*

Launch day, 18 September 1989, dawned clear and warm. High tide was due just before noon and the launch had been scheduled accordingly. The *Aurora Australis* was majestic – if slightly awkward – clear of the army of workers and the cranes, scaffolding and pipes that had veiled her during construction. Five thousand spectators inundated the Newcastle shipyard; many looked up with awe as they walked around the cordons placed under the beached behemoth. Music drifted over the gathering. In the barren shipyard the heat radiated with intensity off the *Aurora*'s steel hull; and without water to protect her sides from the sun, below decks was like a sauna.

There were plenty of vantage points around Carrington's launching basin to choose from. On the bank adjacent to the launching ways people stood atop truck trays or at the water's edge; still others picked their way through and over piles of scrap metal that lay discarded on the ground on the far bank. Directly in front of the *Aurora* a large crowd gathered around the official platform, which was dwarfed by the immense orange bow that loomed above it. Tugboats and pleasure craft on the Hunter River added to the festivities, watching with interest at the mouth of the launching basin.

A bottle of champagne was suspended in readiness from a thin rod protruding from the orange bow. A taut white ribbon sliced the air between the podium and the bottle. Despite the grandeur of the occasion, this was but a humble bottle of champagne: Don and the Carrington team had learned not to use expensive bottles when one had obstinately refused to break during a previous ceremony.

Try as they might, after half a dozen attempts the bloody thing had refused to shatter, simply bouncing back off the bow. Don had eventually called for the spare, cheaper bottle to be brought down to the ship (one was always kept on hand, just in case). The resulting shatter was magnificent. Later, the misbehaving bottle was scored and cut open and the glass was found to be almost a centimetre thick. From that day on, Don ensured the champagne used for christening ceremonies were always 'el cheapo bottles – they smashed beautifully, making a lovely splash against the bow'. The good stuff would be saved for the official reception.

The official party were beginning to arrive. The ship was to be launched by Hazel Hawke, wife of the Prime Minister. Hazel was greeted by Don's granddaughter Jennifer, who curtsied shyly and presented Mrs Hawke with a bunch of flowers. Senator Graham Richardson was beaming as he arrived, clearly pleased to be back at the shipyard to see the Antarctic flagship launched. The Antarctic Division, P&O Polar and Wärtsilä Marine all had representatives in attendance, as did many of the subcontractors involved in the project. Don and the Carrington managers warmly welcomed the visitors to the yard and the party made their way along the red carpet to the podium.

The music faded, and an attentive hush came over the crowd. The ceremony began with the usual friendly welcome and introductions by the General Manager of Carrington Slipways, Keith Lynch. Senator Richardson then stood forward and spoke grandly of the innovative attributes of the ship; in particular her hull design, complexity and research abilities. He also spoke passionately about what the *Aurora* represented to the Australian people, echoing his words from the keel-laying ceremony:

> It represents a nation's pride in its past and confidence in its future. It represents the countless hours of skilled labour by the people of Carringtons – demonstrating once again that Australian shipbuilding challenges the world's best. It is a tribute to the skill, dedication and diligence of the Carrington workforce under its manager, Don Laverick . . .
>
> *Aurora Australis* also represents a landmark in the proud history of Australian involvement in Antarctica. Since the first Australian voyages to Antarctica nearly a century ago, we've used European expertise and technology to break the barrier of Antarctic sea ice . . .

We've learned much about the Antarctic and travelling through sea ice, and we've developed clear ideas about what we want from our ships. In the 1980s we have become firmly committed to a marine science program, and essential to this is a ship with icebreaking capacity able to spend long periods of time cruising the pack ice.

That ship is the *Aurora Australis*. There's no doubt that future years will see it cement its pre-eminent place in the history of Australian Antarctic seafaring and help to maintain Australia's place as a world leader in Southern Ocean and Antarctic research.

The Senator stood aside and the *Aurora* was blessed by Father Stan Willey from the Mission to Seamen. Hazel Hawke then stood forward. The gentle lady spoke stirringly about the environmental issues facing Australia:

Antarctica is now beginning to assert its proper importance on people's minds. In particular, the old belief that Antarctica was unimportant because it was geographically remote has taken a heavy battering from this new wave of public awareness. What was once dismissed as a beautiful but irrelevant landmass now seems closer, and more relevant to our future. Issues involving Antarctica have begun to touch the daily lives of Australian people . . . Our ability to grapple with the emerging environmental issues in Antarctica will be greatly enhanced by the studies which this ship can undertake and support.

At the conclusion of her speech, Hazel pointed out that the name *Aurora Australis* 'has clear historical links, reminding us of Sir Douglas Mawson's earlier voyages to Antarctica . . . and it is a name this vessel will wear with pride out on the bleak Southern Ocean.'

'May she sail long and well, and may good fortune go with all who sail on her.'

With those words, Mrs Hawke cut the ribbon and the champagne bottle swung free and smashed, sending a glittering cascade of white effervescence down the orange bow.

There was a momentary pause as the jacks under the cradles engaged, pushing the inboard side of the rockers higher and higher so that this beamy ship could safely make her trip down the ways. When the *Aurora* had almost reached six degrees, there was a sudden groaning of timbers and the icebreaker began to slide down the greased launching ways. The crowd cheered and the tune of 'Advance Australia Fair' jubilantly filled the air.

Spectators watch on as the *Aurora Australis* is launched with a splash.

The *Aurora*'s belly plunged into the water first at amidships. As her starboard side rapidly followed down the ways she heeled over so far that her portside main decks were submerged in her own colossal wake. The tsunami that followed was a tad unexpected. Spectators on the far side of the launching basin were engulfed in the mighty wave and drenched from head to toe – and those people were standing on truck beds. To the glee of local children, a monstrous eel was found writhing on the bank on the far side of the launching basin, taken by surprise by the surf that had suddenly materialised in its tranquil home. The *Aurora* bobbed uncertainly for a moment, then regally settled into the water. The delighted crowd roared with cheers, whistles and sodden laughter. Horns and whistles of spectator boats resounded over the yard. The *Aurora Australis* was afloat.

Chapter Two

A SHAKY START

After the big splash of the *Aurora Australis*'s launch, the officials and invited guests made their way to the launch reception at Motto Farm Homestead. The colourful flag of P&O Polar fluttered proudly atop a long marquee that was hosting the launch reception, and the official party were handed glasses of champagne as they filed into the elaborately-draped pavilion. Hundreds of invitees followed, a cheery buzz rapidly filling the space. The ringing chink of spoon against glass soon quietened the crowd for the formal speeches.

Senator Graham Richardson stepped forward, giving words of congratulation to the shipyard and P&O Polar. Noting the unseasonal weather that had hampered the *Aurora*'s construction, he sympathetically stated:

Weather is something no Antarctic expeditioner can ignore. Nor could it be ignored here at Newcastle; I know weather conditions have been a problem in getting the ship to this stage and thought you might be encouraged to hear the entry in Douglas Mawson's diary on this day in 1912: 'Strong cold wind. We have had many days of minus 16 degrees lately . . . Good Auroral display this evening.

With satisfaction, the senator concluded, 'Today too, has seen a fine display of an *Aurora Australis*.'

At the conclusion of the formalities, Don called Hazel Hawke forward to present her with a memento in appreciation of her role in the launching. It was a small commemorative plaque that had been hastily mounted with the neck and top of the champagne bottle from the *Aurora*'s christening just an hour or two earlier. Clearly charmed, Hazel triumphantly lifted the trophy, chuckling happily as she proudly showed it off to the gathering.

The presentation of this plaque was the end of the formalities to launch the *Aurora*. Ivan Bear, in his published account of the launching, reported that 'Australia's first icebreaking research/resupply vessel, constructed and manned by Australians, had commenced her life. With her sailing next year will start the development of the personality that will distinguish her from all other ANARE ships.'

But first she needed to be completed. Her fitting out – the installation of instruments on the bridge and in laboratories,

Don Laverick speaking at the launch reception at Motto Farm, with Hazel Hawke in the background.

P&O Maritime Services

Hazel Hawke proudly shows off her unique memento of the *Aurora*'s launch.

cooking equipment in the galley and furniture in cabins and public spaces – was scheduled to take place after the launch. This was because access to completed internal spaces with portable equipment was easier when the ship was in the water, as entry was closer to the water level rather than up half a dozen flights of scaffolding. The final engine alignment and shafting could also not be completed until she was in the water. For once, these technical processes progressed without incident. The ship was a hive of activity, bursting with tradesmen.

In early October, the *Aurora*'s inclining test was conducted. This test involves moving weights by crane to various points on the ship; it determines the ship's centre of gravity at various inclinations, and thus proves that its stability calculations (calculated by the designers) are correct. The results of the test were then sent to Wärtsilä for processing; as the designer, the information and associated formulas required for the calculations were in Wärtsilä's hands. The *Aurora*'s handover date to P&O was fast approaching and Don was eager for the final calculations to arrive as soon as possible.

Then, without warning, Wärtsilä's two representatives at Carrington Slipways were summoned back to Finland, effective immediately. The men had time only to bid a hasty farewell to Don before boarding a plane home within 24 hours. In Finland, Bob Wyble was instructed to return home to Australia, severing the remaining connection between Carrington and Wärtsilä. Don was left stunned. He didn't know what was going on at Wärtsilä, but the rapidity with which this unfolded spelled trouble.

On 23 October 1989, Wärtsilä Marine was publicly declared bankrupt.

As soon as the news reached Carrington, Don went into crisis management mode even while expletives still emanated from the offices nearby. Without the stability calculations from the inclination test, the *Aurora* could not be handed over to P&O, nor sailed in open water. They only needed one set of calculations: one little task that would take someone with the right information, though halfway across the world, a mere thirty minutes to compute.

Don called Wärtsilä repeatedly, pleading for someone – anyone – to supply Carrington Slipways with the calculations they so desperately needed. Eventually, Don was connected to an employee who apologised and explained that while the information sent by Carrington had indeed arrived safely at Wärtsilä, it simply could not be processed. Their office had been shut down.

Don hung up the phone in disbelief. What now? The only alternative was to go to another designer and give them the design plans – such as they were – and the ship, and contract them to work their way through it all. Securing a contract with a firm to do this could take weeks, let alone the months required to do the calculations from scratch. No, that wouldn't do.

Damn it. They'd come so far, overcome so many problems – and now this? It was unacceptable. Don called Bob, who was now back in New South Wales. 'Go home and re-pack a bag', he instructed his colleague. They were both going back to Helsinki.

The flight over seemed endless. While remaining outwardly calm, Don was suppressing a significant amount of anxiety, and found himself fidgeting incessantly. How would Carrington look if this plan didn't work and they could not hand over the ship? While it was clearly Wärtsilä's issue, Don did not want to have Carrington's name dragged into any kind of witch-hunt, media-led or otherwise. Or become the punchline of a joke, he thought, shuddering at the prospect. Don resolved that he would simply not accept no for an answer.

When their taxi arrived at Wärtsilä, the office was unmistakably closed. Don resolutely knocked on the door.

Again.

And again.

Finally a puzzled administrative assistant opened the door slightly to speak with them. The office was closed, obviously; there was no-one else there. At this point Don threw all formality aside. He later recalled that the conversation began with something along the lines of: 'Help! You've got us into a lot of trouble, we need help – how about it?'

At a loss for what else to do and faced with strangers who were stubbornly refusing to go anywhere, the assistant rang a manager that Carrington had been working with, at his home. Don again relayed their predicament and the urgency of the situation. The manager hesitated, then assured them help would arrive before long. Within an hour or two a computer technician appeared. He briskly led them through the deserted office, past rows of desks with computers and stationery still on them. It could easily have been a weekend scene.

They watched the technician boot up several computers and set to work. This man, whoever he was, was about to prevent a debacle before the Australian Government even knew of it. Don also knew that, given the fact that Wärtsilä was bankrupt, this man, and the manager before him, were not being paid for their troubles.

Don had assumed he would have to endure vigorous negotiations and virtually wring the calculations out of Wärtsilä. Yet once a human face was put to their plight, merciful assistance was immediately given, without reservation. Don later recalled, 'We had no problems relating to them; they did as much as they could for us under the circumstances.' Don and Bob gladly accepted the stability calculations from Wärtsilä and hastily made for home.

By December, the finishing touches were being made to the *Aurora* at the fit-out berth at Carrington Slipways. The final structure that would complete her famous form – her mast – would be assembled in Newcastle once she safely cleared the Stockton Bridge on her journey down the Hunter River.

The four Brambles barges were brought alongside the *Aurora* and filled with water until they were almost completely submerged. They were bolted to the lugs at the waterline of the ship, then dozens of brackets rising up from the centre of the barges were attached higher up on her sides to give stability. Once the water was pumped out of the barges, the shipyard had, as planned, reduced the *Aurora*'s draught by just one metre (it was now four metres instead of five), which seems trifling given the effort and planning involved. But it was enough. The transit had been scheduled to coincide with a higher than normal tide, which would allow the *Aurora* to make her way down the five-metre-deep river with a few extra centimetres to spare.

The *Aurora Australis* left her birthplace guided carefully by four tugboats. A marine pilot from Newcastle Harbour was at the helm, while two of the tugs heaved the *Aurora* at her bow and two provided steerage off the stern. The pilot was constantly mindful of the minimal clearance between the *Aurora*'s steel underbelly and the riverbed below. There was only a narrow window of opportunity for the operation; a small period of time before, during and after the peak of the tide that would provide enough water depth for the *Aurora* to remain afloat. If they took too long to get this ship downriver they risked stranding her high and dry.

The *Aurora* advanced sedately down the Hunter River, leaving the paddocks and scrubland of Tomago behind. But before long,

Carrington Slipways/Laverick

The *Aurora Australis* being briskly transported down the Hunter River in late 1989 – note the barges attached to her flank for buoyancy.

the pilot was checking his watch and charts with concern. They weren't making enough progress for his comfort; he wanted to be at their destination well before the tide fell below the critical depth. A hurried management meeting on the bridge resulted in the agreement that the two tugs off the stern should be brought forward to hasten the process.

Like a stagecoach drawn four in hand, the *Aurora* was now briskly transported down the river by her valiant steeds. She made good time along the length of Kooragang Island until the pace was slowed for the manoeuvre under the Stockton Bridge. This area is hazardous for navigation due to eddies in that region known to affect vessels' steerage.

Don and his wife Maureen had driven to a nearby lookout to watch the *Aurora* pass under the bridge. While confident of the plan they had made, Don couldn't help but breathe a small sigh of relief as the *Aurora* passed without incident under the grey concrete arch. It was then just a short trip to Newcastle Harbour, which the *Aurora* reached with time to spare.

Now down at the waterfront, Don watched with satisfaction as the *Aurora* approached. The transit had been a success – another major hurdle overcome by Carrington's 'can-do' philosophy.

The barges were refilled with water, sinking the *Aurora* back down to her natural level. The stabilising braces also needed to be taken off so the barges could be detached from the side of the ship and floated away, and Don, along with several Carrington yardmen, clambered atop the deck of the first barge.

But as the pin was knocked out of the final brace, the outboard side of the barge suddenly shot up, threatening to crush the men between the deck of the barge (which was still attached to the *Aurora*) and the side of the orange ship.

'Oh my God – look out! Get on top!' roared Don even as they all desperately threw themselves against the inclining barge deck in an effort to scramble onto the skyward side. Thankfully, the barge came to a halt at a 45 degree angle to the ship.

The men, shaken, laughed sheepishly. They obviously hadn't put enough water in the barge. By taking the braces off, the previously controlled buoyant force was released, and the unrestrained side of the barge shot up like a cork. The problem was rectified, and the three remaining barges were also filled with more water, just in case.

After her trip downriver to Newcastle, the *Aurora* was put into the floating dry dock to conduct the usual prehandover checks and repairs. These last-minute adjustments included propeller and rudder checks, hull paint touch-ups (for the minor, inevitable scrapes acquired during launch) and fixing anodes to her hull. Shipbuilding Manager Bruce Laverick was often on board at this time, conducting routine inspections across the ship and meeting with contractors.

On the bridge, Bruce and the technicians were spoilt with an expansive view. From this elevated position in the dry dock more than 180 degrees of the inner harbour was on full display through the *Aurora*'s large windows, with an elegant forest of masts at the marina off to the left, and the iconic arch of Stockton Bridge soaring over the Hunter River to the right.

But today, just days into the docking, Bruce was more focused on the interior of the *Aurora* – and it was looking good. Front and centre of the *Aurora*'s bridge stood two plush control chairs, perched in the recesses of an expansive M-shaped console bedecked with buttons, switches, lights and large navigation screens. In the central part of the bridge stood the large chart table and desk for the officers. A separate, dedicated radio room at the rear of the bridge was accessed by a door next to a tiny kitchenette where the officers could make themselves coffee and tea while on watch.

Through the rear door of the bridge, five flights of stairs wound down the main stairwell to decks B, C, D and E, terminating at the main engine room entrance door. Immediately below the bridge, B deck contained the cabins for the captain, officers, engineers, bosun, chief steward and the VL and DVL. Down a level, C deck housed the cabins for the stewards, chefs and Integrated Ratings (IRs, or deck crew), as well as the AAD doctor's cabin, the ship's gleaming operating theatre and the crisp hospital beds of the sick bay. Outside and to the rear at this level was the *Aurora*'s emerald-green helideck, with its contrasting white ring and yellow 'H' of the landing pad.

D deck housed the 34 cabins for expeditioners. Each was in a three- or four-berth configuration, running athwartships. Most cabins had a rectangular porthole between the bunks, but the few windowless cabins in the central part of the ship (also known as the 'bat caves') would quickly become coveted cabins for those working on night shift, or anyone who wanted to shut out the protracted daylight hours of the Antarctic summer. Also on D deck were the expeditioners' and ship's laundries, each with rows of shiny washing machines and dryers bolted to the decks. Located at the rear of D deck was a large expeditioner recreation room, complete with lounges, bookshelf, TV and sound system.

The galley and restaurant, or mess, were down on E deck, where circular portholes cast bright shafts of light across row after row of tables and chairs. Bottles of sauce and other condiments would soon snuggle safely in the timber racks secured to the centre of each table. In a novel move for ships of this nature, the *Aurora*'s restaurant had been designed so that everyone would share the same cafeteria-style eating space regardless of rank (prior to this, officers and expeditioners generally ate separately from the deck crew on Australian-chartered Antarctic ships). Behind the starboard side of the restaurant there was a cabinet which housed the ship's library.

Beyond the restaurant doors, the aft end of E deck was more utilitarian: here the wet lab, oceanographic lab, acoustics lab, conference room and several multipurpose laboratories (including a krill lab) were located. Outside, sitting between the wet and oceanographic labs on opposite sides of the ship, was the trawl deck. Several trawling winches sat like colossal spools of thread at the forward end of the deck. Bollards, winches and pulleys dotted the deck and framework, and a travelling gantry to convey instrument packages out beyond the stern was attached to the underside of the helideck overhead.

Back inside the accommodation, and down the rearmost flight of stairs to the lowest level, F deck, were the *Aurora*'s gym and sauna. Further along the alleyway was the entrance to the lounge bar, before the passageway ended at a rear entrance to the engine room.

Down on E deck, Bruce, bustling between meetings, hurried through the restaurant toward the aft end of the ship. But as he reached the back of the mess the ship suddenly – inconceivably – began to roll. Losing balance, Bruce grabbed a nearby pole and clung to it in alarm.

He assumed the only thing that seemed plausible: that the *Aurora* had somehow come off its blocks on the floating dock. 'God, what damage would be done?' Bruce thought, horrified. The lights went out. He felt the *Aurora* steady, then become stationary once again. He groped his way through the now pitch-black passageway to the aft stairwell and made his way up and out of the accommodation area. Blinking in the bright light of the helideck he saw people emerging in shock from all areas of the ship, trying to make sense of the situation.

One thing was immediately clear: the *Aurora* was still on her blocks. Bruce strode to the rail and scanned the dockyard, seeing powerlines lying on the ground nearby. He looked across the water to Newcastle and gave a startled shout. Clouds of dust and smoke were rising from the city.

'I think we've had an earthquake!' someone behind him exclaimed incredulously.

It was 28 December 1989.

Bruce turned and recognised the man as one of their contractors. They looked at each other in disbelief for a moment, each hoping the other would think of something that could refute that horrifying statement. But they couldn't. The entire floating dry dock had rolled with the earthquake, ship and all.

Sirens began to wail across the city.

Bruce walked over to a burly foreman and some leading hands on the other side of the helideck.

'Does anyone have a radio?' he asked.

A portable radio was produced from the hangar and switched on. The instant barrage of news reports confirmed their fears – Newcastle had been hit by an unprecedented earthquake. The devastation of the earthquake was widespread and at its worst in the city. The Newcastle Workers club had collapsed, with probable fatalities. Awnings and fascias had fallen off buildings on Beaumont Street, injuring and killing people. Cars lay crushed under piles of rubble. Thousands of homes were damaged, as were schools and businesses. Power and telephone lines to many areas were cut.

THE 1989 NEWCASTLE EARTHQUAKE

At 10.27 am, as people were innocently going about their morning business, a magnitude 5.6 earthquake struck the city of Newcastle and surrounding areas. The destruction of the Newcastle Workers Club and collapse of awnings on Beaumont Street were nothing short of devastating in their effects, and further damage was evident across the region in the form of collapsed roofs and walls. In total, thirteen lives were lost and over 160 people were injured. Across the Hunter Valley 50,000 buildings – including homes, schools and commercial buildings – were damaged, with three hundred having to be demolished. The damage total was estimated to be in the region of $4 billion, making this one of Australia's worst earthquakes.

As far as those on the ship could tell, the *Aurora* was unscathed. Once over the initial shock, the worry set in. Many phone lines were down so people would have to physically locate their families in order to know they were safe. Bruce and the foremen ordered that all on board be accounted for, the ship secured, then everyone was to go home immediately to tend to their families.

Equipment was squared away, the gas turned off. The *Aurora* was left on her own to watch over a city in crisis.

By mid-January, following the earthquake, life in Newcastle had somewhat returned to its normal ebb and flow. But for many the shock of the disaster would never completely recede.

The *Aurora*'s mast had now been installed, and she was off dry dock and alongside Merewether Wharf at Newcastle. After a brief period of final fit-out, the *Aurora Australis* was ready for sea trials.

Liberated, the *Aurora* raced up and down the New South Wales coast, undergoing testing to ensure all her operational statistics either matched or outdid the specifications promised to the owner. Among other tasks, Carrington, AAD and P&O representatives had the *Aurora* do the measured mile: they checked her speed, endurance and performance, monitored her fuel consumption and conducted a 24-hour trial, some of which was done at full speed. For the most part, sea trials were unremarkable. Initially there were some minor issues with the arrangement of the two engines; however, these problems were soon rectified with the help of engineers from Wärtsilä (Wärtsilä Diesel, the engine manufacturers, was still solvent and operational, and had sent mechanics to assist with the trials). Some glitches with the data storage system provided by electrical experts Qubit also kept the AAD staff busy.

On 30 March 1989, the *Aurora Australis* was officially handed over to P&O Polar. The impressive icebreaker would soon set sail for her new home port: Hobart, Tasmania.

Contrary to many reports, the *Aurora Australis* was not Carrington Slipways' last build. They built and launched the *Searoad Tamar* in 1990 before the yard was lost due to financial problems caused by a competitive international shipbuilding market (unlike Australian yards at that time, many international shipyards were heavily subsidised by their governments).

However, the losses the shipyard made on the *Aurora*'s construction certainly exacerbated the problem.

Yet even decades after the fact, in Don's mind the *Aurora Australis* would remain Carrington Slipways' single greatest achievement – in no small part due to the challenging problems they had overcome during the icebreaker's construction. Her build was not only a 'technological achievement, of which Newcastle's many skilled people should be justifiably proud,' as NBN News noted, but it was also a testament to the sheer grit, determination and skill of the Carrington workforce.

'Shipbuilding is about taking plates of steel and turning them into something that will have an active life of its own,' said *The Carrington Slipways Story* in 2014.

And what a life the *Aurora Australis* would have.

Chapter Three

TO THE ICE EDGE AND BEYOND

On 3 April 1990 the *Aurora Australis* steamed luminously up the glittering, sunlit Derwent River toward her new home: Hobart. The colonial houses nestled on the hills of Battery Point gazed down at the ship as it motored regally past. It was a striking sight: the *Aurora*'s orange flanks glowed red in the warm light of the autumnal afternoon, and the rippling water radiating from her hull was stained the same unique, vivid shade as her skin.

The 6th Military District Band, waiting on Princes Wharf, struck up a trumpeting welcome as Australia's new Antarctic flagship turned confidently into Sullivans Cove. While the brassy strains of 'Advance Australia Fair' and 'Waltzing Matilda' sounded festively over the gathering, children peeking out from between their parents' legs smiled and waved at the approaching icebreaker.

The *Aurora* slowly manoeuvred herself alongside the wharf, her thrusters causing eddies and vortices to erupt muddily from the depths beside her. The sun slowly dipped behind Mount Wellington just as the wharfies secured the *Aurora*'s braided lines around the weathered bollards, then the gangway* was slowly lowered to the wharf.

---

* The *Aurora*'s gangway is technically an 'accommodation ladder' but the more colloquial term 'gangway' is generally used by the crew, and as such 'gangway' is used throughout this book.

The waiting crowd erupted into cheers and applause. The *Aurora Australis*, the first icebreaker in history that was Australian-built, Australian-crewed and Australian-operated, had officially arrived.

The icebreaker's unmistakable orange hull towered over the yachts, cafés and pubs on the Hobart waterfront. The brand new, technologically advanced ship also made an imposing statement about Hobart's place in the world as a gateway to Antarctica, and the locals were as proud as punch to have the icebreaker in residence. 'New research ship broadens horizons' boasted a *Mercury* article after her safe arrival. 'Ice ship captures hearts of Hobart' affectionately cried another headline, after 10,000 Hobartians toured the ship on its public open day, four days after arrival.

The AAD were also thrilled with the arrival of their new icebreaker, and the possibilities it brought to Australia's Antarctic operations. 'The capability of the vessel is such that the Antarctic program can now run up to six months and we can actually get where we want to go when we want to,' declared AAD Director Rex Moncur proudly in one of the articles. 'Nearly every season something will go wrong, but with the icebreaker capacity of the vessel it will mean we can plan a much tighter schedule and get more done.'

The *Aurora* was officially commissioned into service on 30 April 1990 by minister Ros Kelly, and was ready to begin life on the open seas.

Thanks to the weather and design problems encountered during the *Aurora*'s construction, the *Aurora*'s first voyage was scheduled to commence on 4 May 1990, at the end of the 1989/90 season. Richard 'Dick' Williams, head of the Biology section of the AAD, would be the VL: a man of medium build with neat chestnut hair and a matching short beard, possessed of a warm, British-tinged accent that quickly put people at ease. In the days leading up to the scheduled departure, Dick bustled between the ship and AAD headquarters in Kingston, talking

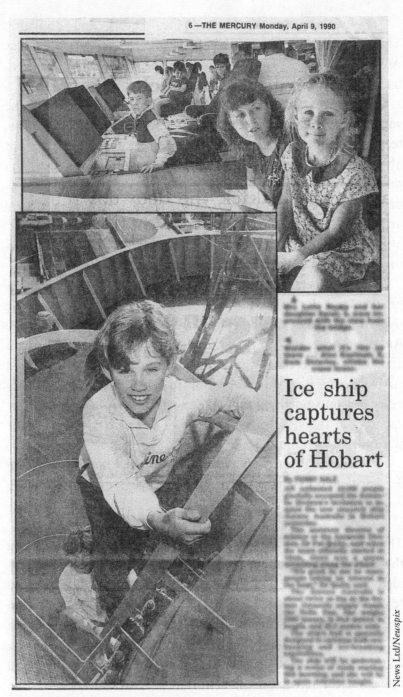

Ice ship
captures
hearts
of Hobart

News Ltd/Newspix

The Mercury, Monday 9 April 1990.

with scientists and crew who were making their final preparations for departure.

'This will be interesting', thought Dick, as he arrived back to the ship on one such visit. He was acutely aware of the challenge of a taking a new ship, with new crew and new equipment, on a midwinter voyage to an area with some of the wildest seas on Earth. A short trial voyage up the east coast of Tasmania had gone pretty well, considering it was the first real test for the brand-new ship and team; the trawling systems and equipment had worked perfectly. And although Dick had some reservations about the oceanographic system, the cutting-edge data storage system that had caused some serious headaches for the technical team during the harbour testing had also run smoothly.

There had been one heart-stopping moment during some wild weather, when Dick and his Deputy Voyage Leader (DVL) Rick Burbury discovered about a dozen oil drums noisily clanging around in the helihangar. The drums had broken loose from their lashings, spilling their contents in an oozing mess that stretched the width of the hangar floor. The incident caused a few red faces onboard, but at least the spill had been contained to the hangar and was cleaned up relatively easily.

On the whole, Dick was very taken with the *Aurora Australis*. The trial voyage had demonstrated she had more facilities than they'd ever dared to dream of in the days of the *Nella Dan*. Now Dick was just impatient to get going. He had high hopes for the voyage, but, being her maiden trip, he knew it would also be a shakedown of all the *Aurora*'s brand-new systems. It was all very well to play around in sheltered coastal waters for a few hours: the real-world scenario would be much tougher on both the ship and her charges. He knew there were bound to be problems along the way. He wasn't wrong.

Just before the *Aurora*'s scheduled departure, her reserve autopilot was found to be malfunctioning and there was no choice but to delay while repairs were hastily conducted. The *Aurora*'s crew and scientists, stifling their bristling impatience, had another few days to get to know the new ship better. After three days waiting in limbo, the *Aurora Australis* and her complement were given the all-clear to leave Hobart for the icebreaker's first official voyage.

Despite being the *Aurora*'s maiden voyage for ANARE, Dick had deliberately kept the new icebreaker's departure low-key. Wanting to get some runs on the board before openly lauding the new ship, he'd given just a small handful of interviews for local media (this later created some confusion, causing some people to think that the *Aurora*'s first voyage was the following trip to the Antarctic ice edge in the 1990/91 season). As a result, when the *Aurora Australis* finally pulled away from the wharf on 7 May 1990, she was farewelled by just a small knot of AAD staff and the families of those on board.

Dick waved cheerfully as the *Aurora* slipped quietly away into the afternoon light. This was it. They had survived the trial voyage, and he was optimistic about the voyage ahead. It was time to see what the *Aurora Australis* could do.

Captain Roger Rusling stood at the helm, the tall, fair man guiding his brand-new ship and her complement into the midst of the tumultuous Southern Ocean. In preparation for his role as captain of Australia's new icebreaker, Roger had undergone additional training at the Australian Maritime College, and had also worked part of the German crew on the *Icebird* as an observer and as mate over several Antarctic trips. The trips on the *Icebird* had been invaluable in getting to know the fickle temperament of the icy realm, and Roger was looking forward to putting the *Aurora*, with all her additional icebreaking and seagoing capability, through her paces.

Their objective was to survey the relatively unexplored area around Heard Island; a program instigated in response to increasing enquiries by member nations of CCAMLR into establishing an icefish fishery in the region.

Located in the remote emptiness of the southwest Indian Ocean, about four thousand kilometres southwest of Western Australia and a thousand kilometres north of Antarctica, Heard Island is situated at the centre of the 'Furious Fifties' – so named for the vicious winds that rage around the globe unchecked by any land at that latitude. The island is a desolate, dark speck in a brutal part of the Southern Ocean that scarce few have inhabited, except for the handful of hardy sealers who lived on the rugged island in the late 1800s, and intrepid Australians that formed the first Australian National Research Expedition (ANARE) between 1947 and 1954.

The voyage's course southwest to Heard Island set the *Aurora* against the prevailing weather, and it wasn't long before the orange icebreaker was beating into relentless wind and swell. She pushed resolutely onward, her decks humming with the uninterrupted rumbling of her Wärtsilä engines. Her wide bow rose and fell with sickening, repeated inertia: one moment the *Aurora* launched herself toward the heavens, then paused for a stomach-lurching, gravity-defying instant before plummeting headlong into the next wall of wind-streaked water. The resulting barrage of spray hammered her bridge windows ferociously.

As the *Aurora* pitched and rolled, a haunting metallic wailing periodically shrieked throughout the accommodation decks. It was the Aurora's anti-roll stabilisers, warbling a melancholy aria as they fought against the tempest.

Despite these stabilisers making the ride much more comfortable than it would have been otherwise, many on board quickly succumbed to the dreaded 'mal de mer', or seasickness. Once seasickness sets in, the typical approach is to simply get oneself horizontal and wait in miserable hope for it to subside. But the queasy expeditioners found that retreating to their bunks did little to help them escape the violence of such heavy swells. Some took to wedging life jackets under the outside of their mattresses to stop themselves being unceremoniously catapulted from their beds. Others surrendered the battle entirely and slept on the floor.

As the voyage went on and the weather subsided, people began to gain their sea legs. Gradually new, slightly hesitant, faces began to join the more robust old salts in the mealtime queue at the galley. It is a universal seafaring phenomenon that shipboard life revolves around mealtimes, and on the *Aurora Australis* it was no exception. Breakfast, smoko, lunch, smoko, dinner, supper – all provided ample opportunity to sample the delectable fare prepared by the *Aurora*'s skilled chefs and cooks. And if that wasn't enough, in a corner of the restaurant lurked an open kitchenette containing a veritable buffet of biscuits (would you like chocolate, plain or cream?), breads, spreads, fruits, cereals, tea, coffee and hot chocolate; all of which regularly lured the hungry to its irresistible, 24-hour siren song.

Meanwhile, the scientific regime had already begun and after a steady start, trouble soon eventuated. Just one day out from Hobart, a CTD unit had been lowered into the deep for the first time, and this continued to occur once a day for the duration of the transit.

THE CTD: REVEALING THE HIDDEN MYSTERIES OF THE OCEAN

The CTD is an instrument named for the variables it measures in the water column: Conductivity (a proxy for salinity, or saltiness), Temperature and Depth. These simple-seeming variables can reveal much about the world's oceans through their physical and chemical properties. The CTD itself is a sensor mounted in the centre of a large cylindrical steel frame that also incorporates an array, or 'rosette', of grey Niskin sampling bottles: these have a cap at each end, so, when open, they are simply large plastic tubes that water can flow through. The entire CTD unit is sent down to within a few metres of the ocean floor, all the while transmitting data back up the cable to the ship in real time, revealing any anomalies or depths of interest to the oceanographers on board. Then, as the rosette makes its slow ascent back to the surface, the oceanographers can 'fire' Niskin bottles one at a time, remotely closing the end caps to capture water samples at chosen depths throughout the water column. These samples are like liquid gold and are distributed between a limited number of pre-approved research projects. If bottles misfire it is not uncommon for heated discussions to develop over the distribution of the last few precious drops of the Southern Ocean's hidden depths.

The smaller, twelve-bottle CTD rosette is brought aboard by the *Aurora*'s crew after a CTD cast.

After the daily cast on the fourth morning at sea, the CTD rosette hung on its pulley beneath the open CTD door, waiting a moment as the salty water streamed off its frame before it would begin its usual trundle back inside the ship. But without warning, the pulley jerked, then shot toward the CTD room. Thrown off balance, the entire CTD swung wildly on its wire and hurtled toward the ship, crashing roughly into the *Aurora*'s hull before vanishing through the CTD door. A lonely grey Niskin bottle plummeted into the abyss.

The mate on watch swore and immediately snatched down the radio, asking the crew if everyone was okay. A curt response profanely indicated that the crew were all fine, but were slightly unhappy with the recent turn of events. Evidently the CTD gantry had stripped its gears.

The rosette was a bit dented and was missing a bottle, but it was the gantry that was the main problem. The science support team repaired the rosette while the crew busily jury-rigged a system using the second winch, and the following day another CTD cast was attempted. It was a deep one, to four thousand metres. Much to the scientists' and crew's relief, the deployment went smoothly, and as soon as the massive CTD door was sealed closed, the oceanographers and plankton biologists pounced. They eagerly stepped into the damp CTD room, clustered around the rosette frame and carefully tapped each grey plastic bottle, ever-cautious of squandering the pristine, crisp liquid through unnecessary spills. Before long they had filled dozens of vials and bottles with their treasure from the deep.

But while the scientists were happy with their successful CTD deployment, the crew had discovered that the CTD winch's cheek plates had buckled seriously during the cast. VL Dick quickly arranged a discussion between the engineers, scientists and technical team, and it was reluctantly agreed that all drops should be limited to 750 metres for the remainder of the voyage.

A few days later, electrical engineer Jonathan 'Jono' Reeve waited in the CTD room during the last stages of a cast, chatting easily with Rick Burbury, the DVL and gear officer, while they kept half an ear on the oceanographers' radio countdown. When the countdown indicated the CTD was nearing the surface, the crew stood back, and Rick settled his shoulder against the inside of the *Aurora*'s steel hull on one side of the opening. He motioned for Jono to do the same. Jono obediently took the spot on the opposite side of the door to Rick, and minutes later, the monotonous whine of the winch stopped, and he heard the sound of water running off the CTD outside.

The next thing Jono knew, he was on his knees, hands over his head shielding himself from sharp plastic shards raining down on them. Pure instinct had driven him to the floor in response to the deafening clap that had ripped through the CTD room a second before. As the cascade subsided Jono slowly peered around the room. An auxiliary wire rigged to the gantry had snapped and whipped straight through the middle of the small room, viciously shattering the overhead light fitting.

'Jesus Christ,' thought Jono incredulously, 'if I'd still been standing there, I would have been cleaned up!' Wide-eyed, Jono and Rick looked at each other across the CTD door opening, then at the crew still standing in shock on the inboard side of the room. Then the pair laughed, breaking the tension. At the very least, the group had an interesting story to tell at dinner. As their heart rates slowed, and the adrenaline slowly subsided, they began to inspect the damage.

Meanwhile, Dick had begun to run some numbers. During the recent near-miss with the CTD, another five rosette bottles had been lost, which meant the cost of the damage was now running into the tens of thousands of dollars. But he had other problems to work through as well. The weather was improving, yet the *Aurora* was still making painfully slow progress between the CTD stations on the way to Heard Island. Concerned, Dick went up to the bridge to find out why, but Roger simply shrugged and smiled, then explained to the VL that, while the *Aurora* had large engines, it is hull shape that limits a ship's speed. With her huge, blunt, icebreaking bow, the *Aurora* lost a lot of her energy ploughing into swell.

'I could burn up the fuel to try to make it go faster,' Roger admitted, 'but all we'd have are more bubbles out the back.'

Concerned, Dick made his way down to his desk to make some calculations. With the accumulated delays of departure and transit, it seemed there wouldn't be enough time to complete all the research scheduled for the voyage. Something had to give, and Dick decided to cancel the midwater trawling, which was the lowest priority of the scientific projects.

Their somewhat sluggish journey to Heard Island had also revealed some friction among the complement. Some of the new crew, more used to working on large commercial ships or fishing vessels, seemed to view the icebreaker as their realm, and the expedition scientists as impositions. A small number of crew were openly referring to their AAD colleagues as 'lodgers' or 'human cargo', which offended some of the scientists and was certainly affecting morale. Most of the crew were nothing but friendly and helpful, but the actions of the small number of persistent stirrers meant that Dick and other senior scientists had to regularly, and diplomatically, smooth ruffled feathers.

Finally, fifteen days and several decent Southern Ocean squalls into the voyage, the *Aurora* reached the wind-battered shores of Heard Island in the early hours of the morning. The rugged volcanic outcrop jutted defiantly from the Southern Ocean, adorned by an immense snow-capped volcano. But as well as being home to one of Australia's two active volcanos, most of Heard Island is covered in immense, ash-speckled blue-grey glaciers. In fact, the island had fleetingly been mistaken for a large iceberg when it was first discovered in 1853. Captain Heard's wife, onboard the *Oriental* at the time, had noted '. . . it must be a twin to Desolation Island; it is certainly a frigid looking place.'

At the coastline the craggy glaciers were interspersed with dark rugged cliffs and black sandy beaches. Vibrant green mosses and soft cushion plants clung to the uneven black rock like lumpy carpets, and tufts of hardy grasses kept a fierce grip on the volcanic soil.

Despite its bleak appearance and severe climate, Heard Island can teem with vibrant, noisy life sustained by the plentiful resources of the Southern Ocean surrounding it. In spring, hundreds of wandering albatross, black-browed albatross and light-mantled sooty albatross soar majestically down to the clifftops to reunite with their mates and perform their elegant courtship dances. Thousands of smaller petrels and other seabirds also concentrate on one of the few land masses dotting the expansive Southern Ocean to breed, and any vessels visiting

The *Aurora Australis* just offshore of Heard Island during her maiden voyage, with the island's peak, 'Big Ben', behind.

the area usually find themselves shadowed by a plethora of avian companions. In summer, hundreds of thousands of feisty, squabbling penguins amass in ear-splitting hillside colonies to breed and raise their fluffball chicks. At the same time, thousands of southern elephant seals and fur seals cram the island's beaches and spill over into the lumpy coastal vegetation. Male seals compete in fearsome barking, belching and bloodletting battles even while females sleepily suckle their bleating, wide-eyed pups nearby.

But the *Aurora* had arrived at Heard Island in the somewhat more sedate winter period, when the domestic dramas of the island's residents are replaced with an idle calmness.

Dick watched as the *Aurora* lowered one of her huge anchors just off Spit Bay on the northeast side of the island. 'It's a glorious dawn,' thought Dick as he took in the scene from the bridge. The skyline to the east was painted a deep orange, and ascended through a palette of peach, pale rose and violet into a crisp cobalt blue. Immediately to the west, the mountainous, ice-capped island loomed high and proud against the sapphire sky. Mawson Peak, the very pinnacle of the island's volcano – known as 'Big Ben' – was even making a very rare appearance, and Dick allowed himself a minute or so to take in the spectacle before turning back to his duties.

This morning's task was to ferry four seal researchers and their equipment onto the dark shore of Spit Bay. This small research team were going to spend a few weeks on the island examining the winter diets and foraging ranges of the fur seal population, which was still recovering from near-annihilation from sealing in the nineteenth century.

By the time the three rubber workboats had been lowered down to the water, the sky had lightened to a uniform, pale blue. It was a perfect day for boating: the air was calm, the sea smooth. The boats were quickly loaded with gear and launched, and by lunchtime the seal team and all their equipment had been safely deposited on the island. The four researchers waved farewell from the steep beach as the workboats turned back toward the waiting *Aurora*.

But subantarctic weather is fickle, and by the time the *Aurora* had weighed anchor and turned away from Spit Bay, the tranquil atmosphere had been replaced by an angry squall that sent raging gale-force winds and churning grey water pounding against the island's coastline.

Those remaining on board the *Aurora* now turned their minds toward the science program, and the icebreaker slowly made her way toward the first fishing study site, where trawl nets were finally lowered into the water and the biological sampling commenced. The scientists and crew worked with gusto, repeatedly deploying the trawl nets and frequently sending the CTD down into the depths of the Southern Ocean.

As each trawl neared the surface, the deck crew, wearing bulky red wet-weather jackets that clashed magnificently with their orange boiler suits and hardhats, waited casually with their hands thrust into their pockets, their heavy boots planted wide on the green steel deck. They shifted their weight unconsciously as the *Aurora* gently pitched and rolled beneath them.

Soon after, the long, sock-like net was hauled up the *Aurora*'s stern ramp, and the oceanic treasure was emptied into plastic fish bins that were then manhandled into the wet lab for sorting. The *Aurora*'s crew clustered eagerly around the laboratory benches as the scientists sorted the catch, wanting to be among the first to view the fruits of their collective labours. Like gulls armed with forceps, the biologists deftly flocked around the catch. They busily sorted, identified, weighed and measured the fish and other animals, organising their haul into tray after tray that lined up along the steel benchtops.

But while the research hauls were plentiful, this was unfamiliar territory for fishing, and treacherous for the gear. Over the next three weeks, the nets were regularly snagged on boulders that lurked unseen on the ocean floor, keeping the gear officer and the *Aurora*'s IRs busy mending the nets, sometimes after every trawl.

Savage Southern Ocean squalls also interrupted the science program regularly. The trawl deck was frequently swamped in 'greenies' – aquamarine waves that would break onto the rear of the *Aurora* as she pitched back, and then submerge the trawl deck under metres of turbulent whitewater as she pitched forward once more. The *Aurora* also rolled ferociously, her clinometer's pendulum swinging over thirty quease-inducing degrees from side to side. People walked like swaying metronomes down the *Aurora*'s corridors, each and every one unconsciously keeping time to the Southern Ocean's irregular beat.

Nevertheless, Dick was thrilled with the *Aurora*; she looked like she was a tough character who could withstand just about everything the Southern Ocean could throw at her. She was even able to hold station for CTDs and trawl in forty knots of wind, which was an unprecedented capability for the ANARE program. In his VL report, he listed the ship's operational abilities then summed up with satisfaction:

These abilities mean that the ship is able to use its available time very efficiently, as demonstrated by the fact that only twenty per cent of the available time in the Heard Island area was lost to bad weather, despite being in one of the roughest ocean areas of the world in the middle of winter.

In contrast, there was an old joke that the *Nella Dan* would 'roll on a wet lawn'.

Despite the nets needing regular mending from their rough treatment on the uncharted ocean floor, by mid-June, six weeks into the voyage, the science team had successfully collected fish from more than seventy trawls. And similarly, despite the early glitches with the CTD system, the oceanographers and biologists had managed to collect data and samples from another 72 CTD casts, with Jono and others keeping an eagle eye on operations. All in all, Dick was pleased with the performance of the ship and her crew and scientists so far. Yes, there'd been a few glitches along the way, but that was to be expected.

However, calamity was about to strike, and the *Aurora* and her complement's ability to perform under pressure was about to be put to the test.

The team on the island had made great headway with their seal research, and conducted a number of other studies such as bird counts, meteorological observations, glaciology work and rubbish collection. By June they had completed a long list of tasks and had begun a seal census, counting and identifying seals currently on the island.

On 6 June, the team's vet, Matthew Stewart, was trying to read the small plastic ID tag attached to the tail flippers of a pudgy juvenile elephant seal. Matthew stepped carefully around the indifferent, dozing seal and slowly bent down to read the number, squinting to make out the digits. Suddenly, he felt a painful, rough wrench, caught a blurred glimpse of fur and sky . . . and realised he was inexplicably flying through the air.

A huge male elephant seal behind him had wheeled and belligerently snatched the hood of Matthew's jacket, then angrily flung him toward the sky.

The breath whooshed out of Matt's lungs as he landed hard on the rocky beach, smack in the middle of a seal harem. Struggling for breath, he staggered to his feet, but the irate seals surrounding him lunged, snapping viciously at the unexpected intruder. Matthew felt stabs of white-hot pain as the long teeth of the elephant seals ripped through his clothes and into his arms and legs.

On the outskirts of the group, biologists Ken Green, Vera Wong and Geoff Moore shrieked and bellowed, waving their arms wildly at the seals to distract them from their frenzied attack. It worked. Dazed, Matthew stumbled out of the herd, inwardly cursing himself and the seals in equal measure.

It was a long, painful walk back to the camp at Spit Bay.

Discounting the searing pain of the seal bites themselves, contracting 'seal finger' – a rare but painful infection that can actually occur anywhere on the body – from a seal bite was a real possibility. Once common with sealers and seal-meat handlers in the early twentieth century, seal finger caused swelling and throbbing pain and could lead to joint problems, mobility issues and even result in death. Historically, the clinical pathogen of seal finger had been unknown, and the traditional remedies had ranged from magic spells, to poultices, to amputation (it was common for those infected to demand amputation of the offending finger, not only to relieve the pain but more importantly to allow them to continue working). Nowadays, the suspected cause was bacterial and the recommended treatment was antibiotics.

Jaw clenched, Matthew cleaned wounds to his calf and hand as he sat in his tent. They had antibiotics in their medical kit, and he quickly swallowed a dose. He bathed the wounds and applied bandages, and sat in deflated misery while he waited for the swelling to subside. But a week later, Matthew felt that things were on the mend, sardonically writing in his own medical report:

'Limb function improved rapidly with a judicious program of therapeutic exercise.'

This 'therapeutic exercise' involved walking along uneven beaches, capturing and manhandling grubby, sand-covered seals while otherwise living in the spartan comforts of a rugged beach camp in the unforgiving wilds of the subantarctic.

Back on the ship, fresh from a busy but successful sampling regime, Dick and Roger turned their minds to the trip home. They calculated that to arrive back in Hobart as scheduled, the *Aurora* needed to leave Heard Island by midday on 21 June. And before they could leave, they needed to retrieve the seal team from their camp at Heard Island; also meaning they needed a window of calm weather where they could operate the boats safely on the steep beach.

Bearing the recent weather patterns in mind, Dick instructed the research party to be ready to depart the island as soon as the conditions became favourable after 16 June. It could have been up to a week before they might get an appropriate break in the weather, so Dick was pleasantly surprised when on 17 June the weather gods smiled and presented them with a suitably calm day to pick up the shore party. The *Aurora*'s flaming orange hull appeared off the dark shores of Spit Bay at 12.30 pm, and just twenty minutes later the red workboats glided away from the ship.

Dick watched the boats motor toward the island. While the heavy grey sky cast a dull, weary light across the rugged island, and the air temperature was a bracing –1°C, the southerly that had marked the previous few days had now almost completely died out. The water rippled in a mellow ten knot breeze and a low surf lapped gently at the sandy beach at Spit Bay.

Gear officers Rick and Andrew Tabor – or 'Fishbuster', as he was known – were in the larger AAD boat, which would work in the surf zone and transfer the people and cargo to the two smaller Zodiacs waiting safely beyond the breaking waves. Their outboard motor buzzed happily as they motored toward the shore. Rick held the tiller, and Andrew sat on the opposite pontoon, watching the rugged island loom increasingly large as they approached. But about halfway to the island, Rick frowned. The wavelets on the steely water were beginning to break with occasional whitecaps, meaning the breeze had picked up since they launched the boats.

But the surf at the beach was still less than one metre high, and Rick carefully navigated their boat between the waves toward the dark shore. The seal team's field leader, Ken, had waded out in his black drysuit, and greeted Rick and Fishbuster cheerily as the boat arrived. Together, they pulled the boat up the steep slope, toward a waiting pile of samples, supplies and camping gear on the beach.

The team packed small loads of their gear into the boat, and, working as part of a production line, Rick and Fishbuster ferried the loads out to the waiting workboats, which in turn transferred the gear to the *Aurora*. But with every trip, the wind became increasingly abrasive against their reddening noses and cheeks, and more whitecaps churned on the ocean's surface.

Finally only the seal team remained on the beach, waiting in their drysuits and jackets with a couple of seal skulls and small cases of samples at their feet. Snow flurries were now swirling around them. The boat approached for the last time, and Fishbuster dropped into the water, holding the craft steady while the four researchers waded out and clambered over the rubber pontoons. In one strong motion, Fishbuster shoved the boat away from the rough beach and hauled himself into the vessel.

Rick idled the boat easily over the small, broken waves near the shore, maintaining position in the white aerated water of the shallows. He gripped the tiller and watched the swell before him intently, waiting for a gap between sets of waves. He felt each broken wave wash under the bow with a soft bump and heard its bubbly rushing swash on the beach behind him.

Seeing his chance, he twisted the throttle. The boat revved and accelerated, racing the next set of swell rolling toward the surf zone. The first wave of the set rose steeper and steeper as the Zodiac streaked toward it. A small lip began to break from its crest, and Matthew clung tightly to the pontoon ropes as Rick launched the boat up the face of the wave. The red bow punched through the top of the face, showering the occupants in cold, salty water, then plunged down the back of the wave. Calf-deep water sloshed around in their boat, which now sat low and heavy in the water; but they were through the surf zone. They bobbed over the next few rolling swells while the water drained out over the transom.

But as Rick watched their frigid bathtub slowly empty, a low wave awkwardly slapped the boat, momentarily dunking the motor under the water. It gurgled and stalled.

Rick turned and hastily pulled the starter cord. The engine spluttered pathetically, but then went silent. He yanked the cord repeatedly, pulling harder and harder while their rubber boat slowly began to drift back toward the surf zone. Nothing. Throwing his shoulders into it now, Rick heaved the cord again – and reeled backwards, suddenly finding himself standing with the end of the starter cord dangling uselessly from his hand.

Shit.

Matthew shivered under his drysuit. The bitter wind was still rising, and sea spray joined the snow, which was now flying almost horizontally. One of the *Aurora*'s smaller boats motored toward them, and Second Mate Ian Shepherd threw a rope over, gesturing and calling against the wind that they would tow them away from the surf zone. Both boats were dangerously close to the breakers and were rising and falling over increasingly steep swell.

But as Fishbuster hastily tied the rope to their tow bridle, a large wave rose higher and higher, inexorably bearing down on them. Seconds later, Rick cried out in horror as the wave effortlessly lifted the smaller boat and viciously tossed it straight toward them. Matthew vainly threw his arms out to fend the boat away, but with a sickening squeal of rubber against rubber, the smaller boat, with its engine still running, swept completely over the top of the AAD Zodiac.

The AAD boat tipped sideways and capsized, flinging Rick and his passengers into the frigid whitewater.

Ken, Geoff, Matthew, Rick and Fishbuster quickly bobbed to the surface in their buoyant drysuits . . . but Vera was nowhere to be seen. Matthew, trying to swim over to where the boat had flipped, frantically called her name. After what felt like an eternity, Vera's head popped above the surface, and she gaspingly reported that she had been thrown under the upturned boat.

By now, the six of them had drifted nearly all the way back toward the shore, and had been joined by Ian and another crew member, who had dived out of the smaller tow boat just as it had washed over the AAD Zodiac. The group staggered up the rocky beach, their gasping breath steaming in the snow-filled air swirling around them. Miraculously, the tow boat was still afloat in the shallows, but further down the beach, the upturned AAD boat washed lifelessly onto the shore.

With two boats now ashore, and one rendered completely inoperable, they agreed it was too risky for the third boat to come to shore to collect the seal party. Instead, they agreed, it would actually be safer for the seal team to swim out to the other Zodiac still waiting beyond the surf zone. The four researchers awkwardly kicked and crawled their way through the wash and managed to grub their way through the surf zone without incident. Blue-lipped and numb, they were hauled into the waiting workboat.

Rick watched the boat as it buzzed away, then Rick and Fishbuster dragged the AAD Zodiac up the scrappy beach and heaved it back over, sitting it upright on the uneven shore. Thankfully the *Aurora*'s workboat was still working fine, and once again, the tow rope was attached between the two boats.

The four men sat silent and tense in the tow boat as they began to make their way toward the surf zone. But the weight of the AAD Zodiac pulled the *Aurora*'s tow boat dangerously low in the water, and almost immediately, its motor dunked under and stalled. The two boats drifted back toward the sandy shore among the white hissing remnants of broken Southern Ocean waves. Ian pulled the starter cord repeatedly, but the engine only gave off small puffs of smoke and more spluttering. Finally, it coughed and gasped to life.

But the wind and snow were still howling around them, and the once-glowing *Aurora* was rapidly fading into a grey mist.

'That's it,' said Rick, 'leave the bloody thing here. Let's get the hell out of here while we still have one boat that works.'

With that, they cut the AAD Zodiac loose and pointed their bow toward the hazy *Aurora*. The abandoned boat washed forlornly to shore.

On the bridge, Dick saw the little red boat appear out of the mist, and he hurried down to the trawl deck to greet the crews after they'd clambered (and, in Rick's frozen state, were pulled) up the rope. But the boat drivers were in no mood for homecoming welcomes from the VL.

'They came back looking daggers at me,' remembered Dick. 'They thought it was all my fault. In a sense it was. I took the responsibility to send them off to do that . . . in retrospect we shouldn't have tried it.'

But Dick also felt it was a bit of a lose–lose situation: he would also have been criticised for not taking advantage of the weather window while it had presented itself. In any event, they all knew that they had been incredibly lucky that no-one was hurt. Both Dick and Captain Roger, shocked by the abrupt turns of weather during both the deployment and retrieval of the Heard Island team, recommend in their voyage reports that rubber boats should not be used for any future landings at Spit Bay.

With all personnel back on board safely, and soon showered, saunaed and comfortably warm, the *Aurora* left Spit Bay to conclude the Heard Island fishing program. After the final trawl had been sorted, and the superfluous fish were thrown to the flock of grateful albatross that constantly followed the ship, it was time to head toward the French territory of the Kerguelen Islands, where they were going to pick up a French fisheries observer, and sample icefish for genetic studies.

The break from the unrelenting research schedule was welcome, and many of those on board enjoyed some well-earned downtime during the transit. By now, the social side of shipboard life had settled into a routine, and down on D deck, predinner drinks were regularly held by generous hosts. Sometimes up to twenty people crammed into the small cabins, laughing and joking and enjoying the experience of being thrown together doing something new and exciting. After the crew 'knock-off' time, expeditioners and crew would gather together in the *Aurora*'s bar, chatting below a fog of cigarette smoke that hung from the ceiling. The stereo boomed, and they danced the night away, unsteadily moving as the *Aurora* rocked and rolled around them, frequently sending people flying across the space to land on the floor in a tangled, giggling pile of arms and legs. Gradually, the bar would empty as people became mindful of the work that still needed to be done tomorrow.

But it was not all relaxation and ease on board. Shortly into the transit to Kerguelen an expeditioner quietly approached Dick and furtively advised him to go take a look around the tween deck, vaguely commenting that the crew may be up to something he might want to know about. Intrigued, Dick walked through the galley, past the large steel hotplates, past the supermarket-like dry store, and into the cool, echoing span of the tween deck hold, his eyes coming to rest on the deck before him.

A large banner was laid out, its freshly painted lettering blaring a robust protest against the French nuclear testing in the Pacific.

Dick later remembered, 'This was absolutely not the thing we wanted to have happen on at least a partially goodwill trip to Kerguelen. It would have gone against all the understandings of working in Antarctica; of keeping politics out of relationships with other Antarctic Treaty nations – we even rubbed along well with the Russians, with whom we were still embroiled in a cold war.'

Dick stared down at the banner, swallowing his hot anger and disappointment. While perhaps well-intentioned, a political protest like this could cause an international incident, and – if he wasn't careful in how he handled it – a nasty dispute with the formidable Seamen's Union. How was he going to deal with this? He stood in the quiet for a few moments, then strode back through the galley and jogged up the stairs toward the captain's cabin.

But Roger had no interest in potentially being involved in a union dispute. The crew were not avoiding their onboard responsibilities, he pointed out, nor were they breaking the law. He had no real power to curb their free speech and stop the protest, he advised Dick. He could, however, arrange a meeting for the next morning between Dick and Rick and the union delegates, if that was what Dick wanted.

So the next morning, Dick, Rick, Roger and the union delegates sat around the table in the captain's office. Dick looked at the burly crew sitting across from him, took a deep breath and made his appeal, pointing out that the Antarctic Treaty means that Antarctic activities are about science and conservation first and foremost, regardless of the political activities or views of member nations. France and Australia had already been hugely successful in joint Antarctic conservation initiatives, Dick pointed out: 'look at the joint initiatives of the French President and Australian Prime Minister in destroying the treaty for mining in Antarctica'. But seeing the gruff, unimpressed faces before him, Dick hardened his tone. 'If you continue to do [it] we just aren't going to Kerguelen. And if that is the case I have to tell my director why.'

The crew soon filed out of the room to discuss their thoughts in private. Dick later wrote in his VL's report:

After some discussion and a full union meeting they agreed not to make any protest, but to send letters to the Prime Minister, Minister of ASETT, the French Ambassador to Australia and others declaring [the] *Aurora Australis* to be a peace ship and denouncing French nuclear tests.

With that fire out, Dick moved rapidly to douse the possibility of any other incendiary action. He swiftly called a meeting with all ANARE staff, who reassured him that no other protests were planned for the visit.

Two days later, the *Aurora* arrived off the French research base, Port-aux-Français, at the Kerguelen Islands. The Kerguelen Islands is an archipelago, and its islands and peninsulas fan outward from the main island Grande Terre like the sinuous fins of a fighting fish. The base itself is situated on a long, bare hill in the southeast of the main island that is punctuated only by the numerous pastel outbuildings that make up the station. Across the gulf, the rugged snow-covered peaks of Ronarch Peninsula shouldered together and gazed down upon the station.

A small boat buzzed toward them from the station, and soon two French visitors climbed up the *Aurora*'s boarding ladder. One was a fisheries observer, who came to monitor the *Aurora*'s fishing activities in the area. But the other visitor was the French base's doctor, who had come on board at ship doctor Peter Gormly's request.

Days before, after the seal team had reboarded the ship, Matthew had reported to the *Aurora*'s surgery to present his elephant seal bites for medical inspection. After answering Matthew's knock at the door, the small doctor invited Matthew into the immaculate room. Below the portholes on the opposite side of the surgery sat a long line of steel drawers, all with labels meticulously describing their contents. Facing the portholes was a wall of glass cabinets with stocks of bandages, instruments and supplies. A hard, padded surgery table stood gleaming in the centre of the space, and a consulting bed sat in the starboard-side corner near the door.

Matthew took a seat on the consulting bed and Dr Gormly peered closely at the back of Matthew's outstretched hand. The laceration had healed satisfactorily, and the doctor nodded and murmured approvingly. Next, Matthew rolled over to lie face-down on the table. Peter carefully peeled the dressing off Matthew's calf, but this time there were no corresponding sounds of approval from the doctor. The chunk out of Matthew's calf had healed well enough, but it was a very open wound and the triangular flap of skin at one end had died and would have to come off. Peter sat back in his chair, pulling off his gloves, and told Matthew he needed a skin graft, and that he needed it sooner rather than later.

The *Aurora*'s surgery was well-equipped and capable of hosting the procedure, but the one thing the doctor still needed was a dermatome, a tool to harvest the skin graft. Dr Gormly went to speak to Dick and Roger.

So, after the *Aurora*'s arrival at Kerguelen, the French doctor boarded the icebreaker with the grater-like tool in his bag. Soon after, Matthew was again laid face-down, this time on the black surgery table and given some local anaesthetic. The masked and gowned doctors draped him with blue surgery sheets, before taking a paper-thin slice of skin from Matthew's upper thigh and applying it to the open wound. It was all over quickly, and Matthew was ordered to stay in his bunk for the remainder of the voyage.

Meanwhile, the *Aurora* steamed northwest of Kerguelen and began trawling. To the delight of both the Australian and French fishermen, the very first trawl hauled onto the deck contained more than fifty icefish. While the scientists got to work sorting the catch and taking genetic samples to compare these fish to their Heard Island brethren, the crew deployed the net again.

By that evening, despite the initial sullen response by the crew to collaborating with the French observer and doctor, the international relationships onboard were faring well. Dick wrote, 'The Frenchmen's reception was rather frosty from some quarters to begin with, but during the evening on our return to Port-aux-Français the atmosphere improved considerably, even among those who had been planning the protest.'

The following day, with both the skin graft and fishing successfully completed, the *Aurora* returned to Kerguelen. A shared objective and a shared meal had worked wonders, and the *Aurora*'s crew even hosted a goodwill tour of the ship for ten of the French station expeditioners.

The *Aurora*'s scientific duties were officially over, and she departed for Hobart with the crew in good spirits. During the transit home Dick worked at his desk, writing his VL's report. Despite the odd hiccup, the *Aurora Australis*'s maiden voyage had been a resounding success. The *Aurora* had handled the tough conditions with ease, and the crew had acquitted themselves well:

> The deck officers were very competent and helpful, and the engineers worked very hard to keep all the systems working, especially the CTD winch and gantry and the seawater pump. The seamen worked very well, particularly on the trawl deck, often in very poor weather conditions, and contributed much collective experience to the fishing operations.

Eighty-five trawl stations and 96 CTD stations had been completed, which was astounding, given all the net hook-ups and problems with the CTD system. The surveys conducted during this voyage documented the basic biology of fish in the area; things like size, age and growth of species. The scientists found that there were good quantities of icefish in areas of the plateau, but also showed that, interestingly, there were no orange roughy in the region. All of the information gathered from this remote part of the subantarctic region was new and exciting for the scientific community.

Most impressive of all, this voyage later resulted in the earliest assessment of fish stocks in the Heard Island region. It was a hugely valuable achievement for Antarctic ecosystem management: this was the first instance – anywhere – that fish stocks were assessed by CCAMLR before commercial fishing took place in an area. And the *Aurora*, with her commercial trawling capability and impressive seagoing abilities, had made it possible.

The *Aurora* arrived at Princes Wharf in the afternoon on 4 July, with the *Aurora*'s complement thrilled with their accomplishments.

'Polar ship back after testing maiden voyage' cried the headlines in the *Mercury* the next day.

But it was the next voyage, the first of the 1990/91 Antarctic shipping season, that would be the *Aurora*'s first test in the polar ice that she was built to break.

The captain, once again Roger Rusling, and the VL, Ian Marchant, were both looking forward to putting the shiny new ship through her paces in the ice-laden waters of Antarctica. The icebreaker would be visiting all three of Australia's Antarctic research stations – Casey, Mawson and Davis – to deliver cargo and summer personnel to each base.

On 9 October 1990, expeditioners tramped up the gangway at Macquarie Wharf No. 3 and were briefed in the D deck lounge by the Master and VL about onboard safety, drills, and the voyage's objectives. The *Aurora* pulled away from the wharf later that afternoon, with the crowds on the wharf and lining the ship's rails waving their mutual farewells.

In contrast to the winter voyage to Heard Island, the conditions for this transit south were good and the *Aurora* made excellent time, despite being slowed temporarily by thick fog in the Furious Fifties. During the transit, the expeditioners happily occupied themselves in the various facilities of the luxurious new ship. The lounge bar downstairs hosted regular parties, where the smoke-filled space was rocked with music and after-shift drinks were poured with cheer. Crew and expeditioners mingled at the bar, trading Antarctic tales and adventures. The sauna was fired up and enjoyed by many enthusiasts, and the extensive VHS library onboard was utilised for group movie screenings in the D deck lounge. And the all-important fare served up by the cooks and stewards was once again exceptional, as Ian wrote in the sixth situation report (sitrep) to AAD headquarters: 'Last night 65 lobsters, 50 steaks, 100 punnets of fresh strawberries, 15 ltrs of ice cream and 6 ltrs of cream were consumed. Beware the catering is superb.'

The first iceberg was sighted a week into the voyage, much to the delight of the expeditioners, who snapped frame after valuable frame of the uneven piece of ice on their film cameras. The open expanses of water gradually became dotted with lonely pieces of floating ice that ranged from being smaller than a dinner plate to larger than a car, then field-sized patches of low and sludgy ice remnants began to break the vast expanses of open water.

Suddenly, the *Aurora*'s constant movement from side to side ceased. The *Aurora* had reached the edge of the pack ice: the sea ice that floats freely on the water and rings the Antarctic continent.

As excited expeditioners pushed through the bridge door they immediately squinted in the intense bright light reflecting off the frozen ocean. The entire sea was white, and it was flat as a tack from horizon to horizon. It was covered in large broken ice floes interspersed with slushy brash, and the *Aurora* effortlessly pushed the pieces aside as she motored through. The jumbled ice floes were crumpled at their peripheries from jostling against their neighbours, and their lumpy edges were the highest points above sea level for miles, except for the immense icebergs now lingering on the horizon.

As the *Aurora* sailed on through the frozen sea she approached the sleeping giants. Some were huge tabular icebergs that dwarfed the *Aurora*, with electric-blue ice caves that punctuated their sides and gaped at the ship like open mouths. Others, rugged and gnarled, sent towers and pillars jutting into the sky between deep, craggy fissures and snow-covered knolls.

The *Aurora* continued to sail past colossal icebergs and through an array of Antarctic pack ice. She motored through vast bands of new 'pancake' ice: small, flat-centred pieces of circular new ice that had raised rims from lapping against their fellows. She nudged through patches of thick, weathered floes that harboured the odd resting penguin or seal, and avoided the occasional stealthy pieces of lone, hard ice known as 'growlers'.

Then, just nine days after departure, the *Aurora Australis* faced the unbroken Antarctic 'fast ice' for the first time. The solid sea ice at Newcomb Bay clung to the Antarctic coastline, and was the final barrier standing between the icebreaker and the rocky outcrop of Casey station.

But the fast ice was not thick, and Roger urged the *Aurora* onward using only one of her engines. Her orange bow lifted on top of the floating mass and she surged easily forward, the sheer weight of her body crushing the ice beneath her. Crumbled pieces of ice slithered and bobbed down her sides, and the *Aurora* advanced into the fast ice in one long lunge, coming to a halt about a mile later. The *Aurora* sat in place snugly, with solid ice around her bow and sides, and a string of open sludgy ice-water extending out behind her.

Smiling in satisfaction, Roger deployed the *Aurora*'s thrusters to hold her safely in her position in the fast ice. The *Aurora Australis* had just set a record for the earliest arrival by a ship at Casey station.

The *Aurora*'s helicopters were bladed up on the helideck, then ferried passengers the short distance from ship to shore, and several Hägglunds – colourful, dual-cab snow vehicles – rumbled out to the ship on their caterpillar tracks to pick up expeditioners and building materials that had been lowered directly onto the ice by the *Aurora*'s cranes.

But it was the departure from Casey that stood out for Roger; he was delighted when the *Aurora* performed beautifully, executing an impressive three-point turn in the solid fast ice, allowing the icebreaker to exit the ice forwards rather than reversing all the way back through the broken channel.

The *Aurora* was then scheduled to visit the fast ice edge off Mawson station and drop off some Hägglunds, but, as Roger wrote in his Captain's report, when they reached the ice edge off Mawson it was more than three metres high, and was treacherously ridged: 'It appeared that an iceberg had drifted along the edge of the ice, pushing the ice into the tortured shape it was seen in.'

It would be impossible to land the Hägglunds on this thick, 'tortured' ice; instead, helicopters were dispatched from ship to shore, carrying sling loads of cargo to the station in a 'fly-off' resupply.

Meanwhile, out on the decks, the *Aurora*'s intrepid crew were working in subzero temperatures and thirty knot winds, which, as Roger wrote proudly, 'meant that the men working on the open deck were in fact exposed to temperatures of approximately minus fifty when the wind chill factor was taken into account, the fact that they did this work uncomplainingly is most heartening for the future conduct of the vessel'.

With the Mawson resupply complete, the *Aurora* turned to Davis station. The fast ice was slightly thicker than at Casey, and an engine coupling failure partway through the transit between Casey and Mawson had left one of the *Aurora*'s engines inoperable, so Roger took the ice carefully. Despite only operating on one engine, in just five easy lunges the *Aurora* cut through four hundred metres of 1.4-metre-thick ice, approaching close enough to successfully resupply and refuel Davis station.

'It bodes well for our next real test, that of breaking in to Mawson through a greater extent, possibly many miles of fast ice,' wrote Roger, already thinking of the *Aurora*'s next voyage. That would display the *Aurora*'s true icebreaking capabilities: it would also be the earliest attempt in history for a ship to break through the notoriously tricky fast ice off Mawson station.

That next voyage also saw the *Aurora* face 1.4-metre-thick fast ice, but unlike the previous voyage this ice had also been overlaid with fifty centimetres of fresh snow.

But this time the *Aurora* was powered by the full horsepower of her two Wärtsilä engines. As Roger prepared to press the *Aurora* forward, a cyclonic roar filled the trawl deck, sending throbbing vibrations up through the feet and into the chests of some of the crew, who were enjoying a smoke out on deck. The sea behind the icebreaker erupted into boiling whitewater, and bright blue aerations pulsed in its depths as the *Aurora*'s propeller drove her forward toward the ice. There was a shudder, and the *Aurora* lurched slightly as she lifted up onto the ice, but, engines still roaring, the icebreaker resolutely continued to advance. The air was filled with sharp snaps, resonating 'ka-chunks' and dull booms like far-off cannon fire as cracks and rifts were cut deep within the solid ice below. The *Aurora*'s advance slowed, and then her bow dropped gently, settling to a rest in the ice.

After a pause, the *Aurora*'s engines roared again. Her orange bow slid smoothly off the ice as she withdrew, leaving a V-shaped 'footprint' out ahead. The broken ice, released from being piled against the *Aurora*'s hull, sighed softly as it slipped back into the crystal-clear channel now cutting into the fast ice.

Once again, Roger gathered the *Aurora*'s power, and the *Aurora*'s formidable icebreaking process was repeated from the beginning.

After making initial inroads, the *Aurora*'s progress stalled. The fresh snow layered over the ice was causing friction against the *Aurora*'s hull, and despite all her efforts, the sticky white substance slowed her lunges, sometimes so much that she seemed to advance mere metres, rather than shiplengths.

'It's like trying to break ice through a jam sandwich,' admitted Roger to ABC 'Quantum' reporter Megan James, after eleven hours of seemingly futile icebreaking.

The *Aurora* had advanced only three miles over eleven hours, and the attempt to break in early to Mawson was abandoned.

It wasn't essential to break into the station to conduct the resupply, and the *Aurora*'s huge exertions were consuming vast quantities of fuel, so the usual fly-off resupply was conducted instead. But even though the *Aurora* had struggled against the ice, her capabilities had been on clear display. Never before had ANARE dared to attempt this kind of icebreaking. They had asked the new ship to break more ice than she was rated to and, as Megan reported, the Antarctic Division would 'reserve judgement of the new icebreaker for a fairer test'. While disappointed the *Aurora* couldn't break through, VL Martin Betts was nevertheless impressed with the new ship: 'Given the fact that this was the third voyage of the ship with the ANARE, and only the second station-related passenger and cargo operation, it must be said that from a charterer's point of view the ship performed to a very high standard.'

In an expeditioner survey conducted by the AAD at the conclusion of the voyage, the ship was almost universally praised, with comments such as:

> This thing is just a floating hotel, compared to those intrepid days of the little *Nella*. How can you improve on excellence? . . .
>
> Life on the *Aurora Australis* is so pleasant that I shall be sorry to leave her tomorrow. She is a ship of which ANARE and P&O should be justly proud . . .
>
> I have found the voyage much better than any other because of AA crew. They have been friendly and helpful and generously allowed me to participate in a number of activities that have been useful to me . . .

And, of course the inevitable:

> Nice paint job!

The *Aurora Australis* had made a good impression, and the 'Orange Roughy', as she was soon nicknamed, had only just begun to make her mark on Australian Antarctic operations.

Chapter Four

WOES

By the 1990s, increasing awareness of Antarctica's unique and fragile position as an unspoiled wilderness meant that global attention was now being paid to the effects of human activities on the frozen continent. In 1991 the celebrated Madrid Protocol was signed, which classified Antarctica as a 'natural reserve, devoted to peace and science', with signatory parties agreeing to take measures to conserve Antarctic fauna and flora, assess all activities with a view to environmental impacts and prevent marine pollution. But part of the Madrid Protocol included the requirement that all non-native animals should be removed from the Antarctic by 1 April 1994. Sadly, this included Australia's beloved husky sled dogs, which had faithfully served Australia's modern Antarctic program since 1954.

As a result, in the 1992/93 season, 22 huskies, including three pups, were brought back to Australia during an emotional voyage of the *Aurora Australis*. Four rows of timber crate kennels lined the *Aurora*'s helideck, each complete with 'street' signs designating them with names such as 'Aurora Alley' and 'Barkville'; and a mother along with her three lively pups were safely housed in the wet laboratory, which was temporarily transformed into a nursery kennel. The voyage was nicknamed MONGREL.

As the *Aurora* pitched and rolled her way across the churning Southern Ocean, the dogs frequently raised their noses in bouts of wild pack howling that ascended from the helideck to be whipped aloft by the oceanic breeze. Handlers and volunteers took turns walking the dogs along the *Aurora*'s snow-dusted, then windswept decks. The *Aurora* arrived in Hobart with her canine passengers on 23 November 1992.

The last huskies on the deck of the *Aurora Australis*, just after arriving in Hobart on the MONGREL voyage.

Jan Dallas/Australian Antarctic Division

ANARE veteran Gordan Bain later described it: 'As the ship got closer we saw, heard and smelled husky dogs on the helideck . . . everyone on the dock clamoured to see the dogs. A very special treat was seeing the three husky pups at the guard rails on the deck in the care of returning wintering expeditioners . . .'

After their poignant departure from Antarctica, the huskies went on to be repatriated in America, where two of the Mawson handlers spent months familiarising the dogs with their new homes and handlers. Incredibly, just six months after leaving

Mawson station, five of the huskies were reportedly part of an expedition that traversed the Arctic and successfully reached the North Pole. The remaining five huskies in Antarctica (older dogs who had passed their working ages) were transported back to Australia onboard the *Aurora Australis* in late December 1993, after which they enjoyed a life of retirement.

In addition to Australia's new Antarctic maritime capability arriving in the form of the *Aurora Australis* in 1990, the arrival of the Cooperative Research Centre (CRC) for the Antarctic and Southern Ocean Environment to Hobart in 1991 had added a level of oceanographic research capability never before available to ANARE. This newly-formed collaboration between the CRC and the Antarctic Division meant that the research conducted onboard the *Aurora Australis* was truly interconnected as well as cutting-edge; it now combined oceanography (looking at currents, temperature and saltiness) with the type of detailed biological work (studying plankton, krill, fish, seals and birds) that the Antarctic Division had focused on since the early 1980s. Onboard the *Aurora*, scientists from multiple fields worked side by side, and the fruits of their labours were shared openly, allowing them to examine how the Antarctic ecosystem was linked together, rather than separately examining elements within it. It was an exciting time to be involved in ANARE.

By the 1992/93 season, the *Aurora*'s crew and scientists had successfully conducted five marine science voyages, including krill and fish studies, oceanographic experiments and geological sampling around Heard Island and off the Antarctic continent. As VL Graham Hosie wrote in his report after one such voyage:

> . . . it was very pleasing to see the ship's crew and the marine science expeditioners all working as one integrated marine science team to achieve the aims of the voyage . . . The friendship and cooperation that has developed between crew and

expeditioners is a major factor contributing to the success of *Aurora Australis*.

Come that autumn, the *Aurora* was about to conduct a dedicated marine science voyage that would unusually consist of four separate 'legs', each focusing on different areas in the Southern Ocean and within the Antarctic pack ice.

This was Dr Steve Nicol's maiden voyage as VL. Steve, a fresh-faced, dark-haired man who spoke with a tinge of cheery Irish lilt, was looking forward to the voyage. A krill biologist at the Antarctic Division, Steve's own research would take place on the second leg of the expedition. 'It would be a busy voyage,' remembers Steve, 'especially for a first-time VL; but with clear delineations between each of the research legs, it all seemed quite do-able, really.'

VOYAGE 9 1992/93: A VOYAGE IN FOUR PARTS

The four legs of Voyage 9 were varied and covered different disciplines, involving:

- Leg one: an oceanographic transect from Tasmania to East Antarctica, where the CTD unit would be deployed at thirty nautical mile intervals to collect data and water samples across the Southern Ocean along what was known as the World Ocean Circulation Experiment SR3 transect, that runs in a straight line south-southwest from Tasmania down to East Antarctica.
- Leg two: would take place just outside Antarctica's ice edge, where the *Aurora*'s echo sounders would be used to conduct an acoustic survey for krill, investigating their distribution and abundance in the region.
- Leg three: this leg involved a number of disciplines within the pack ice, including glaciologists looking at the processes involved in new sea ice growth and the characteristics of pack ice in autumn, as well as biologists studying the seals of the pack ice.

- Leg four: there would be another oceanographic transect (the WOCE PII transect, located longitudinally about halfway between Tasmania and Macquarie Island), scheduled for the end of the voyage while the *Aurora* made her way back toward Hobart.

On the afternoon of 10 March – departure day – the *Aurora* sat patiently alongside the wharf, a thin wisp of exhaust rising from her stacks, while below deck the expeditioners underwent predeparture training, in which representatives from various sections of the AAD gave talks about roles and responsibilities of their staff and conducted safety briefings. Steve chuckled as Dr Gormly gave his ever-graphic 'cold can kill' medical presentation, where images of bloodied and frostbitten limbs served as stark warnings to the horrified expeditioners of the dangers of living and working in Antarctica. The captain, Peter Bain, gave a brief overview of the *Aurora* and a rundown on safety and housekeeping matters on board, before wishing everyone a smooth and successful voyage.

That evening, the expeditioners excitedly lined the *Aurora*'s rails as she was made ready for departure. A crowd had gathered on the wharf, and streamers were gleefully tossed by expeditioners from the ship, falling like shooting stars into the outstretched hands of friends and family below. The rainbow of paper tendrils billowed gently in the breeze as the *Aurora*'s shore lines were cast off and, with a rev of her engines, sounding of her horn and puff of diesel exhaust, the ship pushed away from the wharf. As the watery gulf between the ship and wharf widened, the streamers lengthened, then stretched taut. One by one they snapped; and when the last flimsy connection to shore broke, smiles reluctantly fell into tearful farewells. The *Aurora* turned her mighty orange bow to the sea, and the waving crowd soon blurred into the falling darkness.

In the first few days of the voyage the *Aurora*'s complement became familiar with the smiling faces appearing in the mealtime queues, and the CTD teams soon launched into their routine sampling regime on the SR3 transect. The *Aurora* sailed through a remarkably calm Roaring Forties; but immediately upon entering the Furious Fifties she was hit by storm after furious Southern Ocean storm. White horses constantly charged over the top of huge swells, the misty manes of the jostling herds swept back in their wake by the howling wind. The *Aurora* pitched like a rollercoaster over the mountainous seas while the trawl deck was swamped by walls of foaming blue–white water.

A hairy muster on the helideck in heavy swells during the WOES/WORSE voyage.

'This is one hell of a way to get south,' thought Steve one afternoon as he gripped his desk in his cabin, then clenched his teeth, straining to stay upright while the *Aurora* executed a particularly nasty roll. Conducting an oceanographic transect is slow work; they were supposed to lower a CTD to the ocean floor every thirty nautical miles, but with the weather as foul as it was, the ship's crew had been forced to turn the ship hove-to on more than one occasion, and it seemed to be taking them an eternity to get south.

Finally, twelve days into the voyage, the Southern Ocean's unceasingly rolly days finally gave way to a gloriously still evening. Another CTD was being cast, and, as was his routine, Steve made his way to the bridge to check all was in order before retiring for the night. He pushed open the bridge door and saw that the curtains between the helm and the chart table were drawn. A single light cast a warm glow over the nautical map laid out on the chart table, but the area in front of the table was completely enclosed by the heavy curtain that now divided the bridge. Steve parted the curtain and stepped into the forward part of the bridge – and was instantly enveloped in suffocating darkness.

Unable to see anything, Steve groped his way blindly to a forward rail. Two voices came out of the black to one side, murmuring quietly in the darkness. Was it the mate, talking with the nightwatchman? He had absolutely no idea how many people were invisible in the blackness. Unperturbed, Steve silently looked toward what he could only assume was the front end of the ship while he waited for his eyes to adjust.

Slowly, he began to make out the scene before him.

The *Aurora* seemed to float upon a silken, inky emptiness that stretched silently to the horizon. It was broken only by the faint light reflected by the *Aurora*'s bow and rails, and the lonely, shimmering beam cast by the open CTD door behind them. A few celestial glitterings pierced the dark autumnal sky above, but as Steve's eyes continued to adjust, more stars steadily appeared, and more, until the sky seemed impossibly crowded. After a few minutes the busy throng of the Milky Way was revealed in all its glory, streaking like a fine cloud across the blue–black heavens.

But there were no signs of an aurora appearing in the sky to offer some distraction. Having just endured over a week of constant motion and interrupted sleep, Steve decided he should take advantage of the gentle seas and get some proper rest. He took one last look at the breathtaking celestial display, then went down to his cabin, crawling gratefully into his bunk not long after.

Just as he pulled the doona up to his chin and sighed comfortably, there was a knock at the cabin door. Steve groaned. That'd be right.

'Yes?' Steve called across the dark room, sitting up.

A bright shaft of light cut into the cabin, and Steve saw the lanky silhouette of Jono Reeve pause outside the curtain separating the VL's office from the bedroom.

'You'd better get up,' Jono said cryptically to his VL.

With a few good-humoured utterances, Steve hoisted himself out of bed, threw on some clothes, and hastily followed Jono out of his cabin. Eventually, Jono led Steve down to the internal watertight door of the CTD room. Steve peered into the steel-walled compartment and quickly followed the eyes of the crew to the gantry overhead.

A frayed wire hung limply from the gantry and swayed pathetically across the empty space where the pride and joy of the AAD oceanics section should have stood.

'How the hell did that happen?' choked Steve as he stepped through the frame of the watertight doorway. The entire CTD rosette had dropped off its wire, somewhere about 110 metres below the surface.

Jono, DVL Andrew McEldowney and the whole science technical support team were flabbergasted. They'd checked and double-checked the wire after some previous minor problems and had followed all the proper procedures. Just before the loss, the crew had spotted two more broken strands poking out of the wire. They had rightly paused the retrieval to deal with the broken strands, but then the CTD alarm in the computer room had begun to shriek, stridently proclaiming that the data connection to the CTD had been lost.

The numbers weren't pretty. They'd lost 24 of their highly-specialised sampling bottles, not to mention the CTD instrument itself, which was worth upwards of $125,000. There was a spare, smaller CTD on board but there were just thirteen sampling bottles left, and several of the bottles had been damaged during the earlier mishaps and would need to be repaired before being pressed into service. And they had no idea how the CTD system had failed.

Steve remembers the moment clearly: 'Everyone was running around looking for someone to blame. But nobody knew who to blame. The fact was, the CTD had just dropped off.'

Steve immediately called a meeting with the science teams to talk over their best course of action. In the end, they decided that they would have to use the smaller spare twelve-bottle rosette, and 'double-dip' each CTD station so that all 24 samples could still be collected. But it would increase the allocated sampling time by a third, meaning the *Aurora* would need to stay longer at each station – and once again a string of low-pressure cells had ominously appeared on the weather maps.

The technical support team got busy repairing the cracks and dings in the remaining sampling bottles and the CTD wire was carefully repaired. But, rather than immediately using the now-irreplaceable twelve-bottle CTD rosette, a test run was conducted down to four thousand metres using a heavy weight. The mock cast showed no signs of any issues; the twelve-bottle rosette was eventually rigged to the wire and the SR3 transect was resumed; with the *Aurora*'s crew, technicians and oceanographers keeping a nervous watch on the system.

A week later, tensions had eased. To the complement's collective relief, the double-dipping had been successful and the oceanographers and biologists had happily collected samples from about eleven CTD stations, crossing the Antarctic polar front. Adding to their cheery dispositions was the knowledge that the krill acoustic survey would shortly start, giving the CTD teams a welcome break from their relentless sampling regime.

But up on the bridge, Steve looked out at the grey wildscape and sighed. This was not the ideal way to start his krill research. So far, the echo sounders had not shown any signs of krill in what was supposedly a krill-rich area. The echo sounders don't work very well within the pack ice, and if they didn't find any krill north of the ice edge, he wasn't entirely sure what he should do.

By the time they'd reached the second-last CTD station, Steve had almost given up hope of finding any krill. And now, a bright patch of cloud in an otherwise grey sky dashed any remaining hope he had. It was an ice blink: a reflection of light off sea ice, just beyond view. The pack ice wasn't far away now.

As Steve glowered at the ice blink with a mixture of hopelessness and resignation, the bridge's internal phone trilled. It was the acoustics lab downstairs: a red blob had appeared on the echo sounder display, they reported, and there might be krill beneath the ship. Steve's face immediately lit up, and, suddenly animated, he excitedly asked the crew to prepare to deploy a trawl. Within minutes the midwater net was lowered into the water and it trailed behind the ship, sinking down to the depth of the acoustically detected target. As soon as the retrieval began, Steve quickly donned his gumboots and wet-weather jacket, and stepped onto the trawl deck to watch the net return.

He waited expectantly with the crew, staring at the wires extending out into the *Aurora*'s choppy wake. The aquamarine wash behind the ship hissed as it slipped away from the stern, while the regular thrumming vibrations of the *Aurora*'s engines and propeller rose through the soles of Steve's feet. The massive trawl drums rotated slowly behind him, and Steve flinched now and then when a metallic squeal or ear-shattering grating jarringly punctuated the monotonous hydraulic drone of the winches.

Finally, a horizontal bar appeared between the two trawl wires, and the dark, saturated net rose out of the sea. The net was winched up onto the gantry and backwards onto the trawl ramp, then came to a dripping halt in the middle of the deck, and the crew carefully detached the hard, cylindrical cod-end. Steve peered into it and breathed a sigh of relief. They had captured several hundred krill – the first autumnal krill collected from East Antarctica – and they would be examined in detail to determine how they were preparing themselves for the long dark winter.

A few krill were still flapping about in the net itself and they were gently emptied into waiting buckets of seawater, before the cod-end and buckets were hurriedly carried to the temperature-regulated krill lab. The krill were carefully tipped into holding tanks, and immediately began swimming around their new home; their long feeding legs held forward, folded neatly under translucent orange heads with dark, bulging eyes. The swimming legs beneath their long abdomens undulated frantically and propelled the crustaceans around the tanks with surprising grace and fluidity.

Once the voyage was completed these krill would be transferred to the Antarctic Division's krill laboratory in Kingston, Tasmania, for growth and age studies. Meanwhile, the small passengers would be comfortably accommodated in the specialised seawater tanks of the *Aurora*'s krill lab, where the researchers would spend countless hours seeing to their charges' every need.

While Steve and his research team were occupied in krill heaven, the *Aurora* and her complement sailed into the ice-laden waters of the pack to deploy the final CTD of the SR3 transect. Sixteen hours of floe-nudging later, the diminutive twelve-bottle unit was once again sent into the deep. As the *Aurora* held station among the rutted floes and jumbled bergy-bits of the outer pack, small pieces of ice bobbed and floated past the CTD wire.

The oceanographers quickly saw that the water was incredibly cold in this region. So cold, in fact, that the CTD sensors froze, rendering them useless. The CTD cast was aborted and the rosette brought back to the surface. Nevertheless, the SR3 transect had been successfully completed, much to the joy and relief of the oceanographers, plankton biologists, science technical support team and crew. One quarter of the voyage's objectives had been met.

In another promising development, while en route to the final CTD station, krill had again showed up on the echo sounders. Steve and Captain Peter turned the *Aurora* around and steamed overnight back toward the shelf break, where they would officially start the krill acoustic survey.

The following morning, as they sailed toward the open water, Steve sat working at his desk in his cabin. There was a knock at the door, and he smiled when he saw Dr Peter Gormly's bearded, shorts-clad form step into his cabin.

'You've got to come with me now,' the doctor said gravely. 'One of the crew is really ill. Vomiting blood.'

Steve's welcoming smile instantly fell from his face. Oh god.

'Okay,' Steve said, wrinkling his forehead as he tried to think. 'I need you to tell me what needs to be done.'

Dr Gormly gravely locked eyes with Steve.

'You need to go into the man's cabin and take some photographs,' he said, holding out a Polaroid camera.

'What?' asked Steve incredulously, the blood draining from his face.

'I need photographs.'

Steve hesitantly took the camera from Dr Gormly's outstretched hand, then looked up at the doctor's face, searching for a further explanation for this strange task. But Gormly's features were characteristically expressionless, and he offered no clarification to the perplexed Steve. Gormly simply told Steve that the sick man, IR Ross McCallum, had already been carried to the surgery by the crew and that he'd advised the captain of the situation. He had examined Ross and stabilised him as best he could, and now he was about to call the doctors back at AAD headquarters.

'But we still need those photos,' he said pointedly, looking at Steve from under his bushy brows before walking out of Steve's cabin.

Steve stared after him, still gripping the camera. Snapping out of his shock, he leapt up and jogged down the stairs to the IR's cabin on C deck. He stood at the door for a moment, gripping the handle with his free hand, then resolutely pushed the door open.

The thick, metallic smell of blood struck him full in the face. Steve gasped, turning away. He took a choking breath and held it, then slowly stepped into the cabin.

It was like walking into a slaughterhouse. To his right, bright red blood gaudily splashed the pale cabin walls. It dribbled thickly down the bulkheads and formed sinister, sticky pools on the light, carpeted floor. Steve's eyes followed the bloody gore around the cabin: there were violent, smeared streaks along the wooden desk and dark stains spattered over the soft green doona. The entire floor was covered in an indiscriminate crimson spray, accompanied by a few smudged footprints.

Steve snapped a couple of hurried photos of the grim scene, and lurched out of the cabin, letting out an explosive breath. He bustled around the corner to the surgery, and wordlessly handed the photos to the doctor, who was about to make some calls on the bridge.

Dr Gormly glanced at the few Polaroids Steve had taken.

'Yep – need some more,' he said curtly.

Steve opened his mouth, but a sharp look from the doctor told Steve this a was non-negotiable request.

So back into the cabin he went. The camera flashed and popped, and tongues of pale film appeared with a blink and whir. Finally, Steve returned to the surgery, clutching a handful of developing photos, waiting for Dr Gormly to return.

'We've got to go,' said Dr Gormly as he walked through the door. 'We've got to get back to Hobart as soon as possible, or this man will die.'

The doctor's words hung ominously in the room. The hairs on Steve's arms stood on end as he looked at Ross's pallid, blood-stained form lying motionless on the hospital bed.

There was no decision to make.

Steve turned and sprinted up the stairs to the bridge, running on equal parts fear and determination. He rushed past the expectant captain with a quick word, then disappeared into the radio room. He needed to call AAD headquarters for formal authorisation to break off the voyage. It was immediately given, the director confirming he'd been advised by Polar Medicine that a crew member was critically ill and needed urgent medical attention to survive.

Captain Peter turned as Steve emerged ashen-faced from the radio room and hurried over.

'We have to go back,' Steve said, panting. 'Now. At full speed if we can.'

Already expecting the order, Peter began turning the *Aurora* in a wide arc. He dialled the engine control room and commanded the engineers to flash up the *Aurora*'s second engine and bring it online as soon as possible.

Just fifteen minutes later the *Aurora* was racing back toward Hobart with both her engines blazing. She valiantly tore across the Southern Ocean, leaving a churning trail in her wake.

Downstairs in the *Aurora*'s surgery, Dr Gormly bustled around Ross's hospital bed. Ross had already lost a huge amount of blood. Such a catastrophic loss would almost certainly lead to shock; his blood pressure was already low and if it dropped much further his organs could begin to shut down or he could suffer a cardiac arrest. One thing was certain: Ross wouldn't survive the transit to hospital without blood transfusions to keep him alive.

Thanks to the stringent medical testing required of expeditioners and crew before Antarctic service, Dr Gormly already knew that several of the complement were close matches to Ross's blood type. The AAD had a 'walking blood bank' system, and Dr Gormly tapped each possible donor on the shoulder, asking if he could test them again to find Ross's most compatible match. All agreed without hesitation.

After some quick tests, it appeared that Chief Engineer Ross Jenkins was the closest match to McCallum's blood type. Dr Gormly quickly made Jenkins comfortable on the narrow consulting bed and hooked him up to a blood donor bag. The life-giving blood spiralled slowly down the tube into the bag, which the doctor held low to the floor. Over the next few days, Jenkins and the others all gave a number of donations. But the chief engineer gave more than most. He tried to keep Ross's spirits up with cheeky jokes and talk of paying back the blood debt with the equivalent volume of beer on their return home.

Meanwhile, all the rest of the complement could do was wait and hope their efforts would save Ross's life.

'So here we are,' wrote Steve in a letter to his parents, 'flying along at seventeen knots . . . with both engines on full and the ship juddering and bucking in a swell as we make for Hobart . . . Surprisingly, morale is extremely good and people are welcoming the chance to get ashore for a day.'

After taking three weeks to reach the ice edge, it took the *Aurora* just five short days to sprint back to Hobart – a record-breaking feat. Just before lunch on 4 April, the *Aurora* pulled up at Selfs Point, the refuelling station just up the Derwent River from the Hobart CBD.

Ross was carefully stretchered out of the *Aurora*'s external surgery doors, off the ship and into an ambulance waiting at the end of the pier.

On arrival at the hospital Ross had yet another horrific and bloody vomiting episode, but soon underwent surgery.

They had arrived just in time. Eventually, Ross made a full recovery.

With Ross safely in hospital, the voyage complement planned their return to Antarctica, hoping to continue the science program largely unaltered. In his typical laconic style, Steve wrote in his letter to his parents:

> One of the blessings in disguise is that we'll be able to pick up
> spare instruments for the oceanography in Hobart . . . Still,
> what with all the delays and comings and goings, it looks
> like we'll spend an extra week or so at sea. Not an auspicious
> debut for me as a VL is it? I did offer to ceremoniously fall

on my sword but they wouldn't hear of it so I'm stuck with
having to do the second leg of this voyage too.

But Steve still had to face the fallout from the loss of the CTD at
a meeting with the program leaders and AAD Director on board
the *Aurora*. Steve was stubbornly adamant: no-one was at fault,
he argued, procedures had been followed by both the AAD staff
and the crew. Every precaution had been taken. There was simply
no easy explanation for why the CTD dropped off like that, and
as a result no single person could be blamed.

It was clear that Steve had dug his heels in, and the meeting
swiftly moved on to discuss the plan for the remainder of the
voyage. There was still some ship time available for the research
program, but despite the AAD Director giving an additional three
days to the voyage, there was not enough time to conduct every
project.

'So I gave [my krill project] up,' Steve remembers. 'But it
rather took away my original reason for being on the ship in the
first place!'

Finally, Steve was free to go home to his family for the night.
The use of the CSIRO's brand new CTD had been approved, and
it would be brought onboard before departure, along with new
wire, spooling gear and some spare bottles.

Just after 6 am the following morning, the *Aurora* steamed once
again down the Derwent River. But it was now mid-autumn,
almost a full month after their original departure, and the Southern
Ocean greeted the *Aurora* with an even worse demeanour than
before. The voyagers endured days of stop–start operations as
squalls washed over them and, as they slowly moved south, the
weather maps showed that an intense low-pressure system was
barrelling in from the west.

By the time it reached the *Aurora*'s location on 14 April it was
a colossal, hurricane-force storm that sent leaden clouds boiling
across the sky. The mountainous, foam-streaked swells of the

Southern Ocean heaved and rolled like a leviathan's hide that towered threateningly above them one moment, then fell sharply away into oblivion the next. It sent the *Aurora* rolling drunkenly from side to side; and her bridge-wing windows staggered sickeningly between facing the ocean's surface and reeling up toward the dizzy heights of open sky.

Work was impossible. People sitting at desks were spat from their chairs and those working in labs were hurled mercilessly from bench to bench. As Steve later wrote to his parents:

Well, there I was at the helm, the wind ripping around us at 120 knots, the waves as big as small conurbations, the ship being thrown around like a (insert your own metaphor here) when I asked myself 'what would Captain Cook have done at a time like this?' Of course, I did what any sensible person who is scared witless by the sight of hurricane-force winds at sea would do – I went and lay down on my bunk, put my pillow over my head, my thumb in my mouth and hoped it would go away. This seemed to work as it <u>did</u> go away and we were able to continue our long journey into the frozen heart of the Antarctic winter.

After three days, the cyclonic gales had abated to a mere 35 knots, and the scientific work resumed. But the *Aurora* and her complement were regularly struck by more foul weather as they continued their slow transit across the Furious Fifties and Screaming Sixties. Steve and glaciologist Tony Worby passed much of the time the *Aurora* was 'hove to' playing cribbage down in the restaurant, alternating between grasping their cards, gripping the table and protecting their coffee mugs from sliding off the surface. The complement endured a number of disquieting safety musters on the helideck, while the *Aurora* seemed to buck and rear on the mountainous swell surging around her.

Finally, the anger of the Southern Ocean was tempered by the tranquillity of the Antarctic sea ice, as the oceanographic transect came to an end. The *Aurora*'s second engine was started, and Peter put her into icebreaking mode.

Steve looked out at the infinite expanse of water that was now dotted with low, lumpy floes and chunks of ice. The flat, frozen sea seemed alien to someone now all-too familiar with the mountainous seascape of the Southern Ocean.

As the *Aurora* continued to glide south, Steve decided to take advantage of the calm conditions and enjoy a brief immersion in the freezing wilderness. He climbed up the rungs of the ladder to the forecastle and emerged at the top, his breath steaming in the sharp, cold air. He fumbled with his camera, struggling to take off the lens cap with his gloved hands, then looked out at the pristine Antarctic wilderness.

A thin crust of dark nilas ice had formed on the motionless sea. Over the rail the wafer-thin shell gently bent over the rolling surface of the *Aurora*'s bow wave; but further out the near-transparent ice was unable to withstand the increasing pressure and it cracked, breaking into rectangular fingers that smoothly interlocked, silently sliding over and under each other. The *Aurora* passed through a patch where the crust was slightly thicker and lighter, and here the ice cracked with an audible snap, sending thin, dark fractures streaking away from the bow like lightning.

Before long, Steve's cheeks and nose began to feel the familiar, sharp nip of exposure, and he was goose-bumped under his freezer suit. His numb fingers were struggling to grip his camera, so Steve tucked it back into its case and threw the strap over his shoulder, content with his reacquaintance with the Antarctic landscape. It was time to go back up to the bridge and warm up.

By that afternoon, the ice floes were becoming thicker and more closely packed, and the *Aurora* began to shudder and lurch slightly as she made her way through them. As glaciologist Tony Worby stood chatting easily with Steve on the bridge, his eyes shone. It was time to start the glaciological part of the voyage.

A large flat ice floe several hundred metres across was chosen for the first of the sea ice studies. Using a steel man-cage connected below the large arm of the *Aurora*'s forward crane, Tony and his glaciologists were carefully lowered down onto the floe. Conspicuous against the blank canvas in their garish yellow freezer suits, they picked a site slightly away from the waiting man-cage then lifted a red ice corer – literally an oversized, hollow drill bit called a hand auger – to the vertical position. They took turns heaving with their backs, shoulders and arms, twisting the steel T-bar. The drill cut around a circular tube of ice as it progressed downward, and then came to a stop. Kneeling, the team heaved upward, freeing the ice from its former home. They walked around the floe, measuring thickness and temperature profiles of the ice, and taking snow samples from hastily dug snow pits. All of this information would be used to look at the age and origin of ice cover and help uncover the ecological role of sea ice in autumn.

While the sea ice team got on with their ice sampling, CSIRO biologist Peter and his assistants had been lowered onto the ice. They lifted their large brown hoop net and set off for the other side of the floe, where a resting crabeater seal had been spotted.

The aim of the seal project was to look at the movement patterns of the seals in the Antarctic sea ice, and to look at the seals' blood characteristics. To do this they would need to catch and sedate seals, then attach satellite trackers to the fur of two seals and take small blood samples from others. But unfortunately, the first seal never recovered from the anaesthetic administered to sedate it, and it died. Devastated, the lead researcher arranged for a post-mortem of the seal onboard the *Aurora Australis*.

Dr Gormly (also known as 'Dr Death' in such situations) conducted the post-mortem on the *Aurora*'s trawl deck, but the cause of the seal's death could not be definitively concluded. Tissue samples and measurements were taken for analysis back in Hobart.

The seal team is lowered over the side of the *Aurora* during WOES/WORSE voyage.

The *Aurora* sailed around the pack ice for a week, transiting between areas with thick ridged floes and areas with young pancaked sea ice, with the glaciologists enthusiastically taking samples at five-mile intervals by day and, with the aid of the *Aurora*'s powerful spotlights, by night. Helicopters flew overhead on transects to take aerial images and also to conduct ice reconnaissance missions; looking for 'leads' of open water within the ice, which would make the going easier for the *Aurora*.

They had another reason to look for open water within the pack ice. A new, world-first experiment was about to get underway.

The 'TADPOLE' – a modified, disarmed ex-military torpedo – was about to be deployed for its maiden Antarctic test run. Equipped with an upward-looking sonar that would sense sea ice thickness, the test was scheduled to run for about two minutes, with the torpedo running a small loop. The helicopters found a suitable lead nearby, and the ship headed for it.

VL Steve and Captain Peter watched from the bridge as a workboat towed the TADPOLE aft of the *Aurora*'s stern. The field scientist, Kelvin, received permission from the captain to conduct his experiment and, sitting on the small rubber boat with some of the *Aurora*'s crew, he released the torpedo and waited expectantly. After two minutes, however, neither the torpedo's elongated form or blinking light could be seen. The minutes ticked by.

Steve and Peter trained their eyes on the surrounding waters, but saw nothing. The helicopters, just returning to the ship from the sea ice array deployment, were tasked with circling the area to search from the air. But as time dragged on, Kelvin became increasingly nervous for his $35,000 piece of equipment, and he anxiously looked up and down the lead as night began to fall.

About ten minutes later, Kelvin's radio hissed, and the bridge relayed that a blinking light could be seen under some thin ice not too far from the ship. The torpedo was located and then lifted back on board as the last of the daylight faded from the sky.

The following day, the seal team returned onto the ice. Two crabeater seals had been spotted on a floe which was to also be sampled by the glaciologists. Unfortunately, the second attempt at anaesthesia resulted in the same ill-fated conclusion as the first, with one seal very slow to come out of the anaesthetic and the other dying. The lead biologist's voice was clearly shocked as he radioed back to the bridge that a second seal had died. Like many who worked in conservation, he had great affection for his subjects. Devastated at the deaths of two seals, he called veterinary experts back in Hobart to ask for their guidance.

On their advice, the dosage rates for the seals were reduced. The next day, the helicopters spotted five seals on a floe not too far from the ship, and the ship made her way over to them. The ice and seal teams were once again lifted down onto the football field–sized floe.

Thankfully, the captures and anaesthesia went well. The satellite tags were carefully glued to the short, thick fur of two seals. However, the seals were frisky under such light sedation, and the weighing and measuring had to be halted as it was becoming unsafe for the scientists to handle the increasingly conscious seals.

Over the next few days, the sea ice sampling from the ship continued successfully, and the science team even had a chance to trawl for krill, with no success. However, Captain Peter and Steve were becoming wary: the pack ice was now starting to consolidate. The floes were several hundred metres in length, and the pack was becoming harder and harder for the *Aurora* to penetrate.

On 3 May, the day after Steve's 40th birthday, the *Aurora* reached another large lead in the pack ice, which otherwise stretched uninterrupted from horizon to horizon. Kelvin was keen to deploy the TADPOLE once again, but Steve had his reservations.

'Conditions were not ideal,' he wrote in his VL report, 'as there were many patches of ice on the surface of the lead and ice was continually forming on the surface and the lead was not as large as might have been desired.'

But Kelvin was adamant, and Steve consented. It was Kelvin's gear, and his choice.

This time, the torpedo was programmed to conduct a three kilometre round trip in a large loop that would begin and end in the lead. The TADPOLE was soon lowered down to the waiting workboat, which puttered through the newly forming grease ice to a spot just behind the ship.

Steve and Peter stood on the bridge, Steve listening with interest at the operations and the captain waiting patiently for the request for the launch to take place. The next thing they knew, Kelvin's voice sounded over the bridge radio notifying the ship that the torpedo had been set loose.

Peter's jaw dropped, and a vein began to throb on his forehead. They'd done what?

'There's a f#%king torpedo!' Steve remembers the captain exclaiming over the radio. 'And you've fired a torpedo off near my ship, without telling me!'

Horrified at the thought of an ex-military torpedo circling unseen and uncontrolled in the immediate vicinity of his ship, Peter hastily motored the *Aurora* out of the firing line to a point about a kilometre from the launch site.

Twenty minutes later, all eyes were trained on the thin strip of open water, waiting for the TADPOLE to resurface. But the minutes ticked by without sight or sound of the metal contraption. The torpedo's radio beacon, sonar transducer and distress light were silent and invisible.

The short Antarctic day was coming to a close, and Steve and a still-seething Peter quickly organised a search for the torpedo using the workboat, the *Aurora*, and the two helicopters. But after two hours the search was abandoned. It was clear that the torpedo was not in the open water of the lead but had absconded to an unknown location, probably under the ice.

'Torpedo lost below the Antarctic ice' chortled a headline in *The Canberra Times* after the voyage's return, relating the story and the 'red faces' on board.

'The torpedo itself did not matter,' noted the article. 'It was one of two disarmed and obsolete pieces the Navy sold to the Antarctic Division for $150 each. It was the valuable equipment attached to the torpedo which made for a fair amount of wincing when the craft "did an Optus satellite" and vanished.'

Steve rubbed his forehead. He'd thought Voyage 9 had been bad enough, but Voyage 9.1 had gone from bad to worse.

Thankfully, over the next few days, the scientific focus returned to the more routine work. The *Aurora* remained in the same lead, while the sea ice team puttered around in the workboat or dangled from the man-cage beneath the crane, collecting pancake ice that was forming on the open water. Another seal appeared and was successfully captured, with simple measurements such as length and weight taken.

They had neared the end of the research program, and, according to Steve:

> . . . just as the clock was running out and people were jockeying for position to claim the last few hours of our allotted time, the weather got a bit ominous, the choppers were grounded and the captain made noises about wanting to be well out of the ice before the storm hit.

The *Aurora* was some eighty miles south of the ice edge, and Captain Peter knew that under pressures from the storm, the pack ice could close in and trap, or worse, crush the *Aurora* under the monumental pressures of its vast weight. It was best to be out of the region before the storm hit. Steve agreed and, as the science field programs officially concluded, Peter turned the *Aurora* north.

But while the *Aurora* had easily cut through the ice in the area just days before, she now struggled to make her way through the pack, even with both engines blazing on full power. As predicted, the winds steadily increased, and by the time they cleared the ice, the sea had been whipped into a heaving frenzy by sixty knot winds.

Once again, the *Aurora*'s windscreen wipers swung frantically across the bridge windows, but their efforts were in vain. The sleet, sea spray and low cloud combined forces, forming an impenetrable visual barrier beyond the orange bow of the ship. Peter grimly gripped the wooden rail in front of the radar screen. They were still moving through an area where large floes occasionally appeared on the radar, and the seas were increasingly heavy. With the low visibility and treacherous conditions there was little to do but heave to. Peter put the *Aurora* on a north-easterly heading, making the turbulent ride as comfortable as possible for those down below, and kept the *Aurora* slowly heading into the wind while he and his officers watched the radar screens like hawks, looking for stray chunks of glacial ice.

Meanwhile, with every rise and fall of the *Aurora*'s bow, sea spray whipped over the ship.

They were only just north of the ice edge and, in the subzero temperatures of the Antarctic autumn, the spray and sleet almost instantly solidified on the *Aurora*'s steel surfaces. The *Aurora*'s foredeck became encrusted in a layer of ice, and icicles dripped from the rails like fine teeth. A white shell encrusted the crane and foremast, then thickened to a solid armour. Snowdrifts piled up in corners and against bulkheads. Peter wrote in the captain's report that the entire ship was blanketed by a metre of ice and snow. But it was thickest at the bow, where up to two metres of the rock-hard ice clung to the inside of the port-side rail. The steel staircase leading down to the foredeck was 'completely encased in solid ice'.

But the 'weather gods' free freight' as Peter put it, while spectacular, was causing serious problems for the *Aurora* and her captain. Peter estimated there was now approximately three hundred tonnes of ice and snow frozen to the ship, and the *Aurora* was struggling under this mighty weight. She was riding much lower at the bow than usual, and was heavy and lethargic in the swell. Peter removed three hundred tonnes of ballast water from the *Aurora*'s forepeak and the ship straightened once again.

When the storm finally subsided she resumed her course for Hobart on a relatively even keel, faintly resembling an iceberg herself. But it was two full days before the ice melted enough for the crew to access the front of the ship to assist with ice removal, and they were four days into the transit north before the last of the ice melted away.

Meanwhile, as they motored north and the meltwater still streamed out of the scuppers over the *Aurora*'s side, Steve sat at his desk writing up his VL's report.

Despite the twin voyages living up to their newly dubbed nicknames of WOES (conveniently fitting the acronym Wildlife Oceanography Ecosystem Survey) and WORSE (Wildlife Oceanography Retry Survey of Ecosystem), they had actually compiled a satisfying list of achievements. The two WOCE oceanography sections had been completed; these two CTD sections were now among the most detailed transects ever completed across the Southern Ocean, even though 'nearly six weeks of continuous CTDs put a strain on both the scientific party and on the crew.' The glaciologists had achieved many of their objectives, including collecting 29 ice cores, 91 snow samples, and seventeen nilas and pancake ice samples, as well as deploying some drifting ice buoys. The voyage had shown that it was possible to work in newly forming ice within the pack in autumn, and it 'gave valuable insights into the ecology of the region in autumn and clues for possible future operations in this zone'. Added to that, a new communications technology called 'email' that had been introduced to the ship had been hugely successful; the once-a-night link-up allowed scientists daily contact with their offices in Australia without ANARE 'Big Brother' monitoring every faxed communication to and from their icebreaker.

As for the *Aurora* and her crew, Steve wrote with satisfaction:

The ship proved once again that it is a world-class platform for oceanographic research in a hostile environment . . . The success of this voyage in trying circumstances can be attributed to a large extent to the professionalism and good humour of the officers and crew of the *Aurora Australis*. Not to be outdone, however, the scientific party managed to maintain their morale and good cheer in the face of long hours, major setbacks and unpleasant weather and this made the job of voyage management comparatively simple. A special thanks should go to our Italian colleagues, Dr Giancarlo Spezie and Dr Giorgio Budillon who lent an international flavour to the voyage and whose irrepressible good cheer and incomparable sauces lifted us up when we were down.

Nevertheless, just a year after the success of WOES and WORSE, the *Aurora Australis* was faced with tragedy. In June 1994, while the *Aurora* was 'on the blocks' undergoing routine maintenance in dry dock at Garden Island, a powerful explosion ripped across the wharf, rattling windows across neighbouring suburbs of Sydney and sending a dark column of smoke into the sky. Four oxyacetylene cylinders had exploded in their container on the dock, right next to the *Aurora Australis*.

The massive fireball blasted the *Aurora*'s side, causing crew working on the helideck above to reel back from a vertical wall of fire boiling up her flank. As dust and shards of metal rained down onto the deck, the shaken crew picked themselves up, peered over the rails and were horrified to see a dozen people lying motionless, their bodies strewn across the wharf.

In the chaotic minutes that followed, first responders arrived and began to check over the injured. Two people were quickly whisked to hospital. Shortly after, shocking news began to filter through that the *Aurora*'s chief engineer, Ross Jenkins, had been caught up in the explosion and had tragically lost his life.

Ross Jenkins was the very same man who, just one year before, had so selflessly given blood donations to his critically ill crewmate Ross McCallum. The same good-humoured man who had affectionately joked about the repayment of a blood debt in equal volumes of beer.

The loss was felt deeply. The entire Antarctic community, from fellow crew members to expeditioners, to staff at P&O and AAD headquarters, was devastated. News of this shocking accident even reached the highest levels of the Australian government. Senator Paul Calvert, who was at a senate estimate committee that met just days later, began the meeting sadly:

. . . I would like to pass on my condolences to the family of the chief engineer of *Aurora Australis*, Ross Jenkins. I was as shocked as everybody else to hear of the unfortunate accident that happened in Sydney. I know it was not related to the *Aurora Australis*. I understand that it was just bad luck that he happened to be in the wrong place at the wrong time.

Senator John Faulkner, usually more used to having opposing views to Calvert, solemnly agreed:

> Obviously those sentiments are shared by myself, as minister, and by the whole department, particularly the Antarctic Division. This is an extraordinarily sad occurrence and I appreciate Senator Calvert's making those comments. I want myself and the division and the department to be associated with it.

The force of the blast had not damaged the *Aurora*, but she wore the stark, blackened mark of the explosion like a mourning band. Days later, the *Aurora* came off dry dock and returned to Hobart, her tightly-knit community emotionally battered and bruised.

Over the next four years, the *Aurora* conducted almost a dozen Antarctic and Southern Ocean marine science voyages, many of which were groundbreaking in their scientific achievements. Despite his good-natured protestations to the contrary, Steve Nicol even returned to lead three more ambitious voyages on the *Aurora*, 'some of which' he adds 'were quite successful'. The tradition of giving the voyages informal nicknames continued, and voyages such as THIRST (Third Heard Island Research Survey Trip), ABSTAIN (A Brave Science Trip Amidst Ice at Night) and BROKE (Baseline Research on Oceanography, Krill and the Environment) were successfully conducted, with the voyage acronyms and meanings aptly summing up the experience of each expedition. The *Aurora*'s scientific accomplishments continued to mount as her teams worked together in good humour and harmony.

But the skill of the *Aurora*'s complement would be tested to the limits, under the most terrifying of circumstances.

Chapter Five

FIRE AND ICE

On a grey winter's afternoon, the Hobart sky was rapidly fading to dusk and hundreds of people, rugged up to the eyeballs in scarves and beanies, braved the chilly Princes Wharf to warmly farewell their loved ones and coworkers. It was 15 July 1998 and the *Aurora* was departing for a rare winter marine science voyage; briefly taking her charges to the wave-lashed subantarctic shores of Macquarie Island, then on to the Antarctic 'oasis' of the Mertz Glacier polynya.

POLYNYAS: THE ICE FACTORIES OF ANTARCTICA

Polynyas are year-round, ice-free areas of water that are caused by the howling Antarctic katabatic winds blowing off the vast ice sheets of the frozen continent. They are essentially ice factories: as ice forms on the water's surface, it is soon blown seaward by the fierce winds. The water that remains uncovered by ice is extremely salty, cold and dense and it sinks to the depths of the ocean floor, generating huge underwater currents that circulate cold oxygen and nutrient-rich Antarctic water to many of the world's ocean basins. Because of their wide-reaching effects, Antarctic polynyas are considered key parts of Earth's climatic system.

The Mertz Glacier polynya was a frigid lake-like body of water surrounded by winter pack ice, closely related to the immense Mertz Glacier tongue present at that time (the Mertz Glacier tongue broke off in 2010 and moved westward into the polynya area, subsequently shutting down much of the polynya's activity). In 1998 the scientists on board the *Aurora Australis* were going to combine oceanography and glaciology studies to examine the Mertz Glacier polynya's icemaking and water current–generating processes. At the same time, biologists were going to examine the polynya's value as a feeding haven for whales, seals, penguins and birds during wintertime. Expectations and excitement around the voyage were high, and on departure day the atmosphere at Princes Wharf was electric.

Jane Stevens, a reporter for Discovery Channel Online, looked with delight on the departure scene before her. It was her first voyage on board the *Aurora Australis*. After eight years of the *Aurora* coming and going from Hobart, the icebreaker's departure had developed its own colourful ritual, and this send-off was no different. As the gangway was raised, colourful streamers were once again tossed down to friends and family standing below. The *Aurora*'s horn boomed over the wharves, cafés and government buildings of the Hobart waterfront, loudly announcing her imminent departure. But the *Aurora*'s thunderous refrain was immediately joined by a high-pitched drone, and Jane turned, surprised, as the melodic airs of highland bagpipes erupted from the rear of the ship. Two pipers, Graham Hosie and Neil Holbrook, on board for the voyage, were bidding their bittersweet farewell to Hobart.

Two days later, the *Aurora* was in the thick of the Furious Fifties and was rolling heavily in five metre swells. The formidable Southern Ocean had taken its toll and many expeditioners were confined to their cabins. Jane was among them. She noted in her blog, 'I'm actually hoping for rougher seas – these large, even heavy swells are just too discombobulating.' But now, just as sick of being cooped up in her cabin for 48 hours as she was from the motion of the ship, she tentatively ventured to the bridge for a glimpse of the horizon.

The calm, relaxed atmosphere on the bridge was in sharp contrast to the ferocity of the weather outside. The *Aurora* pitched skyward then plunged down into the huge swells, but some of the hardier expeditioners laughed as they tried to get a well-timed snapshot of a 'blue water' wave washing over the bow. Cruisy, easy-listening music emanated from the stereo, and the captain, Tony Hansen, a sturdy surfer-type with a relaxed demeanour and good-natured smile, sat casually in his chair at the helm. Pale-faced, Jane tottered unsteadily up to the windows. Tony turned in his chair and cheerily chatted to Jane in an attempt to take her mind off her queasiness. It didn't help. Jane gripped a handrail to steady herself and inwardly thanked god for seasickness pills. It was time to go and lie down again.

Jane was sharing a cabin with Barbara Wienecke, a German-raised penguin biologist with a ready smile and, as Jane put it, 'one of the three great laughs of the ship'. Barb's laugh was indeed unmistakable: it was raucous, gleeful and extraordinarily infectious. Barb was a seasoned expeditioner who had worked in many isolated locations with her beloved seabirds. But Jane was envious for another reason; Barb was completely unfazed by the perpetual motion of the rolling ship.

The *Aurora* approached the rugged green slopes of Macquarie Island on the morning of 18 July. The island had been battered by the winds that had also been assaulting the *Aurora*, and the 'green sponge', as it was affectionately known, had received a white dusting of snow overnight. The *Aurora* took shelter from the winds and anchored in the lee of the island's tabular plateau. The sudden reprieve from the motion was welcome; the glorious stability instantly reviving the expeditioners.

Flying conditions were rapidly improving and the *Aurora*'s helicopters were swiftly rolled onto the helideck and bladed up. Expeditioners smiled and waved through the chopper windows as they were flown off the *Aurora* in small groups, followed by the cargo. Pallets of rubbish were returned from the island for disposal in Australia and, after just eight hours of feverish helicopter operations, the resupply was complete. In all, twelve expeditioners left the *Aurora* and one passenger from the island base joined the ship for the long trip home.

The remaining expeditioners affectionately farewelled the green sponge from the helideck as Captain Tony slowly manoeuvred the *Aurora* away from the island, turning the vessel south, toward the ice edge.

Thankfully, sea conditions had improved for the *Aurora*'s transit to Antarctica. The clear steel-blue water receded rapidly under the *Aurora*'s bow as she motored her way smoothly across the Southern Ocean. The endless expanse of glinting water was at first awe-inspiring for the newer sightseers on the bridge, but after a day or so of unvarying scenery the vista soon fell into tedium. As with most voyages, daytime entertainment for the expeditioners was provided in the form of albatross soaring gracefully around the ship, but even the majestic seabirds appeared somewhat bored with the climatic tranquillity, which was not conducive to effortless gliding. Shortly after inquisitively joining the ship, they would break away from the *Aurora*'s meagre updraft, elegantly descending to the water – almost skimming the surface with their outspread wing tips – and skid to an ungainly halt in a feet-first splashdown. They folded their wings and settled on the water with a hint of miffed disdain.

As the *Aurora* made her transit south, planning meetings were held by the research teams on board and evening science presentations were given. Ian Allison, VL and lead glaciologist, explained in detail the polynya project, and Nathan Bindoff (the owner of another of Jane's 'three great laughs of the ship') gave a presentation on the oceanographic program. The *Aurora*'s bar, having been renamed the 'Husky Bar' about four years earlier in honour of Australia's beloved husky dogs, was also a lively locale in the evenings, where people gathered within the now photo-clad walls; happily laughing, chatting and dancing amid images of Australia's faithful and beloved Antarctic huskies.

Then, on 21 July, the endless expanse of blue water was abruptly mottled with white clusters of slushy brash ice, followed by thin bands of opaque new ice that streaked along the water's surface. By day's end the patches of icy cover merged and extended far beyond the horizon. In the distance, towering icebergs loomed out of the dwindling daylight. The anticipation on board was palpable – they were nearing the sea ice zone and the research teams were eager to get their science programs started.

The *Aurora* reached the first research position in the dead of an Antarctic winter's night. The first operation of the voyage was an extravehicular excursion: some of the scientists were going to be lowered onto an ice floe to deploy a tracking buoy on its surface, to track the location of the ice as it moved and aged. Given that it was the first landing of the voyage, the *Aurora*'s officers and scientists had chosen an ice floe several hundred metres in diameter – it was flat, white and uniform; remarkable only in its unremarkableness. The *Aurora* was parked alongside it with her hull resting gently against the ice. The hatch covers opened to lift three orange ice buoys onto the deck. The three-person ice team stepped into the waiting man-cage underneath the crane's raised arm. They were lifted over the side of the ship at midnight with one of the buoys, in the pitch black and biting cold.

The ice team weren't the only ones excited by the activity over the side. Biologist Barbara Wienecke watched with delight from the roof or 'monkey' deck above the bridge. The ice floe beneath the ship was illuminated by the *Aurora*'s blazing spotlights; the bright snow and ice dazzling against the jet-black backdrop. Slightly awkward in their puffy freezer suits, the researchers moved cautiously around the icy stage, taking measurements and setting up the buoy. Barb was fascinated. It was glorious to watch; but god – it was freezing out here! Despite her layers of thermal clothing, freezer suit, gloves and boots, Barb was chilled to the bone. As she watched, she paced the deck to ward off the cold, her breath a suspended frozen mist.

Barb remained outside, riveted by the performance before her, until she realised she could no longer feel her hands. Thankfully the ice team were winding up and everything looked well under control. She clunked her way carefully down the metal stairs, very much looking forward to defrosting in her bunk.

Barb found Jane still awake in her bed; she too had been in thrall of the operations on the ice and had been watching from the bridge. Barb slid into her own bunk and cocooned herself inside her doona, the spreading warmth positively luxurious after the bitterness outside. After a drowsy chat the cabin-mates both sank gratefully into sleep.

By now, the ice team had been lifted back on board and the *Aurora* had left the first research site, carefully moving through the ice-laden waters to the next waypoint. The bright spotlights extending before her glittered with minute ice flecks suspended in the frosty air. It was just after 1 am.

An angry buzz erupted in a cabin upstairs. Third Engineer Robert Cave woke with a start; it was his shift as engineer on-call and his repeater panel was indicating a noncritical alarm from the engine room. He silenced the alarm and skipped quickly down the four flights of stairs to the engine control room.

The main control panel showed the alarm was caused by a minor issue with the bilge. Rob dutifully pumped the bilge, rectified the problem and made a quick lap of the engine room. All was in order, so he climbed the stairs, went to his cabin and fell back into his bed.

Twenty minutes later another noncritical alarm noisily sounded in his cabin. Rob threw off his covers with an oath.

He silenced the buzzer and was on his way out of the cabin when it sounded once more. He silenced it again, then hastily wound his way down the stairs.

But this time, as Rob stepped through the doorway his stomach lurched: the engine room was filled with a thin haze of white smoke. He dashed to the control panel, searching for an answer. Both engine alarms were oil-related. 'That's smoke and oil,' Rob thought, his pulse quickening. Rob reached out to the phone and dialled the number for the bridge.

'Bridge,' came Second Mate Scott Laughlin's voice down the line.

'Pull it back, I think there might be a fire!' Rob exclaimed. Scott immediately took all ways off and the heavy orange ship slowly drifted to a halt among the loose ice.

Rob quickly clunked down the steep metal stairs of the engine room, wanting to check the engines down on the lowest level. But even as he arrived on the platform deck (a mid-level mezzanine deck between the engine control room and the engine level, which extended around the outside of the engine room), he could see flames rising viciously around the turbo chargers of the port-side engine below. 'Shit! Why aren't the bloody fire alarms sounding?' He raced back up to the control room to call the bridge.

Suddenly, the fire bells erupted with an ear-splitting peal, resounding around the decks of the *Aurora Australis*.

Most of the ship's complement were asleep in their bunks and awoke in startled confusion. What was going on? Was it a false alarm? What were they supposed to do? Captain Tony Hansen knew instantly, however, that the shrill alarm meant something was seriously wrong. He leapt out of his bed and threw on some clothes. At least he couldn't smell any smoke, he thought to himself, as he dashed up the single flight of stairs to the bridge. Scott turned as Tony flung the bridge door open.

'There's a fire in the engine room,' Scott said to his captain briskly. 'I've stopped the engines.' Scott stepped aside as Captain Hansen immediately took command of his ship, releasing

Scott to conduct his muster duty, which meant coordinating the fire team. By now, a dozen engine warning alarms were also anxiously wailing on the indicator panel at the rear of the bridge, joining the deafening din of the ship's main alarm.

Meanwhile, Rob had descended to the very bottom of the hazy engine room. He knew that oil would be a further source of fuel for the fire, so he edged his way down to the oil pumps – which were immediately forward of the engine-high flames – and shut them off at their starter boxes. Just metres from the fire, Rob now realised that diesel fuel was spraying down on him from somewhere, the stinking liquid falling like rain onto his orange overalls and the area directly behind where he was standing. The engine room was rapidly filling with dark grey smoke, and visibility had dropped to about six metres. Rob fled back up to the control room, his adrenaline pumping.

On D deck, Barb rolled in her bunk and pulled the doona over her head. Sleepy, Barb hadn't quite registered that the shrill noise was a fire alarm; having been so cold earlier she just wanted to stay warm, thank you very much, despite whatever racket decided to infiltrate from the hallway. Jane, however, got up. She opened the cabin door and peered into the hall, wondering what to do. She saw some expeditioners rushing toward the back stairwell that led up to the helideck. Suddenly, the fire alarm stopped, and Jane stood still, uncertain. She jumped as the bells pierced the silence again; the relentless ring of the fire alarm replaced now by the more raucous general alarm: seven short and one long ring of the ship's bells, repeated over and over. It sounded throughout the ship.

Suddenly, the captain's voice came over the PA system: 'Attention please, there is a small fire in the engine room. Please muster to the helideck.'

Spurred into action, Jane hurried back to her slumbering cabin-mate, shaking her.

'Barb. Barb! Everyone is running down the corridor, we need to get up!'

To Jane's relief Barb's eyes flew open and she rolled out of her bunk. They both knew – thanks to the safety briefings at the start of each voyage – that the biggest threat to any ship, besides sinking, is fire. They had already lost valuable seconds and it now seemed to take an eternity to get dressed. Barb jumped into her freezer suit, simultaneously stuffing spare socks and gloves into the pockets, while Jane donned several layers of clothes. They grabbed their boots and lifejackets and hurried out of the cabin. At the last instant Jane turned, snatching her flashlight off the shelf, just in case. Together they bolted for the rear stairwell and up to their muster station on the helideck.

As the pair stepped onto the snow-covered deck they were confronted with dark hulking figures in full firefighting gear, their breathing apparatus prepped and ready. Jane and Barb hurriedly joined the expeditioners gathered under the bright deck spotlights. The ominous smell of smoke hung over the deck. Barb looked at the uncertain figures clustered around her. She immediately noticed that quite a few people hadn't brought their freezer suits. Or socks, she realised in astonishment, looking down at the feet of one of her already shivering colleagues. Barb handed him a pair that she'd stuffed into her pocket. He was wearing just jeans, a jumper and shoes, in this cold! She could feel the temperature had dropped even further than during her midnight sojourn outside; it was now minus fifteen Celsius. 'Hopefully we won't be out here in the snow too long,' she thought to herself, worried, as Kieren Jacka began the rollcall for their muster group.

In the engine control room, Rob had successfully shut down the main engine fuel supply to stop spread of the fire, but that also meant the ship's generators would soon be starved of fuel. He needed to switch the generators to their auxiliary fuel supply before they too shut down, cutting power to the ship. Rob's anxious thoughts were interrupted as Chief Engineer Jimmy Mackenzie and First Engineer Phillip Kennedy burst into the control room. Rob hurriedly explained the situations with the fire and the generators. Jimmy's eyes widened in alarm.

Without these generators the ship would be completely dead in the water! The Scotsman rushed out, raced down to the bottom level of the engine room and switched the fuel supply.

Rob and Phillip immediately followed. Rob stopped at the platform deck and grabbed a portable foam monitor from the wall to attack the fire below. Phillip seized a fire extinguisher and went toward a ladder at the opposite side of the engines. Standing just above and behind the engines on the starboard side, Phil could see flaming cinders dripping from the turbo chargers and flames rising from the bilge below. He aimed his extinguisher at the flames and let fly.

Hearts pounding, the two engineers resolutely fought the blaze. The fire was grudgingly beaten back by the dual onslaught, then finally the flames were extinguished altogether. The engine room was now filled with choking black smoke and the stench of diesel fuel. But the extraction fans were helping draw the smoke up and outside, and Rob, relieved the fire was out, went down to the bottom of the engine room to find some clearer air. Phillip walked around the platform deck at the front of the engines, finishing off his extinguisher as he went. He met Jimmy about halfway along the port side of the engine and told him that the fire was out.

With a thunderous roar, an explosion tore through the engine room. Seconds later, the *Aurora*'s lights flickered and went out.

Tony Hansen felt and heard the dull thump of the explosion on the bridge. He looked up as the ship went dark, but saw nothing except a momentary glimmer of snow hitting the windows as the lights on the bridge flickered, and went out again. His mind raced as fear and doubt set in. They were isolated, in the ice, in subzero temperatures and the ship was on fire and without power. He drew a steadying breath, pushing his feelings aside.

His first obligation was to keep the people on board his ship safe. Numbers and scenarios continued through his head. There were 79 souls on board, with, as far as he knew, three crew at the scene of an explosion. They were about one hundred nautical miles from the French Antarctic station, Dumont d'Urville. The best chance at extinguishing an engine-room fire was to deploy halon gas, which was a standard firefighting system in ship engine rooms: it fights fire in a chemical reaction that breaks the chain between ignition source, fuel and oxygen. It is an effective firefighting medium, but causes toxic fumes once exposed to the heat of a fire, so the engine room would need to be cleared of personnel first. Halon is also a one-shot system; they would have one chance, and one chance only, to extinguish the fire using the gas.

On the helideck, the expeditioners were also plunged into darkness. Barb heard a few startled cries of alarm, then nothing but an eerie silence as the group silently struggled with their thoughts. The pitch-dark sky and sea had merged, surrounding them; the snowy lumps and rafts of ice around the ship had disappeared into inky obscurity. The *Aurora* hung helplessly, suspended in the dark void of an Antarctic night that was suddenly vast and overwhelming. One thing was abundantly clear to them all: their vibrant sanctuary, the *Aurora* – always comfortingly lit, always gently humming – was now a lifeless speck adrift in the immense Antarctic wilderness. Fear and uncertainty bore down on them from the immeasurable blackness.

After a few stunned moments Barb realised she could hear the sea ice groan as floes jostled and rubbed against the side of the ship.

'Don't panic, ladies and gentlemen, please stay together and we'll be just fine,' Les Morrow's blessedly calm, authoritative voice came out of the shadows. The unflappable third mate had been sent to the helideck by the captain to take control of the passengers. Les instructed the expeditioners to cluster together close to the hangar, to give them some shelter from the breeze. He then directed those in warmer clothes to huddle around those without enough warm clothing on.

Just like penguins, Jane noted to herself as they all bunched together mutely in the darkness. Shivering, Jane switched on her flashlight and handed it to Kieren. The rollcall began again.

In the engine room, Jimmy and Phillip reeled back from the fireball. Jimmy glanced down at the engines, the forward end of which were completely obscured by flames. This new fire was huge and clearly beyond their ability to fight without help. But where was Rob? The flames were rising now, spewing more smoke into the already suffocating engine room. There was no choice but to retreat, and Jimmy and Phillip fled the engine room, climbing a ladder to the rear watertight door on the level above. Once outside, Jimmy urgently messaged the bridge that he and Phillip were safely out of the engine room, but that Rob was missing.

Jimmy, hoping that Rob had somehow made it past the fire to the engine control room, hastily made his way inside the *Aurora* toward the main entrance of the engine room. At the bottom of the central stairwell he found First Mate Peter Dunbar, standing outside the engine room door with an IR, Jason, who was wearing breathing apparatus. Jimmy placed the back of his hand on the door. It was cool. He cracked the door open and shone a light through the dense black smoke. He could just make out the door of the control room three metres away.

'Go in and make sure Rob's not in there,' Jimmy instructed Jason. Jimmy waited nervously as Jason made his way inside.

'It's empty,' Jason finally reported from the depths of his mask. He lumbered back out of the engine room and they quickly sealed the door behind him.

Upstairs, Second Mate Scott heard Peter Dunbar's voice crackle over the radio: Rob was still missing, but he was not in the engine control room and they hoped he was evacuating by the shaft tunnel at the rear of the engine room. Scott knew the shaft tunnel ends with a vertical escape trunk that eventually emerges on the trawl deck. Concerned, he radioed the bridge and told them he would check the tunnel exit and make sure Rob was safe. He hurried down to the trawl deck.

The trawl deck was dark and eerily silent. There was no sign of Rob at the escape exit. Scott waited a moment, then opened the hatch and climbed down the ladder into the shaft tunnel. It was smoky, but he could see well enough through the haze with his torch. He walked swiftly forward, looking down into the bilges below to make sure Rob hadn't fallen in there. At the forward end of the shaft tunnel, Scott saw that the watertight door to the engine room was open. Now he was worried. Rob would have shut it, surely, if he'd come through.

Scott stepped through the hatch into the burning engine room.

The scene inside was apocalyptic. The engine room was full of dense black smoke. Flames, barely visible through the pall, were still burning fiercely at the forward end of the port engine. Scott raised his radio, calling the bridge – they might know where Rob was by now. But there was no response. 'It's the steel,' Scott remembered, 'it screens the radio down here.' He frantically searched the area around the back of the engines, squinting through the smoke. 'Christ,' Scott thought. 'Where is he?' Coughing, Scott retreated back to the watertight door. He stood there, staring intently into the smoke and flames, hoping for a sign of his friend. 'He must be out,' Scott hoped to himself. After a minute or so he heaved the watertight door closed, winding the manual winch to seal the hydraulic door, and made his way back through the shaft tunnel and up the trunk ladder. 'Please be out,' he thought repeatedly as he climbed.

Minutes earlier, behind the engines, Rob had recoiled in shock at the intensity of the explosion. He saw the flames erupt upward – enveloping the platform deck where Jimmy and Phillip had been standing – and realised the inferno completely cut him off from the ladder leading up to the platform deck. Rob turned and ran straight for the watertight door behind the engines, knowing it was his only chance for escape. But as he stepped through the hatch, the *Aurora*'s lights sputtered, and went out. For a heart-stopping instant Rob was completely blind.

Then the dull glow of the battery-powered emergency lighting softly illuminated the shadows – but it was fading fast. Thinking now only of escape, Rob bolted along the rapidly dimming shaft tunnel. He seized the trunk ladder and climbed for his life. Halfway up the ladder Rob realised with horror that he'd left the shaft tunnel's watertight door open behind him. But there was no way he was going back down there without breathing apparatus. He hauled himself onto the unlit trawl deck and groped his way to the forward accommodation door. Unbeknownst to him, Scott had just arrived via the wet lab onto the trawl deck.

As Scott's head emerged above the hatch his radio hissed to life. Rob was safe. Scott exhaled as he felt the weight lift from his shoulders. He radioed the bridge, telling them he'd sealed the aft watertight door to the engine room. On the bridge Captain Tony also breathed easier. All personnel were clear of the engine room.

But the fire was still raging.

The ship's musters were complete and all expeditioners were accounted for; but two crew members were still missing from the crew muster. Dunbar quickly mounted a search, beginning with crew cabins on C deck. Each of the missing crew were found sleeping soundly in their cabins – one wearing earplugs – completely oblivious to the unfolding crisis. Almost laughing in relief, Dunbar quickly shook them awake before calling the bridge: all personnel were now accounted for.

Captain Tony immediately gave the order for the halon to be released. Les, having heard the order on his radio, turned to his knot of expeditioners on the helideck and, as Barb Wienecke put it, 'calm as a cucumber [Les] said "Ladies and gentlemen, the halon will be released. May I please ask you to step back as far as possible because it could get a bit whiffy."'

A number of moans of dismay arose from the group, but they obediently shuffled to the rear of the helideck. The captain's voice came over Les's radio, counting down to the release of halon. Chief Engineer Jimmy, now also on the bridge, raised his hand to the halon control panel. Three. Two. One.

Zero. Jimmy released the halon.

Jane's thoughts turned to her husband as a putrid 'sticky sweet' stench fouled the air over the helideck. She could just make out thick clouds of smoke or halon – or both – rising from the ship's exhaust stack. The helideck was silent as they waited, thinking of loved ones and imagining the scene in the engine room; all hoping – praying – that the halon would work.

On the bridge, having unleashed the ship's main line of defence, Tony now focused on the next task at hand. Their situation was still critical and no-one outside of this ship currently knew anything about their ordeal. He turned to Ian Moodie, the deck communications officer. 'Issue a mayday,' Tony instructed Ian resolutely. A mayday is the most urgent of all the distress signals, one that is strictly reserved for situations of a grave and imminent threat to a ship.

But the bridge was still without power, as was its satellite phone. Ian hurried back to the radio room at the rear of the bridge, flicked on the emergency light and searched the racks and desk. Everything, including the satellite phones and radios, was dead. Instead, Ian set to work preparing the battery-operated emergency radio. It was a short-wave transmitter and right now it was their only hope for communication with the outside world.

On the helideck, the crew began to lower the life boats. Barb heard another whimper of dread as their lifeboat swung into the torchlight; but, ever their rock, Les spoke comfortingly, assuring the expeditioners that the captain had ordered the craft to be lowered as a precautionary measure only, and there was no cause for further alarm.

Nevertheless, as Jane eyed the orange, barrel-like boats she began to brew on her sudden love-hate relationship with the plasticky tubs:

I dreaded the thought of getting into the windowless, claustrophobia-inducing craft . . . that would certainly mean that some of us, perhaps all of us, would die, because the ship would be aflame and perhaps sink. On the other hand, we might survive this ordeal in it. I was scared, as I have never been scared before. We were all scared, from the captain on down. Antarctica doesn't offer many avenues of escape.

Barbara's reaction to the lowering of the lifeboats was somewhat more extreme. 'No way,' thought Barb, 'am I EVER getting into one of those.' Sick to the stomach at the thought of being adrift in Antarctica with help who knows how far away, she fervently resolved that she'd rather go down with the ship and get it over with.

While the expeditioners were on deck contemplating their fate, Jimmy hurried to the emergency generator space behind the bridge. The emergency generator should have kicked on when the power went out – it was supposed to power the emergency lighting and radios if the main power failed – why the hell hadn't it? Inside the cramped space he found Rob's sooty form already bent over the generator, attempting to get it started. After a few moments running checks, they realised there was a minor issue with the fuel supply and quickly fixed the problem. The generator kicked over at the next attempt and settled into its noisy drone.

The *Aurora*'s emergency lighting blinked and shone softly, giving the catatonic ship a small glimmer of life.

Upstairs in the radio room, the emergency power also gave sudden animation to the *Aurora*'s main radio. Ian hastily cast the battery radio aside, quickly dialled in distress frequency 4125 kHz and urgently pronounced:

MAYDAY. MAYDAY. MAYDAY. This is the *Aurora Australis*, *Aurora Australis*, *Aurora Australis*. MAYDAY *Aurora Australis*. Our position is 65 degrees 29 minutes south, 144 degrees 58 minutes east. Our vessel has an engine room fire. We require urgent assistance from any vessel. We have 79 people on board. There are no injuries. Please respond. Over.

He waited. There was no reply.

MAYDAY. MAYDAY. MAYDAY. This is the *Aurora Australis* . . .

Ian reissued the mayday, trying distress frequency 6 MHz. Then another distress frequency. Then another. Again and again, with nothing in return but white noise. After fifteen frustratingly unresponsive minutes he returned to 4125 kHz and pressed the two-tone distress alarm, hoping to get the attention of someone – anyone, anywhere. He let the alarm run for a minute before issuing the mayday yet again.

MAYDAY. MAYDAY. MAYDAY. This is the *Aurora Australis* . . .

Suddenly, a voice sprang out of the static. The *Toanui*, a vessel from New Zealand, acknowledged the mayday, promising to immediately pass their message to the Sydney Maritime Communications Centre (MCC). At that very instant, a new voice hit the airwaves: it was Sydney MCC declaring they had received the *Aurora*'s mayday.

Contact. For the next sixteen hours, Ian remained in constant communication with Sydney MCC.

On the helideck, Les was becoming seriously concerned for the expeditioners. They had been exposed to subzero temperatures for almost an hour, some with very little clothing, and the icy breeze was steadily increasing. Several of the expeditioners were shivering uncontrollably now and Les was worried that they were at very real risk of exposure. He suggested to Captain Tony that the expeditioners should be moved into the helicopter hangar. It would still be cold, but it was out of the wind and lit by the emergency lighting. Tony agreed.

The two helicopters loomed large inside the hangar. Expeditioners picked their way around and between the aircraft, finding spaces to sit on the cold steel floor. Some sat on their life jackets, some leaned against the walls, others sat on netting and materials that the crew had seemingly pulled from nowhere. Called away by the captain, Les left VL Ian Allison in charge of his expeditioners. Over the next couple of hours Ian's radio would occasionally buzz to life and give them a momentary glimpse of the story unfolding downstairs. The chief engineer Jimmy had briefly entered the engine room wearing a lifeline and breathing apparatus. He reported that the fire seemed to be out. The captain downgraded their distress signal to pan pan – still an urgent distress signal but one meaning there is no immediate threat to the ship or to life.

The entire ship continued to wait while the halon took its full effect in the engine room's atmosphere. At about 0430, Tony and Chief Engineer Jimmy decided it was time to assess the situation in detail before they vented the smoke and halon from the engine room. Shortly after, Jimmy and First Mate Dunbar geared up in their fire suits and breathing apparatus and lumbered their way down to the watertight door at the forward end of the shaft tunnel.

'Ready?' Jimmy asked Dunbar in his Scottish brogue.

'Yep,' Dunbar replied in his broad Aussie drawl. He lifted a fire extinguisher and held it out, primed for action.

Jimmy stepped through the door, with Dunbar following as armed backup. Jimmy's torch thrust a smoke-streaked beam into the gloomy haze before them. Sweat immediately began beading on their masked faces from the heat. The pair slowly made their way forward through the silent engine room toward the main scene of the fire. As they approached the *Aurora*'s port-side engine they saw that the walkway plates at their feet were warped and charred.

Ghostly plastic stalactites, formed from molten fluorescent light cases, hung from the deck head above. The paint on the main engine had blistered and peeled, and the charred motor now resembled a forlorn, burnt-out car. But as appalling as the obvious damage to the *Aurora*'s heart was, the scorched engine was not the worst of it. As hard luck would have it, the engine room's main cable run was located directly above the seat of the fire. The inferno below had been so severe that cables and wires had fused together and their incinerated, ropey remains dangled from the run in a black, twisted mess. Jimmy's heart sank. The very nerves of the ship had been destroyed.

Part of the *Aurora*'s engine room after the fire; the electrical cabling overhead is completely destroyed.

The heating, plumbing, cooking, lighting, communications and stabiliser systems – not to mention the engines themselves – were all currently inoperable. And these were just the most basic systems they would need to sail the *Aurora* and her passengers safely across the punishing 1300 nautical miles of the Southern Ocean to Hobart. It would take everything Jimmy and his engineers had in them to get them all home safely.

Upstairs, the group in the helihangar was holding up well, thought Barb, under the circumstances. Other than the occasional muted utterance of fear during the peak of the crisis, no-one had panicked. 'It was quite impressive really,' she thought, watching as the VL tended to his expeditioners throughout the hangar; a quiet check here, a gentle reassurance there. After another hour or so Tony Hansen's voice came over the radio, permitting the group to move out of the cold hangar into the relative comfort of the D deck recreation room.

Only now was there a sign of the strain they were all under: one person flatly refused to go below decks in fear of the fire. The terrified expeditioner remained anxiously in the helihangar with one of the mates, who offered what reassurance he could, while Barb and the others went gratefully down to the shelter of the rec room.

But while their lodgings might have improved, the mood in the rec room was sombre. The expeditioners tried to make themselves as comfortable as they could, strewn over the floor on beanbags or whatever else they could find. But no-one spoke. Many faces around the room were creased with worry. Others were blank, immersed in their own thoughts. The knowledge that halon had been dropped was cold comfort to the uncertainty they still faced. Was the fire really out? How bad was the damage? Could the ship be repaired? Will we be stuck here? Do my family know? It was quiet for a long time. Then Barb heard someone clear their throat, and say, 'Well, a friend of mine told me this story . . .'

Helicopter pilot Simon Eder proceeded to tell jokes to the melancholy group. And as he quipped, a nervous titter of laughter went around the room. The pall of doom lifted slightly. They began to laugh, and then laugh hard; cackling and hooting in both hilarity and relief.

The door squeaked open and two blue eyes peered inquisitively into the room. They belonged to the captain, Tony, who bore a wry smile on his exhausted face. Later, Tony would tell Barb, 'I just didn't know what to do . . . whether to go in there or just lock the door – you all sounded completely out of your minds!'

The expeditioners were coping well, thank goodness. Tony stood forward and wearily addressed the group. Yes, the incident was serious, but the ship was still afloat. The situation inside the engine room was still being assessed, and he promised to let them know when they could go to their cabins. Then, stepping back, he thanked them for their patience. Jane blinked as the group did a collective double-take: he was thanking them? The entire room applauded the captain as he left for the bridge.

They continued to wait. Barb rested her now thumping head against the wall. Her mouth was dry, but there was no water to drink as the pumps were offline. She wished she could just go up to the helideck and collect some snow to slake her thirst.

After an hour or two Tony returned with Peter Dunbar; both came bearing juice and milk for the parched expeditioners. Tony told the exhausted group they were allowed to go back to their cabins, or on the helideck if they wished, but they needed to stay clear of the restaurant, which was currently the crew's mobilisation point for the engine room – and they would need to gather back together when the engine room was vented. Jane wrote, 'He asked if we had any questions. We were silent. Then someone piped up from a corner of the room: "That was a good fire drill." Dunbar's rough, blackened face cracked into a smile. "Was it real enough for you?" And he laughs. He's the third of the three best laughers on the ship, a nasal staccato braying. And we all laughed.'

By now, the frigid Antarctic air had leached into the *Aurora*'s steel superstructure, and a few people went to their cabins to collect warmer clothing to put on. Some decided to get some rest in their cabins, but many found solace in the company of others and lingered in the rec room in small groups, talking quietly. Others ventured up to the helideck and beheld a spectacular aurora dancing in the clearing skies: 'Lime green curtains hung on the stars and undulated slowly on solar winds,' Jane wrote. The aurora flickered and danced across the sky, hints of purple tones occasionally joining the green. But it was still so very cold, and many did not stay out on deck long to view the heavenly spectacle. Ian, satisfied that his charges were still coping, made his way up to the bridge.

He found Tony standing at the satellite phone, attempting to contact the French base, Dumont d'Urville, which was 110 nautical miles from the ship. With the help of two French researchers acting as translators, Tony explained their situation to the station winterers, who offered every assistance they could. But the question remained – could Tony even get the *Aurora*'s complement to the safety of the base if necessary?

Together the *Aurora*'s captain, crew, pilots and VL began to formulate a contingency plan, but it soon became abundantly clear it wasn't going to be simple. Firstly, the helihangar door was operated by the *Aurora*'s main generators; with these offline, the only way to open the massive steel door would be to force it with a forklift. This would damage the door and should only be done in the event of another emergency. The two helicopters were almost empty of fuel, and again, with no mains power on the *Aurora* they would have to be refuelled manually – an arduous and dangerous task. There was also limited aviation fuel on board the *Aurora*, so once flying, the choppers would have to refuel at Dumont d'Urville. In addition, the aircraft could only carry five people at a time; if they did need to get everyone to safety via chopper, the process of relocating 79 people would probably take a few days – and that would be weather permitting. Nevertheless, this was their best option in the event they needed to evacuate the ship. Preparations were quietly made, just in case.

The halon had been dumped, allowed to do its work for a number of hours, and the fire was confirmed to be out. Now Jimmy and Tony felt that it was time to vent the engine room to extract the halon and smoke. But there was concern from Hobart experts that the fire might reignite, and the Tasmanian Fire Service, among a specialist crisis group assembled in Hobart, advised Tony to wait a while longer. The fire service would let the crew know when they calculated it would be safe to commence venting. In the meantime, the crisis group in Hobart requested regular reports of the temperatures inside the engine room. Tony Worby, DVL and glaciologist, provided the crew with an infrared radiometer, a hand-held device which they could use to take skin temperatures of machinery in the engine room. The crew dutifully monitored the engine room and reported to Hobart hourly.

Eleven hours after the fire, permission was finally granted to the *Aurora*'s crew to commence venting the engine room, with strict instructions from the specialists in Hobart to minimise risk of another fire. Tony immediately made the required preparations, the expeditioners were recalled to the D deck rec room and ventilation began.

The *Aurora*'s crew were finally able to enter the engine room without breathing apparatus or a backup team at about 1900 hours. Tony felt he could now lift the urgency or 'pan pan' status with Sydney MCC, knowing they could reissue the distress signal if necessary.

But they weren't out of the woods yet. Now that the engine room was finally vented, Chief Engineer Jimmy was able to fully appreciate the scale of the destruction. Fire and smoke damage extended the full height of the three-level engine room, and the blackened walls seemed to absorb all light they could throw into the space. As expected, the large V16 port-side engine, turbocharger and pumps were a charred mess. However, the smaller, starboard-side V12 engine was relatively unscathed by the fire; if they could jury rig some pumps and some new wiring it might well be operable. But the first priority was to get the basic functions of the ship up and running. Jimmy needed to get electricity, water, sewerage and heating to the accommodation areas as soon as possible. In the meantime, in lieu of working toilets, people were asked to use buckets provided in the public toilets. With the number of people on board it quickly became necessary to inhale deeply before they entered the toilet spaces. Men took to venturing outside, when their circumstances allowed.

The restaurant was reopened to the famished expeditioners. However, the galley was still without power, and food and drink options were limited to sandwiches, cereals and cold goods. Barb stood quietly in the queue waiting her turn. She was watching the stymied chefs bustle around the galley when she suddenly remembered her cooking equipment – a few small gas bottles and some high-pressure cookers – which she had brought to use during her penguin research on the ice. She offered her meagre kit for use in the galley, if it would help. The chefs were ecstatic. The freezers were without power and despite the plummeting temperature inside the *Aurora*, food was going to thaw and spoil quickly. The *Aurora*'s water pumps and desalination plant still weren't working, but several large containers of distilled fresh water were miraculously produced from a laboratory by triumphant scientists. The ship's doctor declared it fit for human consumption and suddenly, coffee and soup were available to the crew and expeditioners. Morale lifted. Barb remembers:

> My god, we lived like kings! All the [perishable] food that was supposed to last us six weeks. Oh my goodness! The galley staff was ever so glad to be busy. It was sort of a competition between us and them – could they cook fast enough, or could we eat it all? . . . Those kinds of things made a huge difference.

Meanwhile, the *Aurora*'s engineers were working tirelessly. Remarkably, from as early as that evening Jimmy and his team began to restore the lights, water, toilets and hot water systems across the ship.

But without heating, the *Aurora* was unprotected from the hostile temperatures of the polar winter and the ship's complement endured a bone-chilling night. Even the captain fell afoul of the freezing conditions. By the time he was able to attempt some sleep, ice had accumulated inside his porthole windows and Tony had wearily gone to bed wearing layers of thermal underwear, tracksuit pants, T-shirt and socks and gloves. But, as Tony noted in his Captain's log:

Awoke at about 0230 shivering, put on another pair of woollen socks, tracksuit pants, gloves, my heavy woollen jumper and woollen hat. Took [20 minutes] to warm up and get back to sleep.

The next morning, *Aurora*'s complement woke to a whiteout. A blizzard had enveloped the ship overnight.

For twelve long hours the ship was buffeted by gale-force winds and driving snow. Snow and ice encased the windows, and a calm, ethereal light shone through the frost-gilt glass. But their sense of vulnerability was acute: the *Aurora* was still incapacitated and almost entirely defenceless against the vicious elements; however, she was actually protected somewhat by the loose pack ice surrounding her. Remarkably, she drifted at less than one nautical mile per hour. They had been lucky in many ways, Jane reported, following the captain's candid briefing the next day:

We had the worst thing happen to us, but under the best of circumstances. If the fire had occurred two days earlier while we were rolling through fifteen-foot seas . . . fuel would have sloshed back and forth, spreading the fire to other parts of the engine room . . . If it had happened one day later – yesterday – we would have had to muster into a blizzard with 40 to 60 knot winds, and a wind chill of up to minus 50 degrees Celsius. If we were in thick sea ice, instead of fairly loose pack, the ship would have risked becoming beset or even crushed. If we were in looser pancake ice, we'd risk being pushed by wind and current into an iceberg.

Meanwhile, the heating had been slowly brought back online, albeit at a reduced capacity. The prolonged period without heating had been uncomfortable enough, but it also gave rise to considerable shipboard complications. While the water pumps had been offline, water lay motionless inside the ship's pipes, and in the subzero temperatures the water in these pipes had soon frozen and expanded. Once the water pumps and flow were restored by the *Aurora*'s engineers, split pipes burst indiscriminately across the ship. Water gushed along the *Aurora*'s decks and alleyways without warning, leaving a sopping mess in its wake.

While the *Aurora*'s rehabilitation had been centred in the engine room, everyone throughout the ship did what they could to help out and keep each other's spirits high. Expeditioners were lending a hand with food preparation and cleaning in the galley. Flooded decks were jovially mopped by whoever first encountered them. The AAD technicians helped the *Aurora*'s engineers install temporary wiring and cabling across the ship. Chief Engineer Jimmy barely slept, and when he did retire he took his radio to his bunk in case his team needed his expertise or help.

But an invisible obstacle still threatened to sink morale. Since the fire, all personal emails to and from the ship had been restricted. This communications embargo was normal onboard emergency protocol and was expected in the initial hours after the crisis, but it did mean that those onboard had not been able to directly communicate with their loved ones back home. Instead, the AAD and P&O had made contact with relatives and friends, advising them of the situation and reassuring them that all on board the ship were safe and well. But the embargo dragged on, and the lack of communication weighed heavily on all of them. Tempers frayed. Ian wrote in his VL's report:

> After the first day the expeditioners (and crew) became increasingly agitated and annoyed ... and I received numerous complaints and delegations about the unfairness and distress of the embargo.

As a result, the embargo was partially lifted that evening and incoming emails were released to those on board. Although, Ian wrote, '. . . this made the situation worse in some ways as many started receiving messages of the "cannot understand why we have not heard from you" kind.'

Incoming email also brought with it copies of media reports on the fire, which were distributed throughout the ship. And now, as well as being isolated and stressed, the *Aurora*'s complement was affronted. Many on board thought that their horrendous ordeal and their current perilous situation had been dramatically played down. Whether this was inadvertent or intentional, it nevertheless caused an element of anger and frustration to enter the fray. It had already been traumatic enough.

Finally, the outgoing communications embargo was lifted two-and-a-half days after the fire, and the anxious expeditioners and crew were able to personally contact loved ones and reassure them that they were safe. Jane Stevens sent her first report on the fire to the Discovery Channel Online. Tensions eased. Later, some even began to see the lighter side of the situation: when it came time to 'name' the voyage, the trip was dubbed 'FIRE and ICE': an apt acronym of 'F*%# It's a Real Emergency and I Can't Email'.

Meanwhile, the engineers had rigged a gravity fuel feed to the starboard (V12) engine. It was time to see if they could get the engine started. The entire complement felt a thrill of relief as the once-familiar vibrations reassuringly reverberated through the ship. The V12 engine was tested for over an hour using the gravity fuel feed; then, once this was shown to work well, the engineers clutched in the propeller. The *Aurora*'s giant propeller slowly turned beneath the loose ice that had accumulated around the back of the ship. The *Aurora* tentatively moved forward in the ice, under her own steam for the first time in days. A cheer went up on the bridge as the engineers announced their jury-rigged system passed the test. The engine was shut off and the engineers now focused all their energy on restoring fuel pressure to the *Aurora*'s engine.

The next afternoon Tony stood at the helm and made a 'bing-bong' announcement over the PA system. He instructed all personnel to hold on to something solid: the engineers were about to start the engine once again. They all held their breath, and downstairs the *Aurora*'s smaller engine revved to life with a shudder and a roar. Tony gently pressed the icebreaker forward and ran her for over three hours: testing, probing, pushing through the ice. Finally satisfied, Tony declared the test a success and immediately set the *Aurora* on a course for Hobart. Four days after the fire, they were going home.

Along with the immediate feeling of relief of being homeward bound came quiet trepidation. Leaving the ice meant also leaving a certain amount of safety; the ice had clearly provided protection to the ship over the last few days. With the *Aurora* in such a fragile state – running on just her smaller engine, with a jury-rigged system and no stabilisers – the trip home through the Southern Ocean was an unknown and entirely intimidating quantity. Tony worried that his wounded ship might not be able to hold up against the pounding that the roughest ocean in the world could dish out.

Meteorologist Kieren Jacka had been constantly providing Tony with updates on the weather; the current forecast showed an intense low-pressure system to the north on their route to Hobart. So instead of making a beeline for home, Tony decided to set a course west-northwest. Keeping the wind safely behind them, he would slowly alter their course more northward once they cleared the low-pressure system.

But despite the considerable combined skill of the captain, chief engineer and meteorologist, the *Aurora* ran into problems. The first came within twelve hours of heading home; a steam line in the emergency generator room burst, flooding the main switchboard. The main engine and both generators immediately shut down, and the ship was once again floating dead in the icy water. Jimmy and his engineers managed to get power rapidly restored, but it was still hours before the navigational equipment was fully operational. Days later, during the dark, small hours of the morning, water pumps that had been temporarily rigged to cool the engine failed. Again the engine cut out. Now in the midst of the mighty Southern Ocean, the *Aurora* wallowed. She drifted beam-on to the swell and was pummelled mercilessly by the surging waves. The *Aurora* rolled violently; drawers flew out of cupboards, people fell out of their bunks and dishes in the galley crashed to the floor. The engineers worked frantically to get the *Aurora*'s systems working, and in just twelve minutes they had the ship underway and on course once more.

For six days the unsleeping chief engineer, captain and crew nursed the *Aurora* carefully across the Southern Ocean, all the while avoiding the worst of the weather systems. At the point Tony was finally able to turn the ship directly toward home he recalls 'we were closer to Fremantle than Hobart'. Amazingly, with favourable winds and seas the *Aurora* made speeds of fifteen knots at times – close to her top speed – running on just the small engine and her patched-up system.

Throughout the entire crisis the complement had successfully sustained morale, but they were nearing emotional exhaustion. They had endured the fire, a blizzard, borne the constant worry and difficult conditions of drifting in ice and had withstood a precarious Southern Ocean transit. But now, thanks to the unceasing vigilance of the captain, officers, engineers and crew, the ordeal was almost over. The final phase of their deliverance was about to begin: the *Aurora* had made it to the mouth of the Derwent River.

It was midnight, and the darkened bridge was packed with silent, shadowy figures. Tony had opened the bridge to the anxious expeditioners so they could watch, on the proviso that they remained quiet and did not hamper the crew or operations. Initially P&O had suggested the *Aurora* should wait for daybreak before coming up the river. Stunned, Tony swiftly rebuked this astonishing instruction and insisted the stricken vessel be taken into port ASAP. Upon hearing the captain's tone of voice, P&O quickly acquiesced.

Barb watched the distant light of the Hobart pilot boat grow steadily brighter, until the small orange boat finally appeared out of the darkness and pulled alongside the *Aurora*. The pilot clambered adeptly up the rope ladder. Two tugboats also arrived out of the darkness; they would be escorting the *Aurora* under tow, as without thrusters the icebreaker had little capacity to manoeuvre at slow speed. A heavy braided tow rope almost as thick as Barb's leg was attached to the *Aurora*'s bow. Up ahead, the tug *Keira* took up the line, and the *Aurora*'s engine was shut down.

The *Aurora* began to glide silently though the water. Suddenly, with a resounding boom, the massive tow rope snapped. It flung across the bow, narrowly missed crew on the deck, and one end slithered away into the dark water, leaving the *Aurora* floating powerless on the Derwent River. Barb watched, incredulous, as their ship drifted inexorably toward the shore. 'We've come so far,' Barb thought, 'and now after everything, we are going to run aground here at the entrance to the Derwent River!'

The tugboat *Storm Cove* motored quickly to the starboard side of the *Aurora* and gently nosed the orange ship away from the shore, holding the icebreaker in position so that another huge tow line could be slung from the bow. Tony asked Jimmy to start the *Aurora*'s engine, and this time keep it running while she was under tow. The *Keira* gradually heaved the *Aurora* up the river. But twenty minutes later there was another thunderous clap: the second tow line had also snapped.

Finally, at 0400 on 31 July – and carrying a complement strained as tight as the tow rope before them – the *Aurora* edged alongside Princes Wharf. There was a painful wait while the gangway was lowered and Customs officers came on board to clear the weary travellers, but eventually the expeditioners were allowed to disembark. Barb smiled as the first expeditioners flew down the gangway and immediately threw themselves into the arms of waiting loved ones, tears of relief rolling down their cheeks. Cheers and applause erupted from the crowd on the waterfront, while the bright lights of the waiting media lit up the wharf as they captured the scene.

Captain Tony Hansen was soon caught up in the media melee. The press praised the response of the crew and the successful return home of the *Aurora*, astonishingly without injury or even a scratch among the crew or expeditioners. When pressed, Tony

Hansen admitted he didn't completely stop being afraid until the *Aurora* was tied up alongside the wharf.

But more than anything else he was intensely proud of his crew and expeditioners, later noting:

> It was very much a team effort . . . by naming some I do not wish to reduce the significance of the role played by others. [Chief IR] Per Larsen worked tirelessly throughout and led the crew with distinction . . . Ian's assistance has been wonderful and I appreciate it greatly. The engineers, well what can I say, but a marvellous effort, to get us home safely is a credit to them all. My Deck Officers . . . I would not swap one for any of the previous hundreds of deck officers I have sailed with in [24] years.

Captain Tony Hansen, Chief Engineer Jimmy Mackenzie and the crew of the *Aurora Australis* had managed the impossible. They had battled an engine-room fire, revived a critically injured ship, and then nurtured her safely across the notorious Southern Ocean. Incredibly, there were no deaths nor injuries. While many on board would harbour emotional wounds (some suffered from repeated nightmares and insomnia after returning home), the scars would eventually fade, with time and support.

VALUABLE LESSONS LEARNED

A number of safety improvements were made as a result of the fire. It was lucky that the expeditioners had mustered on the helideck before the power went out — below decks would have been pitch black once power was lost. From this voyage forward, all cabins were fitted with emergency torches that were kept permanently on charge. Emergency 'grab bags' with additional warm clothing were made part of the Antarctic Division's kit provided to expeditioners — and expeditioners were henceforth required to bring these to every muster.

The subsequent investigation by Australia's Marine Incident Investigation Unit (MIIU) revealed that the fire had been caused by a small split in a fuel hose beneath the engine room footplates. This tiny fault allowed diesel fuel to spray in an arc up and across the engine room, extending several metres from the hose. Some of the fine spray had atomised, and the heat from the engine's turbochargers ignited the fuel, which caused the initial fire. The foam and dry powder used by the engineers to extinguish the first fire would not have had any cooling effect on the turbochargers, and the residual fuel vapour in the air soon reignited on the hot surface, this time causing an explosion and fireball.

Incredibly, the MIIU investigation also found that, due to various issues with power supplies, four of the engine room's ten halon bottles had not discharged, three of which were in close proximity to the fire. As the MIIU report points out: 'The failure of these three bottles to discharge meant that the halon release probably had little immediate effect on the fire.'

The fire was in all probability not extinguished by the dumping of halon, but by being starved of fuel.

The disaster could have been so much worse. Their location in the ice and the action of the quick-thinking engineers to shut down the fuel pumps and restrict further sources of fuel to the fire, while at extreme personal risk, in all likelihood saved the ship and all her charges.

But sadly, in the end there may have been one casualty of the fire after all. P&O manager John Gleeson died of a heart attack just days after the *Aurora*'s safe return to Hobart. John had been a critical part of the crisis response in Hobart and part of the crowd on the wharf waiting anxiously to greet the ship, to personally welcome the crew and expeditioners safely home. Tony Hansen had been in constant contact with John during the ordeal and was convinced John passed away 'no doubt because of all the stress he was under'. Touching tributes were published by the *Aurora*'s shocked crew and P&O Polar, for the man who will 'always be remembered for the energy and dedication with which

[he] steered our ship through the years' and whose 'loyalty and dedication have ensured that our flag flies proudly in Antarctic waters.'

For the expeditioners, after the relief of their safe return, there was bitter disappointment that the science program had ended even before it had really begun. Undeterred, the scientists were unanimously resolved to return next season to conduct their research. Jane wrote: 'We'll go back next year; the odds of this happening again are so remote as to fade into infinity. And we understand, better than ever . . . [that] Antarctica can humble us like no other place.'

Yet fate, it seems, liked shorter odds than that.

Chapter Six

THE 'ANNUS HORRIBILIS' CONTINUES

The mammoth task of repairing the *Aurora*'s fire-ravaged engine room began almost immediately. More than forty contractors worked feverishly around the clock to replace the icebreaker's devastated electrical system, refurbish her charred engines and remove all traces of smoke damage. It would take weeks.

In the meantime, Australia's Antarctic stations were without the critical personnel, fuel and cargo needed for the summer work programs. The reclusive continent only releases her frozen embrace of the Southern Ocean during the height of summer; scarcely opening her arms to visitors before retreating to her twilit, meditative solitude. Every summer day that slipped by without accessing the Antarctic stations was an opportunity irrevocably lost; the Antarctic Division had to act – fast. The Norwegian-owned *Polar Bird* (formerly the *Icebird*, but renamed by new owners when they bought her), a 109-metre-long custom-built Antarctic resupply vessel, was hurriedly chartered to substitute for the indisposed *Aurora*.

The *Polar Bird* pulled alongside Hobart's Macquarie Wharf less than two weeks later. Her tall white accommodation block

Wayne Papps/Australian Antarctic Division

View from Tasman Bridge of polar supply ships at Macquarie Wharf, Hobart in 2000. (L to R) *L'Astrolabe*, *Polar Bird*, *Aurora Australis*, *Kapitan Khlebnikov*.

sat toward the stern of the ship, while her red bow proudly extended before a lengthy forward deck punctuated by two towering cranes that were busily moving over her cargo holds. The holds were soon jam-packed with the plethora of assorted cargo required at Antarctic stations: pallet after pallet of food, equipment and bags as well as three helicopters and a container laboratory. Finally, the heavily laden *Polar Bird* sailed down the Derwent River on 12 September 1998 bound for Mawson, Davis and Casey stations.

By mid-October the *Polar Bird* had traversed the Southern Ocean and successfully resupplied Mawson station. But en route to Davis, the red-and-white cargo ship faced an endless expanse of thick, snow-covered pack ice. While the *Polar Bird* was ice strengthened, she had limited icebreaking capability, and was at very real risk of besetment in the thick, dense pack ice surrounding her. Her progress slowed as she carefully picked her way through the ice, then virtually halted altogether. The helicopters were dispatched on reconnaissance flights that radiated outward from the ship; pilots and crew determinedly searching for favourable course options that could lead them south toward Davis station. But after a number of painfully slow days it was apparent to the *Polar Bird*'s VL John Brooks that there were no ice leads – the 'Superhighways or Autobahns' of the ice, as he called them – leading toward Davis station.

It was futile, thought John. They had a schedule to keep, and another station in need of resupply. After doggedly persisting in the pack ice for as long as he dared, John reluctantly took the only ice leads that were offered to the ship – tiny 'Polish backroads', as he wrote in his daily sitrep, that led to the north, away from Davis station – and grudgingly set the *Polar Bird* on a course for Casey. The forsaken Davis expeditioners and the cargo on board would have to be transhipped via Casey to Davis using a more powerful icebreaker, which ironically would be the *Aurora Australis*, whose repairs back in Hobart were almost complete.

The *Aurora* was declared fully operational a week later and was hastily mobilised under the care of VL Suzanne Stallman and Captain Peter Pearson.

Suzanne was an experienced VL on both the *Aurora Australis* and the *Polar Bird*. She had an approachable, no-nonsense demeanour, warm eyes and a friendly laugh. On 28 October, the day prior to departure, Suzanne stood on the wharf in front of the *Aurora*, smiling at newspaper and television reporters hungry for news about the recovery of the ship and the state of Australia's Antarctic shipping season. Suzanne outlined the *Aurora*'s voyage schedule, which now involved Casey, Davis and Mawson resupplies, a Sansom Island depot changeover and a busy marine science program. Yes, it was a demanding timetable, she admitted, but one that was required after the unfortunate events of this difficult summer. Suzanne deftly diverted questions from the reporters regarding the fire on the *Aurora*'s previous voyage. She was entirely confident in the *Aurora*'s restoration process and refused to be drawn into portraying any sentiments of hesitation about the safety of the ship. Standing under the cycloptic gaze of the cameras, she steadfastly iterated and reiterated *this* voyage's objectives, stressing the importance of the station resupplies and the aims of the marine science program.

The major research project for the voyage, Suzanne explained, was an ice seal survey. It was part of a large circumpolar project called Antarctic Pack Ice Seals (APIS), with several international biological teams around Antarctica conducting the same research, at the same time, in different locations. Australia's component was led by biologist and seal expert Colin Southwell, and it had been years in the making.

'The reason we want to study seals on this voyage,' Suzanne went on confidently, 'is because seals are top-level predators in the Antarctic ecosystem, and like other predators such as whales and penguins, can be used as key indicators for the health of an eco-system.' The travelling and feeding patterns of these animals can allow scientists to better understand how the Antarctic ecosystem works, and give scientists and governments vital information on how to manage human activities such as fishing for krill or fish. But gathering information on any free-ranging marine animal in such a remote and expansive area is no easy task. In Antarctica, at-sea visual counts of whales, seals and penguins are typically done by a team of biologists standing on the top deck of a ship, or from a helicopter or plane. The problem is, marine animals can only be counted in this way when they are at or near the water's surface (usually when breathing, travelling or resting). So visual surveys don't account for animals currently swimming unseen under the water's surface, which, given these animals are feeding on fish and krill, is quite likely to be where they are at any given moment.

However, while ice seals spend a large part of their time underwater travelling or foraging, they also periodically haul-out on ice floes to rest and sleep. As well as conducting the traditional visual counts, the researchers planned to approach seals while they were 'hauled-out' and attach satellite tracking tags to their backs. The data collected from the tags would not only show where the seals go on their travels, but would also help determine how much time the seals spend underwater compared to on the ice. This would allow future visual survey results to be calibrated to better represent the total number of seals actually in an area at a given time, and provide more accurate information essential for effective ecosystem management of Antarctica.

Suzanne also pointed out that other important research projects would take place while the station resupplies or the seal survey were underway. Ice cores would be extracted from sea ice for climate change research, water sampling would be undertaken continually as the ship moved along the survey track, and the nets would be deployed off the trawl deck to sample the zooplankton communities in the region and to study growth patterns of Antarctic krill.

The media's appetite for information was now satisfied and Suzanne was released from her public relations duties. As the cameras and notebooks were being packed away, Suzanne marched back up the steep metal steps of the gangway, eager to tackle the organised chaos of pre-departure logistics. There were ship familiarisations and safety inductions to coordinate, safety drills to participate in, expeditioner queries to deal with and cargo to finalise.

The next day, Suzanne buzzed with liveliness from the relentless bustle of pre-departure coordination. Even while she stood on deck, watching the crowd below gleefully wave and cheer as the *Aurora* and her passengers finally pulled away from the wharf, she was running a mental to-do list. 'But there's no rest for the wicked,' she thought to herself with a resigned smile, soon turning away from the farewell transit downriver and stepping inside the ship. For Suzanne, the journey south immediately became a busy procession of appointments and meetings with the team leaders, the ship's captain and crew, and briefings for shore and ship research teams.

For many of the expeditioners on board, their work would only begin shortly before the station resupplies commenced.

So, in an effort to keep her rowdy wards from weeks of uninterrupted idleness, Suzanne coordinated a number of social activities in between juggling her logistic commitments. Melbourne Cup day was celebrated with a 'fashions on the field' party, where artistic headpieces of questionable couture quality were crafted and paraded with swagger around the restaurant. Every night a movie was advertised and screened in the D deck rec room, and on Friday the Thirteenth a 'fright night' fancy-dress party was held in the freakishly festooned Husky Bar. In addition, the shiny locks of some brave crew and expeditioners were sacrificed for the greater good during a Camp Quality fundraising head-shave. By 5 November, the end of the transit south, Suzanne was ready for a reprieve. She wrote affectionately in her daily sitrep:

> The voyage is a bit like having 108 kids in the back seat of your car – with someone always feeling sick, someone always wanting an ice cream and all of them asking 'When are we going to get there?' At least there's some great scenery now.

The morning had dawned calm and clear, and the *Aurora* had just sailed through the first bands of ice. Almost immediately, excited cries ran through the ship: a pod of whales was also spotted. Their misty blows hung tall in the motionless air, and the rippled rings of their surfacing 'footprints' speckled the water's silver-mirrored surface, revealing the pod's trackline like a join-the-dots chart. The first iceberg was seen later that day, and the lucky winner of the iceberg sweep was announced.

'Captain's decision final: no protests,' Suzanne joked, deftly cutting off several of her cheeky charges.

The *Aurora* arrived at Casey station two days later. The helicopters were readied and the treasured mail was flown in, followed by the station's new doctor and the inbound expeditioners. The choppers returned to the ship laden with cargo from Casey – as well as the additional transhipped cargo from the *Polar Bird*. As each load arrived, Suzanne, her DVL Steven Whiteside and the crew determinedly pieced the complex cargo puzzle together, somehow finding room for it all. Lastly, the remaining expeditioners from the *Polar Bird* were able to end their period of limbo at Casey, joining the *Aurora* to continue their long, roundabout trip to Davis station.

Almost as soon as the *Aurora* turned her bow away from Casey, chief scientist Colin and his seal team took up observations on the bridge. Colin smiled with anticipation as he looked out at the expanse of ice and water before them. After four years of meticulous planning, it was finally time to put all his work into action.

Colin's team took up shifts on the bridge; scanning the dense uneven pack ice in repeated arcs, methodically searching for seals and opportunities to deploy their satellite tags.

The first opportunity came just a day out of Casey station, when a crabeater seal was spotted dozing on a massive, uneven ice floe not far from the *Aurora*'s current heading. Crabeater seals are the most abundant species of seal in the world, and, despite their name, feed almost exclusively on Antarctic krill. In fact, their diet is so specialised that their teeth are remarkably adapted: instead of having solid teeth, each tooth has multiple lobed projections. These lobed teeth act as a strainer: when feeding in krill swarms, crabeater seals take mouthfuls of water containing their prey, then close their jaws and force the sea water out between their sieve-like teeth, trapping the krill inside their mouths.

The grey-brown seal rolled lazily as the ship approached. Behind its tail, the otherwise pristine ice was graffitied with violently vivid streaks of unmistakably krill-red poo.

Colin rapidly assessed the situation. It was a single seal, which was good – no possessive mates to deal with. The ice floe was solid and the seal wasn't too far from the ship, nor too close to the water's edge. It was the perfect situation for tagging. After a brief meeting with Captain Peter and VL Suzanne, the seal team had the go-ahead to disembark. It took the team just minutes to get ready; they quickly stepped into their freezer suits, pulled on thin snow-white hazmat suits for camouflage against the ice, then rapidly laced up their fleece-lined rubber boots.

The six-person seal team was loaded into the *Aurora*'s waiting man-cage along with two red sleds and eskies full of equipment. The long arm of the crane carefully lifted them up over the side of the ship and gently down onto the ice floe.

A seal survey team unloading field equipment on ice beside the *Aurora Australis*.

The team quietly pulled the sleds and gear clear of the cage, and then Colin and three others sat low and silent on the ice. The vet, Damien Higgins, and Mike Heinze, a marine mammal researcher, lowered themselves to their stomachs and slowly crawled their way across the lumpy floe toward the seal.

Damien grunted slightly as he dragged himself prostrate along the ice. As he crept, he held onto the rifle-like dart gun. The ammo and drugs were being kept warm in the thick insulated bag on his back. These days, seals were anaesthetised with reversible drugs, to avoid the unfortunate mortalities that occurred in the early days of ice-seal research, and were tranquilised from a distance rather than captured with a hoop net, to avoid stress on the animal.

It took the pair a painstaking hour of slow, silent and uncomfortable skulking to get into position. Then, lying on his stomach, Damien loaded the rifle and rested it on the ice before him. He peered intently down the sight, put the mottled seal in the crosshairs, exhaled, and squeezed the trigger.

The sleeping seal started as the dart hit its target. It looked up in fright, intently searching the surrounding ice for the sight or sound of a threat. But, not finding any apparent danger, the seal soon settled, resting its suddenly weary head back on the ice.

After about ten minutes, Mike raised himself to a half-crouch and slowly approached the seal. His feet crunched loudly on the ice with every careful, measured step. The animal lay motionless as he drew closer. Its eyes were closed, and its nostrils opened and closed rhythmically with each soft, warm breath. Mike motioned, and the team strode over, dragging the sleds across the ice.

The white-clad team knelt around the sleeping seal and busily got to work. Damien unpacked his monitors and attentively watched the seal's vital signs. Colin took off a layer of gloves and carefully mixed some specialised glue. The others assisted or took notes. The tag, a hand-sized satellite-linked dive recorder, was carefully glued to the seal's short, thick fur. This small box would track the seal on its travels and provide information on its diving behaviour, before eventually being shed with the seal's winter coat during its next moulting period.

It was all over in minutes. The group packed up and retreated, watching intently from a distance as the seal groggily came around, then became more alert. Colin, satisfied the seal had recovered safely from the anaesthetic, directed the group to return to the ship.

Meanwhile, on the other side of the *Aurora*, the ice team had also been lowered onto a floe and had successfully collected an ice core. They clustered around the core, carefully measuring, storing and tagging the cylinder of ice. The core would be processed on board the *Aurora* for analysis back in Australia, to identify the microscopic plankton and organic compounds locked within the ice, which would help inform scientists on relationships between sea ice and local and global climate.

After all the excitement of the ice-based work had died down, the *Aurora Australis* continued along her track line. Within a few hours she steamed into a relatively ice-free patch of water, and the krill team had their chance to begin their research program. This team, consisting of two biologists from the AAD and a visiting scientist from Japan, hoped to catch Antarctic krill and salps (gelatinous pocket-like filter feeders that vaguely resemble jellyfish) for growth experiments.

The *Aurora*'s crew repeatedly lowered the midwater trawl net out into the freezing blue–grey water behind the ship. But after each trawl, the net slithered back on deck virtually empty. After several attempts they had caught half a dozen smaller, non-target species of krill, but absolutely no Antarctic krill or salps. Yet, maddeningly, the team could actually see the odd Antarctic krill happily swimming and flitting around in the water beside the *Aurora*'s hull. In desperation, the scientists, Simon Jarman, Joel Scott and Sanae Chiba, began to think outside the box and attempted to catch some krill using a simple hoop net dropped vertically below the ship. When that failed, they resorted to a humble bucket on a rope. But despite their best efforts, just one lonely Antarctic krill was captured. He was immediately nicknamed 'Bill the Krill', and for now he was the sole occupant of the *Aurora*'s luxurious krill laboratory tanks.

The *Aurora* charged through the last few miles of the ice-free oasis and was soon slogging through heavy pack ice once again. Jumbled chunks and floes of ice completely covered any hint of the water's surface, and the messy white mass stretched unendingly to the horizon.

Suzanne stared unseeing out the bridge-wing windows while the *Aurora* pushed and shouldered the ice aside. Roused occasionally, she smiled and chatted politely with expeditioners and crew on the bridge, but inwardly she was worried. While the scientific work continued with gusto, the *Aurora*'s progress through the ice was painfully slow; the same dense pack ice that had thwarted the *Polar Bird*'s transit to Davis station weeks before was now seriously hindering the *Aurora*. And to make matters worse, Suzanne had just discovered there had been a mix-up between P&O and the AAD prior to the *Aurora*'s fuelling in Hobart, and it seemed that somehow the *Aurora* hadn't been loaded with enough fuel to conduct the full seal survey. Suzanne sighed. If they didn't start making better time, it looked like she might have to cut time from the research program to make sure all the stations could still be resupplied. It's never a nice decision to have to make, especially so early in the voyage.

But while the ice may have been causing some serious logistical headaches, it was perfect ice-seal habitat. The seal team seized the opportunity to tag two more seals, and then prepared to conduct their first visual survey using the helicopters. The aircraft were quickly dragged out of the hangar and bladed up. Colin squeezed himself into the back seat of one of the red-and-white choppers, his long legs wedged in tightly between cameras, recorders, seats and the makeshift lectern on top of which sat his paperwork. He pulled on his headphones, and the pilot's thin, tinny voice came through, conducting final checks and flight confirmation. The cabin soon roared and vibrated with the powerful thrumming of engine and blades.

Before Colin knew it, they were in the air. The *Aurora*'s green helideck with its white H rapidly contracted beneath them. The horizon expanded and the *Aurora* shrank to an unnervingly small red dot in an infinite sea of brilliant white. Colin had to remind himself to restrict his gaze to the arc forward and to the side of the helicopters: they were here to find seals, and for now he and his team needed to ignore the remarkable, immense landscape before them. Before long, Colin was busily recording locations of and bearings to the elongated grey bodies of seals dotting the pack ice.

*

The *Aurora* continued to determinedly slog through the pack ice. Finally, after frustratingly slow progress, she reached a patch of relatively open water and made much better time toward Davis.

The next morning, an ice blink to their southwest interrupted the uniform grey mass overhead. They had almost reached the fast ice, the expanse of thick white ice that extended all the way from Antarctica's coastline.

The *Aurora*'s second engine was re-engaged, and she charged toward the ice. Dozens of Adelie and a few Emperor penguins stood at the very edge of the fast ice, the charismatic birds watching with confident curiosity as the huge orange ship steadfastly approached their solid platform. As the *Aurora* ploughed into the ice, some of the penguins slid on their bellies away from the ship or scrambled into the water. Others simply watched as the ship motored by, squawking the occasional protest.

The icebreaker cut through easily, but before long the fast ice thickened, and the *Aurora* went into reverse, resorting to her more formidable icebreaking process. Once again she reversed in her channel, then pressed forward; a fine, blue ribbon of broken ice slowly lengthened behind the ship.

As the *Aurora* determinedly cut into the fast ice, off in the distance Adelie penguins walked in swaying groups between their ice-locked colony at Gardner Island and a sliver of open water on the horizon. The groups, a long, black medley of follow-the-leader lines and tight clusters, almost looked like the dashes and dots of Morse code along the ice.

The *Aurora* eventually ground to a halt about a mile from Davis station, the fast ice extending around the ship. Under a blue sky mottled with clouds, the crew lowered the gangway down to the ice, and the resupply began.

Like a conductor of an eclectic orchestra, Suzanne stood watching from the bridge while the resupply teams played their parts in a logistic symphony. The 'diesos' ran out the heavy black rubber fuel hose, unfurling it across the granite-like surface to the station. After pressure testing the lines, they began to pump fuel from the ship into the station's cylindrical storage tanks. Quad bikes and skidoos rumbled intermittently across the frozen field. The summer expeditioners were transported to their new home-away-from-home while day trippers from the ship happily stretched their legs and walked with careful steps on 'solid ground' to and from the station, occasionally slipping on the slick, miniature ice-dunes known as sastrugi. All the while the *Aurora*'s cranes rose and fell rhythmically as each precious load of cargo from Australia was deposited on the ice beside the ship.

Despite snow squalls and howling gales regularly interrupting operations, the Davis resupply went smoothly and, four days later, the *Aurora* deftly reversed and then broke her way out of her icy berth.

Suzanne and Peter immediately turned their minds to the next stop on the schedule: Sansom Island. Used primarily as a fuel depot for long-haul helicopter operations between Davis and Mawson stations, Sansom Island is located in a small nook in the southernmost reaches of Prydz Bay, near the edge of the Amery Ice Shelf. Painfully aware of the fuel situation, both the VL and Captain Peter were relieved when the *Aurora* encountered favourable ice and weather conditions and was able to make quick progress to her rendezvous point, 32 nautical miles from the island. The choppers once again buzzed overhead, delivering drums of fuel, crates of food, skidoos and quad bikes to the rocky outpost in rapid succession.

But the good luck was short-lived. The A factor was about to strike again: the voyage meteorologist had detected an approaching blizzard. As the clear sunshine was replaced with a flat, grey gloom, the choppers were secured in the hangar and operations came to an expectant standstill.

Before long, a white cyclone roared around the *Aurora*. The blizzard's winds howled ferociously while driving snow lashed the ship. The *Aurora* sat unflinching against the beating of the furious polar storm, but the icy hand of the blizzard soon left its unmistakable mark: the *Aurora*'s orange flanks became crusted with snow and ice, and her green decks cloaked with a soft white blanket that concealed a slippery, frozen varnish lurking beneath. Her ledges and handrails dripped with translucent icicles.

Inside the *Aurora*, all was calm, but the blizzard's visual static completely obscured the world beyond the portholes.

Taking advantage of a break in operations, King Neptune, resplendent in toga and crown, complete with mop-wig and trident (and accompanied by suspiciously masculine-looking ocean-sprite attendants), paid his visit to the *Aurora Australis*. All souls who had crossed sixty degrees south for the first time were called to kneel before the King and pay their respects, in the ritualistic 'crossing of the line' ceremony. The new expeditioners listened, rapt and giggling, to the sermon of King Neptune (who was actually an unidentified crewmember clearly revelling in his new-found royal status). They were 'anointed' (or, more accurately, doused) with a thick, foul-smelling concoction of unknown ingredients and questionable origin, then, with one reverential kiss of a large, scaly fish and a blessing bestowed by the King, they became South Polar Sea Dogs, who swore an oath to henceforth 'take pride in the brine that will now course through their veins'. They were proudly presented with certificates, irrefutable proof of their Sea Dog status.

After four long, unrelenting days the Antarctic blizzard finally began to ease. But as the whiteout slowly receded, a new problem came into focus.

When the *Aurora* had first arrived at Sansom Island, she had only broken a quarter of a mile into the fast ice. The blizzard's brutal winds had since pushed the pack ice in the north of Prydz Bay southward, and the *Aurora* was now some twenty nautical miles inside the ice edge. She was encased on all sides by harsh icy terrain; with solid fast ice to the south and heavily rafted pack ice to the north. Under the immense pressures of the blizzard's winds and the weight of the pack ice pushing relentlessly against it, the fast ice had become scarred with long, uneven ridges that protruded into the air like defensive battlements. The blizzard had left a thick layer of soft, sticky snow over the ghostly land-scape, and the lumpy, chaotic mess stretched infinitely to the horizon.

Suzanne and Peter stood together at the bridge windows, discussing the sea of jumbled ice surrounding them. It was an unenviable position, but not overly alarming: they were, after all, on board an icebreaker. First things first, they agreed: they had a job to finish. The helicopters were rolled back out on deck and the last of the Sansom Island fuel drums were exchanged. With that resupply finally completed, it was now time to turn their attention back to the seal survey and the transit to Mawson station.

The helicopters were dispatched again, this time on an ice reconnaissance flight carrying one of the *Aurora*'s knowledgeable officers. Shortly after, the officer pronounced over the hissing airwaves that they had spotted a crack in the ice not too far from the orange ship. It led north, to more open water about ten miles away. Their course was altered and the *Aurora* slowly made her way to the lead, once again reversing and thrusting into the ice. Down in the *Aurora*'s belly both engines roared as they powered the mighty ship onward. Clangs, screeches and vibrations of ice hitting steel reverberated throughout the vessel.

Captain Peter sat at the bridge chart table, updating their position on the current map while Third Mate Allan McCarthy stood at the helm. Peter shifted in his chair and looked out at the mess of one-metre-thick ice extending around the ship. Clumps of snow and fractured ice jutted unevenly from the frozen sea for miles. He sighed. It was going to be a slow haul to the lead. Peter turned back to his charts as Allan reversed the ship to prepare for another lunge into the ice.

A minute later, Peter realised he hadn't yet felt the anticipated thrust forward. He looked up to see Allan checking his controls with concern. Peter dropped his pen and strode over to the helm. They could both clearly see that the control and propeller pitch were indicating full ahead, but the *Aurora* was still drifting slowly astern. Something was very wrong. Peter immediately declutched the *Aurora*'s engines, dialled the engine room's number and asked the Chief to please find out what the hell was going on.

Chief Engineer John van Dam, or JvD, a man of small stature with a sunny nature and a razor-sharp mind, hung up the phone, puzzled. There were no alarms on the engine control panels to indicate anything was amiss. Both engines were running just fine. He clambered down the steep stairs to the lowest level of the engine room, to check the oil pressure of the propeller system.

The *Aurora Australis*'s propeller system comprised a single stainless steel, controllable pitch propeller, or CPP, where the blades could change pitch (or angle) by rotating at their base. The chosen pitch of the blades would determine whether the propeller would provide forward or rearward propulsion for the ship.

The pressure needed to change the physical pitch of the *Aurora*'s propeller is supplied through a hydraulic feedback pipe. This is essentially an oil pipe that runs down the middle of the long shaft connecting the *Aurora*'s powerful engines to her propeller. The oil that controls the pitch that propels the ship forward is supplied down the inside of the feedback pipe, and the oil that controls the astern pitch – which moves the ship in reverse – is supplied between the outside of the feedback pipe and the inside of the propeller shaft.

Arriving at the oil distribution box at the forward end of the propeller shaft, John saw that the oil pressure of the system seemed fine; but still, nothing was happening at the 'business end' of the *Aurora*'s propeller. John shook his head. Whatever the problem was, it must be inside the shaft itself. It's a massive job to even check the system inside the propeller shaft, let alone fix a problem in there.

John took the stairs up to the bridge two at a time.

'Well that's it,' John said to Peter, shrugging apologetically. The issue seemed to be located within the feedback pipe, and if it was, it wouldn't be an easy fix. The *Aurora* wouldn't be going anywhere for a while.

Captain Peter stared thoughtfully at his chief engineer while he processed the diagnosis. John was one of the pre-eminent chief engineers in the maritime industry and knew the *Aurora*'s systems better than anyone. If John said it was a serious problem, then Peter had no doubt this was the case. The captain set his shoulders. It was time to make some calls. Together, Peter and JvD went to the satellite phone to break the news to P&O Polar – and discuss their next move.

Over the next few hours, lengthy phone calls between the *Aurora*'s crew, the *Aurora*'s shore superintendent Dave Crane in Hobart and Lips (the CPP system manufacturers) in the Netherlands led to the consensus that the feedback piping within the propeller shaft had probably fractured somewhere along its 34-metre length. Lips felt the most likely scenario was a fracture in the very last length of piping, which was very unhelpfully located within the propeller hub itself. The best option was to remove all nine sections of the thirty-plus metres of piping within the propeller shaft and check every length for a fracture.

John exhaled as his suspicions were confirmed. It would take days.

But Lips went on; if there was indeed a fracture where they suspected, there was absolutely no way to repair it while the *Aurora* was at sea. The icebreaker would be stuck where she was until she could be towed out of the ice and taken to a dry dock for repair . . .

As they sat listening to Lips' grim prognosis, Peter looked at John and shook his head.

'You can't tow a ship in the ice,' the captain murmured to his chief. John shrugged again, this time in resigned optimism. 'Before we worry about that too much,' he consoled Peter, 'we need to find out if we are right about the problem.'

While Peter went to break the news to the VL Suzanne, John clumped quickly downstairs to mobilise his engineers.

Upstairs, Suzanne and Peter called a meeting with the expeditioners. Peter stood before the group and calmly explained the situation with the propeller system. 'Yes, we are stuck, but the *Aurora* is quite safe in the fast ice.' Once again, the *Aurora* had been lucky, Peter remarked. 'If the problem had occurred in the pack ice we would have drifted helplessly, and could have been dashed against an iceberg. But we're quite safe here; we have to just grin and bear it for the moment.' He promised to keep them updated. In the meantime, they would all be allowed a free phone call home to let their families know they were safe.

The meeting ended and nervous chatter filled the room. Colin, however, slumped back in his chair in gutted disbelief. That was it. The seal survey was over before it had really begun. Four years of planning, out the window – just like that. All that work! He knew from experience that the A factor was a force to be reckoned with and worked around, but honestly! Would his research program even be rescheduled to another year? The disappointment was crushing; the uncertainty, dizzying. Colin rubbed his forehead. He felt a throbbing headache coming on.

The one thing he did know was that now was not the time to wallow in self-pity. Instead, Colin focused his time and attention on processing what little data the team had managed to collect so far.

While Colin threw himself into his work, and the engineers were immersed in the oily problem downstairs, the rest of the expeditioners had little to do while they waited. Thankfully, in stark contrast to the howling four-day blizzard, the weather now was clear, sunny and remarkably mild.

First Officer Murray Doyle, or 'Muz', was on watch on the bridge. Not that there was much to do while the ship was parked in the ice. Murray fiddled with the scale of the radar – a jumble of green blobs and scribbles filled the screen, but not a pixel of the Pollockesque abstraction was moving; it was just ice reflecting the radar signal. Muz wandered across the bridge. Beyond the rear bridge-wing windows a group of expeditioners were lounging on the deck, sunning themselves. Muz chuckled, his eyes crinkled in humour. They looked in every respect like they could have been enjoying a Pacific cruise, if it weren't for the icy vista surrounding them.

Meanwhile, beneath her calm exterior, Suzanne felt less comfortable than Peter with their 'secure' location. An iceberg lingered worryingly off their port side, and Suzanne, familiar with the *Nella Dan*'s besetments and extremely close calls, found herself keeping an anxious eye on the offending 'berg. Like a protective parent, she silently worried about their situation even while she reassured her expeditioners. In the meantime, all she and the *Aurora*'s complement could do was wait for an update from the engineers.

After three exhausting days working in shifts hauling incessantly on a chain block, eight lengths of feedback pipe lay on the engine room floor. None had shown any sign of fracture. John and his engineers heaved with renewed energy on the chain to pull the final section of pipe out of the propeller shaft. They grasped the pipe as it finally emerged, and lowered it carefully to the deck.

There it was. The end of the feedback pipe had sheared right off, right at the end of the hub. The problem was exactly where Lips had said it would be.

And according to Lips, it would be impossible to repair.

The *Aurora Australis* was now officially beset in the ice. She was surrounded by ice and icebergs, 72 nautical miles from Davis, 280 miles from Mawson and a sobering 2612 miles (or 4838 kilometres) from Fremantle.

P&O Polar swiftly made arrangements to recover their paralysed icebreaker. One of the world's most powerful salvage tugs, the *John Ross*, was chartered from South Africa to tow the *Aurora* from Prydz Bay to Fremantle. But there was a problem: the super tug was not ice strengthened and could not rescue the *Aurora* from her position locked deep within the Antarctic sea ice.

The Australian Government turned to fellow Antarctic Treaty nations. The Antarctic Treaty was signed by fifteen nations back in 1959 and had come into force in 1961. There were currently

43 parties to the treaty, including Australia. While there are many provisions to the Treaty that each party must agree and uphold, most significantly member parties agree that '*Antarctica shall be used for peaceful purposes only*' and '*Freedom of scientific investigation in Antarctica and cooperation toward that end . . . shall continue*'.

In a nutshell, the spirit of the Antarctic Treaty is one of international cooperation and allegiance, regardless of politics.

In addition, operating in a remote, extreme and often brutal place like Antarctica means that when things do go pear-shaped, the only bodies generally capable of mounting a timely emergency response are other national Antarctic programs. But Antarctic rescues can come at a huge cost to a nation's own Antarctic pursuits. Rescue efforts use up valuable time and resources that had been intended for conducting research or resupplying Antarctic stations. Diverting an entire ship to conduct a rescue can mean dozens of scientific projects and complex logistic programs might be at best postponed, or at worst, cancelled altogether.

However, such unselfish acts of sacrifice do come with a karmic bonus. In Antarctica what goes around often comes around – and one day, a rescuer's own program may find itself in dire need of assistance.

But the question remained: was there even an international Antarctic program currently able to help the *Aurora Australis*?

As luck would have it, the Chinese icebreaker the *Xue Long* (or 'Snow Dragon') was due to arrive in the *Aurora*'s vicinity to resupply the Chinese base, Zhongshan station. China offered her aid: perhaps her ship could break the *Aurora* free from the ice, allowing the *John Ross* to take up the tow at the ice edge and return the *Aurora* to Australia. But neither the *Xue Long* nor the *Aurora* had towing equipment on board, so it was decided the best course of action, for the moment, was for the *Aurora* to stay put. Nevertheless, it was a comfort for everyone on board the *Aurora* to know that an icebreaker was relatively nearby if they urgently needed help.

The Japanese research and navy ship *Shirase* was currently in Fremantle preparing for a trip to Antarctica for the Japanese Antarctic program. The Japanese immediately answered Australia's call and offered every assistance. The offer was gratefully accepted. The *Shirase* delayed her scheduled departure from Fremantle so that a specialised tow rope could be purchased and loaded on board, then she raced her way across the Southern Ocean toward the *Aurora Australis*.

But on board the *Aurora*, Chief Engineer JvD had refused to accept defeat. John was convinced he and his engineers could fix the *Aurora* themselves, despite Lips's adamant claims that a repair was impossible. John, his engineers and the shore superintendent Dave Crane secretly hatched a plan to invent an object that might connect to the failed pipe and screw into the propeller hub. Ideas and designs soon streamed back and forth over the airwaves between Antarctica and Hobart.

The engineers were bent on success. Every idea, no matter how unconventional, was examined and discussed in detail. Dave set up a simulation jig at Taylor Bros workshop in Hobart and tested various options and prototypes. Knowing that resources on board the *Aurora* were limited, Dave only used materials that were available to the crew on board.

It was now abundantly clear to VL Suzanne that the Mawson resupply would have to take place from their current position in the ice, or it wouldn't happen at all. The *Shirase* was on her way to rescue them, and once she arrived the *Aurora* would be entirely committed to the process of getting home.

Suzanne sat at her small desk in the VL's cabin, mulling over their extensive cargo list. The *Aurora* was within range of a fly-off resupply, but the ship was still two and a half hours by helicopter from Mawson. So, including loading and unloading time, the pilots needed more than a five-hour weather window to get a load to the station and come back safely. It was a big ask. Suzanne called a meeting with the pilots, captain and officers. Together they pored over the numbers and maps, calculated the point of no return, and agreed it was practicable, in the right conditions.

Each precious resupply flight would clearly need to be used to its utmost potential, so Suzanne, DVL Steven and trainee deputy leader Gerald began the onerous task of sorting through and identifying every single item of cargo. They made their way between the *Aurora*'s tween decks and the helihangar, fossicking through shipping containers and rows of cage pallets. They sliced boxes open, prised lids off crates and went through every consignment with a fine-tooth comb. Their efforts were soon rewarded. Suzanne was stunned when Gerald suddenly stood, grasping a vibrant green, plastic potted bamboo plant taller than himself. It had been crammed into a cardboard box and packed as 'essential fly-off cargo'. Later, nestled snugly within a timber box, they uncovered a shiny red bicycle, also labelled as essential cargo. Laughing in amazed disbelief, Suzanne grabbed her camera and took photos of the offending items before swiftly removing them from the fly-off list.

The Mawson resupply began on the evening of 1 December. Expeditioners helped to organise and load cargo and cheerily worked around the clock. By the next morning, three flights of the two helicopters had successfully arrived at Mawson station. The resupply continued on and off for over a week, working around weather windows, with Suzanne and Steve keeping an eagle eye on operations, organising cargo and passenger manifests, monitoring the weather forecasts and meeting safety requirements.

Eventually the *Aurora*'s scientists and round-trippers who were meant to have time at Mawson arrived gratefully at the base. The station expeditioners welcomed the new faces – their arrival meant that the uncertainty of their own return date to Australia might soon come to an end (the Mawsonites' return had already been delayed several times because of the *Aurora*'s fire earlier in the season).

But while the choppers were able to fly to the station, and the *Xue Long* was not too far away if the *Aurora* did urgently need help, the reality was that those remaining on board the *Aurora* were largely on their own. Suzanne and Peter had no idea whether the *Shirase* would actually be able to reach them through the dense pack and fast ice that had packed around them during the blizzard. As a precaution, they asked the chefs to review the menus in case the *Aurora* was in for a long wait. Goods such as flour were flown in from Mawson to keep the galley going. Water production was reduced and all on board were instructed to participate in water rationing measures, including limiting showering to every second day. These procedures were precautionary, but they formed a foreboding cloud which hovered threateningly over the ship.

Back home, the news of the Aurora's situation had broken. 'It hasn't been the easiest season, as you would imagine,' AAD director Tony Press told a press conference in Sydney, covered by the *Mercury*. The negative impacts on the AAD's operational and scientific programs after the dual afflictions of the engine-room fire, and now the CPP failure, were all too apparent. 'It's been a bit like the Queen's *annus horribilis*,'* he later admitted to the Australian Broadcasting Commission (ABC).

Peter and Suzanne briefed the expeditioners and crew daily regarding the situation, plans and repairs. Most on board seemed to be coping fairly well, thought Suzanne after a day or so, but there were a few anxious faces in the mix. Suzanne was acutely aware that low morale was contagious and could spread through a ship like wildfire. She needed to keep everyone busy and distracted.

'Club Aurora' was born.

Suzanne instigated a full schedule of social activities: barbecues were regularly fired up on the trawl deck, where the comforting crackle and aroma of sizzling sausages (and vegie burgers) floated in the crisp, clean air while expeditioners and

---

* 1992 was dubbed the Queen's *annus horribilis*: that year three of the Queen's four children separated or divorced (and were involved in a number of related, highly publicised scandals), a tell-all biography about Princess Diana was published and a fire devastated Windsor Castle.

crew gathered together to relax, eat and take in the spectacular polar landscape around them. Hacky sack and deck tennis were regularly played on the helideck, much to the entertainment of the officers who watched the hotly contested tournaments on their grainy closed-circuit screen on the bridge.

Inside, Japanese and Spanish lessons were given by expeditioner nationals on board. Juggling and origami classes were also popular with the troops. Darts, table tennis, cribbage and Five Hundred competitions were conducted, and Suzanne noted satisfactorily the success of 'the ever popular Quiz Nites'. Science talks and slideshows were regularly given by onboard experts, including 'Sex-changing fish on the Great Barrier Reef' and 'Humpy harmonies: whales sing the blues'. Film screenings were advertised and enjoyed every evening. For the physical enthusiasts, as well as the games held on deck, there were aerobics and yoga classes and the regular use of the gym and sauna.

Their perilous situation was never far from their minds, but the mood on board turned noticeably from one of unease to lively optimism. They were also mindful of the sacrifices the Japanese were making to rescue them, and eager for their saviours to arrive.

On 4 December the satellite phone on the bridge rang and Shore Superintendent Dave Crane's voice came excitedly down the line. He'd had a breakthrough. John, Peter and the engineers sat riveted by the phone as Dave explained the piece they would need to construct to fix the CPP system. It was an ingenious fix, but it would be tricky to pull off. The team later explained to the Institute of Marine Engineers, 'The job was like someone trying to pick a lock on a door in an adjacent room, neither of which you had seen before!'

The piece was immediately nicknamed the Gizmo. In essence, the Gizmo was a bit like an anchor bolt: it consisted of a central pipe that protruded past a shorter, covering sleeve. It would be attached to the last section of the hydraulic feedback pipe, then fed through the propeller shaft and inserted into the propeller hub. Then, when the feedback pipe was pulled back slightly, the mating sleeve would expand and lock the bolt into position, thus replacing the fractured section of pipe and allowing oil delivery.

Or so the theory went. John and his engineers all knew the effect of doing this repair on the feedback pipe meant that they would not get a second stab at it. But the *Aurora* was entirely disabled already, so what did they have to lose? The engineers immediately set to work. Phillip Kennedy worked tirelessly at the lathe in the engine room workshop, carefully and meticulously machining the parts they needed.

News of the engineers' repair attempt spread around the ship and the Gizmo was soon the talk of the town.

Days later, John carefully laid a white cloth over a bench in the engine room. This kind of repair had never been successfully completed at sea, and John wanted to photograph the machined pieces for posterity before they were assembled together to form the Gizmo.

It was strange really, thought John as he arranged the components. It was hoped that these five small, unassuming pieces of metal would fix a problem that had immobilised a 94-metre ship. He lifted his camera to his face, focused the lens and wound the film on after every explosive flash.

The engineers made swift work of assembling the pieces, and their invention was soon ready. It took several long, greasy days to insert the Gizmo, but finally it made contact with the propeller hub. John hefted a huge wrench into position and threw his whole weight against it to rotate the inner pipe further and further. He felt the pressure go as it went through the bore, and he kept turning until it was past home. Together, the four engineers attached the chain block for the last time and heaved back on the inner pipe. It pulled the Gizmo into the mating sleeve, which expanded and locked the entire mechanism into position.

John felt a thrill of satisfaction. He was fully confident the *Aurora* could now break out of the ice under her own steam.

John van Dam

The components of the 'Gizmo' prior to assembly.

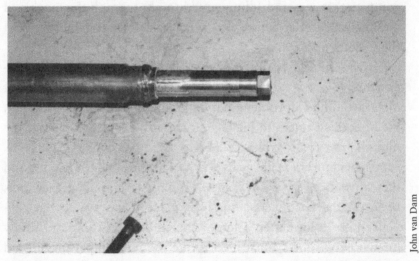

John van Dam

The Gizmo fully assembled (the narrow section to the right of the piping) and ready for insertion into the *Aurora*'s propeller shaft.

But recovery plans had already been made under the assumption that a repair was impossible. The *Shirase* was well on her way; the Japanese had gone to great lengths and had abandoned their own program specifically to help them out. The *John Ross* too was already en route to meet them at a rendezvous point north of the ice edge. They had no choice but to await the *Shirase*'s arrival. John's exhilaration quickly gave way to frustration; they were in the starting blocks ready for a sprint, but the marathon was already underway.

On the morning of 13 December, a blurry green dot materialised at the edge of the *Aurora*'s radar screen.

All eyes on the *Aurora*'s bridge strained toward the horizon. Despite the holiday atmosphere created by 'Club Aurora', there was a tangible feeling of relief when the pale superstructure of the *Shirase* appeared over the skyline. Eventually, the orange hull of the Japanese ship emerged from the fine sliver of horizon between ice and sky, and grew larger as the mighty vessel steamed resolutely toward them.

The *Shirase* was operated by the Japanese Maritime Self-Defense Force (JMSDF), a branch of the Japanese military. At 134 metres in length, the *Shirase* was a third longer than the *Aurora Australis*, and was capable of carrying a whopping complement of 170 crew plus sixty scientists. Launched in 1981, she was eight years older than the *Aurora*; and she had previously rescued the *Nella Dan* from a seven-week besetment in Antarctica.

The *Shirase* sliced through the ice like it was butter. The red sun-disk and rays of the JMSDF flag fluttered brightly above the superstructure as the huge ship steamed in circles around the *Aurora*, effortlessly breaking up the thick jumble of ice around the motionless vessel. Armies of people were out on every deck peering inquisitively at the stricken ship. Suzanne smiled wryly as she counted the number of crew fastidiously laying out the huge tow rope on the aft deck. It almost equalled the entire crew complement on the *Aurora Australis*. 'They don't do things by halves in the Japanese Self-Defense Force,' she thought.

Later that morning, Suzanne, along with Sanae, their Japanese biologist, who was acting as an interpreter, flew across to the *Shirase* to make arrangements for the *Aurora*'s recovery. In turn, a couple of the *Shirase*'s crew came onboard to act as liaison officers on the *Aurora*'s bridge. A small group of the *Shirase*'s engineers also flew across to lend the *Aurora*'s engineers some assistance with repair. This slightly riled JvD, who later wrote:

> . . . they thought we only had a broken pipe and we could not weld (I held a pressure welding qualification and one of our IRs was a former Taylor Bros boilermaker). When they realised what the problem was they asked me to pull our invention out but I assured them this was not possible.

Meanwhile, the *Shirase* continued to steam in circles around the *Aurora*, turning the unbroken mass of white around the orange ship into a churning, lumpy aqua–white soup. Finally, after twelve hours of icebreaking, the Japanese ship turned toward them. Muz watched as she slowly bore down on the *Aurora*, drawing closer and closer to the *Aurora*'s starboard side. The expeditioners standing on the bridge-wing shifted uncertainly as the *Shirase*'s bow loomed larger in front of them. The *Aurora* lurched slightly as the ice bulged under the pressure between the two vessels. Suddenly, the *Shirase* turned confidently hard to starboard; seconds later the two ships were side by side. Muz chuckled to himself as the expeditioners outside grinned at each other in embarrassed relief.

The back deck of the *Shirase* drew alongside the *Aurora*'s bow. The massive hulls of the two icebreakers were now separated by just metres of sludgy ice–water. A line of the *Shirase*'s crew, each impeccably turned-out in their thick navy jackets and yellow hard hats, assembled on the side of the *Shirase*'s helideck. The thick braided tow rope snaked back and forth at their feet. At the rear of the assembly, one crew member pointed a small, red, cannon-like device toward the *Aurora*'s bow. A readying flag was waved, a shrill note blown on a whistle and, with a resonating clap, the device was fired. A rocket arched over the *Aurora*'s bow, trailing a fine white line that draped across the deck. It was

Carrington Slipways

The moment the *Aurora Australis* is christened with champagne at her launching ceremony, 18 September 1989 (left). Pictured below, the *Aurora*, at full tilt, hits the launching basin at Carrington Slipways.

P&O Maritime Services

The *Aurora* navigating a stormy Southern Ocean. Waves can get as high as 20 metres and more.

Graeme Snow

Steve Nicol

'Well, there I was . . . the wind ripping around us at 120 knots, the waves as big as small conurbations, the ship being thrown around like a (insert your own metaphor here) when I asked myself "what would Captain Cook have done at a time like this?"'. Letter from Voyage Leader Steve Nicol, pictured here during a gnarly safety muster on the helideck during WOES/WORSE voyage, 1992/93.

Stay, Australia's unofficial Antarctic mascot, enjoying a few of her many Antarctic adventures and dog-napped capers (from top): going boating at Macquarie Island; diving under the Antarctic sea ice; meeting some friendly king penguins at Macquarie Island, and travelling incognito through Europe.

HOTEL AURORA

Colin Southwell

Murray Doyle

International cooperation has played an important role in the success of many national Antarctic research programs, with air and marine resources redirected without question in times of urgent need. Over her 30-year lifetime, Australia's primary maritime Antarctic resource, the *Aurora Australis*, has both given and received assistance in times of crisis or adversity. Such unselfish acts of valour and camaraderie between the international community have safeguarded the lives of many living and working in the harsh Antarctic realm.

Here we see the *Aurora Australis* under tow by the Japanese icebreaker *Shirase*, 1998 (top), and the CHINARE helicopter coming in to test the ice floe prior to the *Akademik Shokalskiy* passenger air evacuation, 2013 (bottom).

Natalie Tapson

Stay being carefully transported from the CHINARE helicopter across the ice floe to the *Aurora Australis* during the *Akademik Shokalskiy* passenger rescue, 2013.

Edwina Hollander/Australian Antarctic Division

The *Aurora Australis* and *Polar Bird* moored alongside each other at Horseshoe Harbour during the refueling, 2002/03. This untested manoeuvre was the first time in history two vessels would be moored together inside the harbour, which is usually a snug fit for just one vessel.

The *Aurora*'s diverse community is an important part of the icebreaker's personality. Highly skilled and professional, they are passionate about their ship and Antarctica; but they also make sure to take the occasional moment to enjoy the incomparable Antarctic experience.

Expeditioners and crew enjoy a Christmas feast during the HIPPIES voyage off Heard Island, 2003/04.

King Neptune with his attendants, 2017/18.

Rob Easther/Australian Antarctic Division

It's all about perspective: the icescape and icebergs dwarf the *Aurora Australis* in the distance.

Nicole Saunders/Australian Antarctic Division

The *Aurora* departs for the first voyage of the 2005/06 season in the traditional manner – farewelled with a large crowd and streamers. This tradition sadly fell out of practice in line with increased security requirements at the port in the late-2000's, with farewelling crowds subsequently unable to access the secure wharf area.

The *Aurora* allows scientists to study regions of the Southern Ocean that have never previously been explored. Scientists and technicians take full advantage of her unique laboratory facilities and ice-going capabilities, and their work contributes directly to our ever-increasing understanding of the Antarctic and Southern Ocean ecosystems.

Biologist Ty Hibberd sorting out invertebrates including feather stars and pencil urchins in the *Aurora*'s wet lab, 2010 (left). The field team collecting ice cores on the sea ice during the SIPEX voyage, 2007 (below).

A group of glaciologists drill on the sea ice, 1997.

Mike Whittle/Australian Antarctic Division

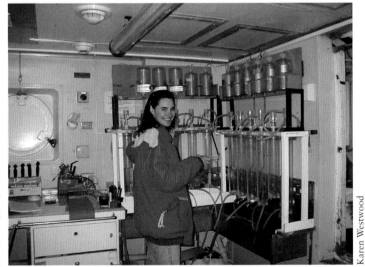

Biologist Karen Westwood conducts some underway sampling in the oceanographic lab during the KACTUS voyage, 2000/01.

Karen Westwood

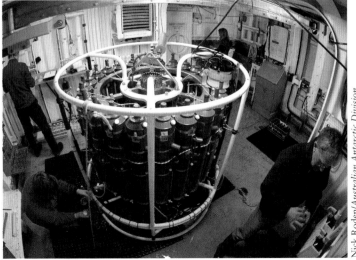

Scientists taking samples collected by the CTD for processing during SIPEX II, 2012.

Nick Roden/Australian Antarctic Division

Expeditioners hauling the refuelling hose ashore on Macquarie Island after resupply, 2013.

It is always a privilege to encounter Antarctica's beautiful and charismatic megafauna such as penguins, seals, seabirds and whales. Ship-based visual and passive acoustic surveys conducted on the *Aurora* have contributed to our understanding of the abundance and distribution of many Antarctic predators, and fishing and active acoustic surveys have helped uncover the important connections between these predators and their prey.

Here, we see (top) a view from Davis beach of the *Aurora* with southern elephant seals in foreground – the seal on right is fitted with a tracking device – and (bottom) a waddle of emperor penguins on sea ice in front of the *Aurora* during SIPEX II, 2012.

Darren Shoobridge/Australian Antarctic Division

Patti Virtue/Australian Antarctic Division

Expeditioners walking in the rafted sea ice in front of the *Aurora*, near the Amery Ice Shelf.

Trevor (Mike) Craven/*Australian Antarctic Division*

The *Aurora Australis* at Atlas Cove, Heard Island, 2008.

a lead-line, and with it the crew of the two ships transferred one end of the tow rope to the *Aurora*.

A messenger line is attached between the *Shirase* and the *Aurora Australis*.

'Geez, I could've lobbed that line over myself,' thought Suzanne with a smile, 'the ships are that close!' But she had to hand it to them; the meticulous efficiency of the rescuers was second to none.

The thick tow line was secured between the two ships and the *Shirase* gently moved ahead. Gradually, the tow line strained taut, and the *Aurora* began to glide after the *Shirase*. Small ice floes and brash ice scraped along the *Shirase*'s side then circled back around in her eddying wake; the ice jostled and bumped together, then clanged loudly against the *Aurora*'s bow. Muz stood at the helm, staring intently at the ship and ice ahead.

But just as he and the other officers began to relax into the tow, there was a colossal, whip-cracking boom. The tow line had snapped.

Murray swore. The *Aurora* drifted quickly to a standstill, slowed by the messy ice. Radio chatter filled the bridge as the two ships swiftly reacted and then made plans to reattach the tow line.

But that evening, just as they'd reattached the line and were about to resume the tow, the *Aurora*'s radio once again came to life. The *Shirase* advised matter-of-factly that operations would now cease for the day; it was time for the *Shirase*'s captain to go to bed. Muz was flabbergasted. Despite the *Shirase*'s huge complement, absolutely no towing would take place while the captain was not on the bridge. Instead, the *Shirase* continued to run circles around the *Aurora*, continually chopping up the ice around the Australian icebreaker while most on board the two ships slept soundly in their bunks.

The next morning, the tow line was secured for the third time, and finally, the *Aurora* was pulled along by the *Shirase*. This time the tow line held fast. But the *Aurora* refused to be towed in a straight line; the heavy, flat-bottomed ship slalomed in wide zigzags behind the *Shirase*. Captain Pearson and his officers did what they could to wrestle the *Aurora* into a manageable tow position, but it was a near-impossible task. Murray later wrote:

> If the *Shirase* went around a big floe the *Aurora Australis* would continue in the old direction until jerked around, like being on the end of a bungy cord, sometimes . . . we ended up at right angles to each other. The other problem was when the tow line became slack it got caught under ice floes and ran the risk of chafing.

There was also another problem. When the *Shirase* came across heavy ice it would slow her down, or halt her progress altogether. But the *Aurora* had no brakes and the threat of running up the back of the *Shirase* was a constant worry. The *Aurora*'s officers, nerves always on tenterhooks, managed to keep their unruly behemoth under control using the *Aurora*'s thrusters. But it was stressful work, and they finished each watch with a distinct sigh of relief.

Sleeping comfortably in his bunk in the early hours of the next morning Muz felt a jolt, and once again the *Aurora* suddenly slowed. Muz rolled over and switched on his radio, listening to the *Aurora*'s chatter. This time, the entire towing bracket on the *Shirase* had sheared clean off the deck. Muz rubbed the sleep from his eyes and rolled out of bed.

While the officers once again conferred urgently over the airwaves, chief engineer John saw the funny side of the bracket breakage, noting with a certain satisfaction that 'at least it gave [the *Shirase*'s] welders something to do'.

The tow eventually recommenced, and by day's end the two vessels were in a band of open water. But it had been a long, hard slog. At the *Aurora*'s helm, Captain Peter Pearson kept a close eye on a few uneven icebergs and 'bergy bits' floating around in the open water. There was a line of more sea ice in the distance. More slow-going ahead, thought Peter as he adjusted the *Aurora*'s thrusters for the thousandth time.

The next morning, 16 December, John paced around the bridge muttering about the ponderous rate of the towing operation. The chief engineer was fully confident that the Gizmo would work and that the *Aurora* was capable of coming to her own rescue, thanks very much. Murray, again on watch, couldn't help but smile. Sometimes, thanks to the friendly rivalry between the crew ranks in the maritime industry, a frustrated engineer is a hilarious sight for an officer to behold.

Murray's amused thoughts were abruptly interrupted by the concerned voice of the *Shirase*'s captain. John stopped in his tracks and turned toward the radio as Murray lifted the handset down from its clip overhead and acknowledged the call.

There was a problem with the *Shirase*, the captain reported; the slow speed of towing the *Aurora* in the ice was causing damage to the ship's massive engines. They could not continue to tow in this manner. Would it be possible for the *Aurora*'s crew to try their repaired system and see if it worked?

Murray grinned and turned toward the *Aurora*'s toey chief

engineer, but the space where John had only just been standing was now entirely vacant. Behind Murray the bridge door slammed loudly. John, finally unleashed, had sprinted down to the engine room. Chuckling, Murray asked the *Shirase* to stand by. He called Peter's cabin and relayed the request to his captain.

'You'd better ring the Chief,' instructed Peter, agreeing instantly.

'He's already in the engine room!' chortled Murray.

John busily warmed up the *Aurora*'s engines while the tow line was brought on board. He dialled an open line to Peter and Murray at the helm stations on the bridge, and confirmed he was clutching in the propeller.

Peter and Muz looked expectantly out the bridge windows. Nothing.

John's heart sank slightly as the officers relayed back that the *Aurora* hadn't moved an inch. But just as John turned to go check the engines, Peter called out.

'Hang on: we're moving!'

The *Aurora* slowly began to push through the broken ice, under her own steam for the first time in weeks. Proud, triumphant relief swept over John. Their determination, hard work and lack of sleep had paid off – the Gizmo worked!

That evening, having monitored the propeller system constantly since they'd clutched in, JvD and two of his engineers trudged wearily upstairs to dinner still wearing their oil-smeared orange boilersuits. As they arrived, the entire complement spontaneously erupted, raucously cheering, applauding and banging tables to show their appreciation of the engineers' mammoth efforts. In response, the weary engineers smiled shyly, and sat down for their well-earned meal.

Sailing in tandem, the two ships broke through to the open water of the Southern Ocean on the morning of 18 December. The *Shirase* was now free to resume its own Antarctic operations; but first, there were farewells to be had. On behalf of the Australian Antarctic Division, P&O Polar and all those on board, Suzanne and Peter gratefully pressed 241 individually addressed *Aurora Australis* Christmas cards – one for each and every member of the *Shirase*'s complement – into the hands of the departing *Shirase* crew and thanked them for coming to their aid.

Other, more official farewells were also taking place. Faxes flew between Canberra, Tokyo, Hobart, and the two ships, with, as Murray later recalled, 'everyone saying thank you . . . and how happy [they] are.' Finally, when the diplomatic niceties had been exhausted, the two ships bid their final farewell.

Suzanne stood among the crowds of crew and expeditioners out on the decks of both icebreakers, waving and cheering their goodbyes and good wishes to the other vessel as they passed each other for the last time. Then the *Shirase* turned and steamed west toward the horizon, heading for the Japanese base, Syowa station. The *Aurora* sat alone at the ice edge, patiently waiting for her escort home.

Just before 2100 the following day, the *John Ross* approached. A massive black-and-white supertug even longer than the *Aurora*, she bore a formidable reputation as one of the most powerful towing vessels in the world. By now the weather had increased and whitecaps crowned short, heaving swells, but the *John Ross* punched easily through the surging waves.

With the *John Ross* acting as escort rather than tug, the two ships began their transit north.

Meanwhile, John was keeping a close eye on things in the *Aurora*'s engine room. Almost as soon as they left the ice, the electric motor that powered the hydraulic pressure pump for the CPP began to overheat. John checked and rechecked the system, but couldn't find the reason for the temperature spike. Well, he reasoned, it was either run or burn. In the worst case, if the electric motor burnt itself out, they had the *John Ross* there to tow them home as originally planned. Otherwise, they may as well push on: there was nothing to lose. John and his engineers simply rigged up some fans to try to cool the motor enough to keep the *Aurora* running.

Upstairs, Christmas preparations were in full swing. Creative

'Kris Kringle' gifts were busily crafted from whatever useful materials the expeditioners could lay their hands on. The galley and restaurant were bedecked with strings of glittering tinsel, and the ship's Christmas tree was unearthed and brightly decorated. Anticipation of the culinary delights the chefs had in store for the complement was building; the *Aurora*'s Christmas feast was usually a huge affair – although this year expectations were somewhat muted because the Christmas dinner had not originally been part of the plan for this voyage.

The complement gathered for carols on Christmas Eve. The merry refrains were sung with gusto and echoed cheerily along the passageways from the restaurant.

At lunchtime the next day, Suzanne walked into the restaurant and gasped. A huge suckling pig sat on the long tables amid platter after platter heaped with sliced meats, whole chickens and turkeys, vegetables, salads and dried fruits. There was a mountain of oysters and a colossal whole salmon. Another table groaned with heart-stopping desserts, and yet another was burdened with beer, wine and sparkling. The complement piled their plates high, raised their glasses for a Christmas toast and tucked in to the feast. There was a cheery, sporadic popping, and bright paper bonbon crowns soon dotted the restaurant.

Just as they were finishing dessert, the sound of bells and hearty laughter belted out from the stairwell. Santa Claus had arrived. He was quickly escorted to the place of honour at the front of the gathering, and, with beard slightly askew, merrily fished Kris Kringle gifts out of a line of kit bags before presenting them to every member of the gathering.

Afterwards, cheeks flushed with Christmas cheer, the expeditioners eagerly climbed up the rear stairs to the helideck in search of their gallant escort, the *John Ross*. Leaning against the rails in a riot of flailing tinsel and waving arms, the group bellowed Christmas wishes at their chaperone until their throats were hoarse. A number of them moved apart to reveal a tinsel 'Merry Christmas' banner, which was excitedly waved toward the tug. They laughed and joked as the oceanic wind simultaneously whipped at their hair and made the fluttering banner near-illegible. But no matter. The message was received loud and clear, and the *John Ross* pulled closer alongside the *Aurora* and tooted her horn in mutual festivity.

The two ships crossed the Southern Ocean at an average speed of twelve knots, and finally pulled alongside the Fremantle wharves on 27 December. A small crowed of AAD and P&O officials waited in the glare while the *Aurora*'s gangway was lowered to the dock below.

Despite the *Aurora* eventually managing to rescue herself, the assistance of the Japanese had been a vital part of the *Aurora*'s successful recovery. The international spirit of cooperation was alive and well. As Captain Peter Pearson noted on a number of occasions during the voyage, 'If the rest of the world cooperated as well as they do in Antarctica, it would be a better place.'

John van Dam was intensely proud of his engineers. They had achieved the impossible. The *Aurora* had once again been rescued thanks to the collective expertise and commitment of her crew; even though the *Aurora* had been beset in the ice for two weeks, there were no injuries or major damage to the ship. Remarkably, all cargo operations had been completed and all personnel successfully transferred to and from the bases. While some of the science projects had been cancelled, they had already been rescheduled to the following season. Others, such as those using the underway seawater sampling system, weren't affected at all. With tongue firmly in cheek, Murray noted in an article in *Maritime Officer*:

> . . . the only casualty [was] Bill the Krill who died on Christmas Day, which was a great blow to Joel Scott who had been sent south to catch thousands and ended up with one and lost all with finish line in sight.

Back in Fremantle, formal congratulations from P&O representatives took place on the bridge of the *Aurora*. The captain, bridge officers and chief engineer were all given firm handshakes and hearty thanks, but the engineers in their orange boiler suits were assumed to be part of the *Aurora*'s deck crew and were overlooked. On many ships worldwide, engineers wear white coveralls, which can help distinguish them from other members of the ship's crew. On the *Aurora Australis*, engineers wear the same distinctive orange coveralls as the rest of the crew. John's only lingering regret would be that the other engineers were not thanked properly on their arrival to Fremantle.

The *Aurora*'s crew, however, were so proud of their fellow engineers that they installed a permanent memorial to their efforts in the *Aurora*'s engine room. The small, unassuming timber shelf bore a brass propeller with each of the four engineers' names engraved on a blade and a matching plaque forever proclaiming 16 December as National 'Gizmo' Day.

The Gizmo was officially named the CvD link (Crane van Dam link), with a *Marine Engineers Review* article about the ordeal and the ingenious repair headlined 'Mission impossible!' Their unlikely fix was so innovative it became legend within the Australian maritime industry: John's name was henceforth widely known and became synonymous with the *Aurora Australis* herself. All the while, John continued to refuse single credit for the success, always honouring the role his engineers and shore superintendent played in the event.

Chapter Seven

THE RULE
OF THREES

On 11 January 1999, two weeks after her safe return to Fremantle, the repairs to the *Aurora*'s propeller system were complete and the *Aurora* was slowly lowered from the dry dock. She passed a sea trial for seaworthiness just off the West Australian coast and, having been declared fit for operation, was once again loaded with cargo, this time at the North Quay container berths in Fremantle. From there, she would depart for a resupply voyage to Casey and Mawson, with a quick stop along the way to retrieve some of the moorings that had been deployed before the fire had erupted.

As the Fremantle twilight dwindled to darkness on 13 January, Second Engineer Robert Cave (the engineer who'd been on duty on the night of the fire) bustled around the lower plates of the windowless engine room. The engineer, wearing his oil-smeared orange boilersuit and black earmuffs, was preparing the *Aurora*'s larger V16 engine system for the departure push from the wharf. He opened the pistons, clearing them of water. 'The engine room's looking good,' Rob thought as he ran his safety checks; the last time he'd seen it, it was depressingly dark and gloomy after the fire. Now the only sign there'd ever been an incident was the conspicuously fresh paintwork of the nine-year-old engine room.

He walked over to the control panel and hit the switch to start the V16. But as soon as the *Aurora*'s large engine rumbled to life, a dirty cloud of exhaust spewed into the engine room. Rob frowned and hurriedly fiddled with couplings and hoses, running checks and searching over the engine; but try as he might, he couldn't find the source of the smoggy leak. Stumped, he phoned Keith Thorpe, Chief Engineer on this voyage, for his opinion. A few minutes later, Keith's tan steel-capped boots clunked hurriedly down the steep ladder treads to the engines.

But even Keith couldn't find the fault. After running his own checks, the chief stood back, twisting his lips as he stared thoughtfully at the engine. He signalled to Rob to shut down the V16. They could go out on the V12 and fix the exhaust leak on the bigger engine while they were at sea. Rob nodded his agreement and set to work preparing the *Aurora*'s smaller engine. He quickly fired it up and it purred happily while it came up to operating temperature.

Shortly after, Captain Dick Burgess stood alongside a Fremantle pilot at the *Aurora*'s helm. After receiving clearance to leave the port, Dick sounded the *Aurora*'s horn in one long, booming blast. Down on C deck, near the raised gangway, a handful of expeditioners vainly waved and called out cheery farewells to the near-deserted floodlit commercial wharves below.

John Kitchener, a plankton specialist from the Antarctic Division, was among them. Despite the empty wharves below it didn't feel right not to farewell civilisation when they were leaving. John stood at the rail, quietly waving. He was looking forward to the voyage. Like many of the crew currently on board, John had been on the *Aurora* during the fire earlier in the season. And now – finally – after being frustrated by the delays from the fire and then the CPP failure, he was able to pick up his research where it had left off.

The *Aurora* motored through the entrance to Fremantle Harbour, and then slowed momentarily to let the pilot climb safely down the wooden rungs of the boarding ladder to his waiting pilot boat. Soon the *Aurora* was humming along at a speed of 11.5 knots, comfortably heading south under the watchful, unblinking eyes of the Southern Cross.

Once again, it was Rob's shift as overnight duty engineer on call. After checking the engine room, he programmed the alarms to the repeater panel in his cabin, went upstairs, hopped into bed and promptly fell into a comfortable sleep.

Just after six o'clock the next morning, the panel in his room shrieked obnoxiously. Rob groggily rolled out of his bunk and stepped over to the blinking light near his door. A noncritical. He silenced the alarm, threw on his boilersuit and tramped blearily down the stairs.

The engine alarm also sounded on the bridge's repeater panel. Captain Dick Burgess – only on his second voyage on board the *Aurora* – had just relieved First Mate Les Morrow on watch. Dick pressed the button acknowledging and silencing the bridge alarm, then waited for the duty engineer to report back to the bridge. Suddenly, another alarm buzzed impatiently behind him. A red indicator light was blinking furiously on the fire panel at the rear of the bridge. Dick quickly strode around the chart table to the indicator panel; it was an alarm for zone 21 in the engine room.

Just as he went to press the button to acknowledge the alarm, another lit up with a shriek. Then another. As a sea of red lights spread across the panel, Dick pulled back his outstretched hand and turned, leaving the alarms frantically wailing, and instead he hurried over to the phone to call an IR to go and investigate.

In his bunk on D deck, John Kitchener had just woken up for the day. He stretched lazily, and idly noticed a shaft of sunlight peeking around the edge of his porthole's blind. He stared dreamily at the swirling dust motes in the bright beam. Then he frowned slightly, suddenly concentrating. The dust was swirling thinly in the air rather than hanging suspended. Something about that wasn't quite right.

Upstairs, Captain Dick stood impatiently listening to the rhythmic ringing of the phone. He glanced at the closed-circuit

TV monitor at the helm, where the black-and-white images on screen were flicking steadily between locations on the ship. His heart skipped a beat as the engine room appeared on the screen.

Flames.

Then the screen went blank.

'No!' Dick yelled to the empty bridge. 'Not another f#%king fire!'

Hardly believing his eyes, Dick pulled the *Aurora* back and simultaneously hit the general alarm button, keeping it held down under his finger for a few seconds. The *Aurora*'s bells erupted into a ringing chorus, and then went mute.

Downstairs John Kitchener jumped as the bells rang out. Shit! A weight instantly dropped like a rock in the pit of his stomach. The terror of the fire on the earlier voyage was still all too vivid in his mind, and he leapt out of his bunk and frantically started getting dressed. There was no way he was hanging around; he knew now that the 'dust' he'd been looking at was smoke – and if smoke was on D deck, a fire was either close, or it was extremely bad.

Meanwhile, as the *Aurora*'s bells rang, duty engineer Rob reached the door to the engine room at the bottom of the main stairwell. The sharp smell of smoke hung threateningly in the air. He hurriedly snatched his steel-capped work boots from the wooden shelf, kicked off his soft indoor shoes and half-crouched, tugging on his boots in preparation for whatever lay before him. As he straightened an IR arrived behind him; and before Rob could even open his mouth to protest, the IR pulled the engine-room door open.

A thick cloud of black smoke spewed out of the doorway and spiralled up into the *Aurora*'s main stairwell. Rob and the IR both staggered back, coughing.

'This can't be happening,' Rob thought, 'not again.' He muttered a curse and then dived toward the door.

'Tell them I've gone in,' Rob barked at the IR. With that, he took a deep breath, shut his eyes and disappeared into the pall, pulling the door closed behind him.

*

Upstairs, First Engineer Kenny Tivendale and all four of the bridge officers had been startled by the strange, short ringing of the bells, and they rushed out of their cabins on B deck, running as a group toward the single flight of stairs to the bridge. They all knew the short alarm meant something, they just weren't sure what. But as soon as they raced into the stairwell, the fetid, smoky air wiped any trace of uncertainty from their minds.

First Mate Les shouldered the bridge door open, and the sound of shrieking alarms spilled down to the others still coming up the stairs. The group rushed into the bridge and found Dick standing at the fire panel.

Nine zones of the engine room now had activated fire detectors, he reported tensely as they arrived. Chief Engineer Keith suddenly appeared behind the group, breathlessly saying that he couldn't get to his muster station down in the engine room – the smoke in the stairwell down there was too damn thick. For a fraction of a second they all looked at each other.

Then they scattered, moving into action. Radio Officer Roger Linbird hurried to the radio room and switched both radios over to battery power. Captain Dick and Chief Engineer Keith went through the process of shutting down the engine room and accommodation ventilation systems from the bridge, and Les leant over the phone, dialled the public address 'bing–bong' number and urgently announced, 'All passengers and crew are to go immediately to their muster stations wearing their lifejackets.'

The clipped, British voice of the first mate echoed hollowly out of the speakers and phones in passageways, cabins and public spaces. He paused, then repeated the message.

'All passengers and crew are to go immediately to their muster stations wearing their lifejackets.' He released the PA button and turned to assist his captain.

In the radio room, Roger called Perth Radio. There was no answer. He tried a second time and paused, but once again there was just static.

Meanwhile, Second Mate Scott dashed toward the muster point on the helideck. But on the way he detoured down to the corridors on D deck, in a frantic effort to make sure the expeditioners knew there was a real fire.

'Get out, get out, get out!' Scott yelled down the corridors as he hammered on door after door, then ran upstairs to coordinate the muster.

John Kitchener's blood ran cold at the stressed urgency in Scott's voice. The fire must be right behind him! Dressed now, John grabbed his freezer suit in one hand, his emergency grab bag in the other and ran for his life, up to the helideck.

Downstairs, having just stepped through the engine room door, Rob blindly lunged for the control room door, holding his breath. He knew it was only a metre or two away. His hand found the handle and he flung the door open, lurched inside, then threw himself back against it.

Rob opened his eyes, taking in the situation inside the control room in an instant. The air was clear; the control panels were a panic of blinking lights and buzzing alarms; and the window pane in the door overlooking the engine room was completely dark. It was black as night back there.

Jesus Christ. Already, this fire seemed more intense than the one he'd survived just months ago.

Rob set to work on the panels. He saw that Dick had shut the engines down from the bridge. Good. Rob's hands were a blur over the buttons, switches and dials as he shut down the fuel pumps, circulating pumps and ventilation fans.

Then he stood over the speaker phone and dialled the bridge's number. A thin haze of smoke now hung in the air above his head.

'It's a major fire,' Rob shouted down into the phone as it was answered by the captain. 'I've shut down the pumps and fans. It's zero visibility in the engine room. It's bad down here.'

Rob glanced over at the window again. If anything, the darkness in the engine room had intensified. There was no way he was going back that way; the putrid smoke would be incredibly dangerous even over such a short distance, without even considering how much was now floating in the stairwell above the engine room's door.

'I don't think I can get out,' he added.

'Get out of there!' Dick commanded urgently. 'Go out the emergency exit and get to your muster station.'

'Okay,' Rob confirmed before quickly hanging up. He turned and sprinted for the control room's emergency escape shaft at the aft end of the control room. He opened the metal hatch, fastened the door behind him and clambered up the cold steel rungs, each tread echoing hollowly through the vertical metal shaft. Finally, he opened the shaft's upper hatch in the bunker station on E deck, just behind the *Aurora*'s restaurant.

He flung the restaurant door open and dashed past the rows of empty tables and chairs, making straight for the ship's central stairwell. He wanted to check it – god knows how much smoke had spewed into the space when they'd opened the engine room door. Rob yanked the door open and dark, foul smoke billowed into the restaurant. He swore. The stairwell was far too dangerous for anyone to use. He knew the crew wouldn't dare risk using it, but the evacuating expeditioners might still try.

Rob slammed the door closed and streaked down the starboard passageway, running past the string of science labs toward the rear stairwell. He bolted up to the expeditioner cabins on D deck and hurried into the alleyway.

He pressed his back against the wall as expeditioners hurried past him on their way to their muster station on the helideck. They seemed relatively calm, except for the alarm in their eyes. But a small group were hovering uncertainly up the forward end of the passageway near the central stairwell. As he rushed up the corridor Rob saw the emergency exit stickers above their heads glowing softly on the bulkheads: the *Aurora*'s power was out, Rob realised. He smoothly pushed past the uncertain group and pointed them toward the rear exit, explaining it was safer.

As they hastily moved off, the last of the expeditioners began to emerge from their cabins, now carrying torches to help see through the increasing smoke. Again, Rob pointed them away from the central stairwell, directing them to use the rear exit. Rob stayed at his post near the central stairwell until he was certain D deck was clear of personnel.

In the radio room, Radio Officer Roger had still not received a response to his calls. He threw his head back in exasperation, looking up at the clock on the bulkhead. It was just after 6.30 am. His eyes widened as he realised that the radio silence period for distress channels was just starting. (At this point in history, three minutes of radio silence were observed on the hour and half hour on distress frequencies to increase the chances of a weak distress message being heard. These periods are no longer required, but are still recommended.) He turned back to the panel, picked up the handset, changed frequencies to 2182 kHz and tried again.

This time, a crackling response instantly came back through the speaker. Breathing a sigh of relief, Roger relayed that a fire had broken out in the engine room of the *Aurora Australis*, and asked Perth Radio to stand by for more information.

On the bridge, Captain Dick stood at the helm listening intently to the *Aurora*'s radio for confirmation from the muster that everyone had been accounted for. Minutes later, the message came back from Scott on the helideck – all personnel were accounted for, except for engineer Rob Cave.

Dick stood anxiously, waiting for further news. The last he'd heard of Rob, he said he would leave the engine control room. Had Rob made it out safely? Or had he collapsed inside? If he made it out he should have reported to his muster station by now. At the rear of the bridge, Keith unlocked the perspex door of the halon control panel and turned the key switch to ready the system. He looked over at his captain expectantly, waiting for the command to release the gas.

Dick wouldn't give it. Not yet. It could kill Rob if he was still down there. But as the seconds ticked by, Dick knew the time was fast approaching when he might have to choose between some-one's life in the engine room, and the safety of the ship and the lives of the rest of the people on board. He felt every heavy thud of his heart as the seconds dragged on.

A minute later, Rob flung open the bridge door, ran over to Keith and breathlessly told the chief engineer that the situation downstairs, in his opinion, was bad.

Relieved, Dick looked over to Keith and told him to deploy the suppressant system. For the second time in a single season, halon was dropped in the engine room of the *Aurora Australis*.

Dick turned to Roger and instructed him to broadcast a pan pan distress message to all ships. Roger immediately strode back to the radio room and sat down.

PAN PAN, PAN PAN, PAN PAN. This is the *Aurora Australis, Aurora Australis, Aurora Australis*. PAN PAN *Aurora Australis*. Our location is 32 degrees 57.7 minutes South, 114 degrees 09.7 minutes East. We are 97 miles from Fremantle. Our vessel has an engine room fire. We have forty people on board. There are no injuries. Stand by. Over.

It was now just 6.34 am.

Smoke and toxic fumes from the fire had begun to infiltrate the highest levels of the *Aurora*, and the air inside her bridge was quickly turning noxious.

Dick, the officers and engineers hastily moved their control station out into the fresh air on the starboard-side bridge wing. They stood together in a tight cluster, grasping radios and clip-boards in their hands as they blinked in the bright light. The glary, sunlit morning seemed surreal after the smoky gloom inside. Above them, thick, fetid smoke and halon poured out of the *Aurora*'s stacks, forming a grave pillar against the clear blue sky.

The rancid smoke had also begun to waft into the radio room, and Roger stood and shut the door to the bridge. He unlatched the portholes, opening them inward as far he could to let fresh air into the space, then slid back onto his seat at the radio desk. He was now the only person remaining inside the smouldering ship.

Once again, it was time to wait while the halon took effect.

Dick was relatively new to the *Aurora*, having come from the offshore industry, but he knew that his officers, engineers and crew all had a huge amount of experience on the icebreaker – and many had endured the last fire. Wanting to use this combined wisdom to its full effect, he held regular 'toolbox' meetings on the bridge wing. He and Chief Engineer Keith agreed that they would wait a minimum of two hours before they would begin venting the engine room.

The next question they had was, how long would the emergency power last?

Keith hurried around to the emergency generator room and found the fuel line halfway up the indicator. He reported back that there was half a tank left, and the group agreed the best option was to shut the emergency generator down, to conserve what emergency fuel they had left.

Keith shut the generator down, and once again, the *Aurora Australis* floated silent and powerless, this time on the Indian Ocean. On this occasion, however, emergency batteries continued to supply power to her radios and communications station.

Although the sun glittered brightly off the sapphire-blue water, the sea heaved with rolling swells. The smoking *Aurora* drifted beam-on to the swell and she rolled so heavily that the expeditioners, sitting on the green steel of the helideck, struggled to stay upright. The sun beat down upon the exposed deck and reflected off the steel decks and superstructure, and the harsh rays began to sting and burn bare arms and faces. No-one had thought to grab hats or sunscreen when evacuating the accommodation. In fact, their pre-departure training had been so effective that John and a few others had even grabbed their freezer suits, forgetting they were still in the temperate climes off the Western Australian coast.

There was nothing the expeditioners could do except wait, and they had no idea for how long. John found a shady nook around the corner near the C deck companionway, rolled up his freezer suit for a pillow and lay down on the deck. His fear had now given way to anger: how could this happen again? How could so many things go wrong in a single season? He crossed his arms and grumpily closed his eyes, hoping that sleep might expedite the incessant waiting.

The crew placed a bucket behind a cage pallet – the most discreet position available on the otherwise bare, open deck – for use as a toilet. Some of the crew, the memory of the first fire still fresh in their minds, had thought to grab large bottles of fruit juice as they evacuated the restaurant, and had taken them up for the expeditioners to share. These were received gratefully, but quenched thirst only for so long.

They were only nine hours out of Fremantle, and not far from a major shipping lane. Occasionally massive cargo ships steamed past in the distance, the expeditioners watching as the imposing vessels appeared and then disappeared over the horizon at breakneck speed. The colossal ships did give them some comfort: at least help wouldn't be too far away if the worst were to happen.

Just before 9 am, two small teams of crew wearing breathing apparatus stood at the dimly lit shaft tunnel facing the water-tight door to the engine room. The first team, Chief Engineer Keith and Dean McPherson, an IR, were getting ready for entry. A fire hose had been rigged and was ready at the door. Another IR stood holding a fire board to record their entry and exit times and the pressures of their air tanks. A second team, consisting of Third Engineer Jon Handicott and Second Mate Scott, were stationed on standby at the watertight door.

The door was winched open, and Keith and Dean stepped into the engine room. The previously shiny metals and pristine, glossy painted surfaces of the engine room had once again been replaced with a dimensionless, matt-black gloom. Engines

Sarah Laverick

The *Aurora*'s engine room as it normally looks, viewed from the mezzanine. The V16 engine is on the left, the V12 on the right. The drum-like turbo charges are on the forward ends of the engines.

P&O Maritime Services

The engine room (above the starboard engine), after the second fire.

and machinery appeared in the swinging, hazy torchlight like ghostly spectres that retreated eagerly back into the darkness. The wiring and fluorescent light fittings on the deck-heads above had melted, just as they had in the first fire. The congealed fibres and plastic dripped from the ceiling like thick spider's webs.

The pair stepped slowly around the engine room. This time, the damage was worst around the *Aurora*'s smaller V12 engine, and heat was still radiating from engine and walkway plates surrounding it. While they could see that the fire was out, they needed to cool the hot surfaces of the engine down so they wouldn't be a starting point for further fire.

The pair connected a fire hose to a nearby hydrant, with Dean grasping the end and Keith manning the valve. But as Keith twisted the hydrant on, a metallic clank rang around the engine room, accompanied by a sodden curse. The brass end fitting had blown clean off the fire hose, sending water spewing wildly from its end.

Keith muttered an oath and turned off the water. He lumbered around the engine room and climbed up to the mezzanine, toward the fire hose he knew was stored on that level. As he climbed, beads of sweat trickled down his nose and cheeks inside his mask. He breathlessly reached the platform above and behind the engines, but the hose there had completely melted in its stowage bracket. It lay in a congealed mess on the metal deck, like an old, discarded snake skin.

The pair radioed the team outside, asking for a spare hose to be passed into the engine room. Once again, they set the new hose to the lower hydrant, ready to cool the V12. But just after Keith opened the valve, a violent cascade of water suddenly gushed around Keith's legs and ankles. What the hell was going on with these hoses? He hurriedly shut the hydrant off. This time, the hose had blown from the end fitting, right at the coupling to the hydrant.

The standby team passed a third hose to the team in the engine room. But their allocated time was running out, so instead of cooling the area Keith decided to complete his inspection of the engines. Amazingly, the *Aurora*'s larger V16 engine, while blackened and covered in soot and ash, seemed relatively unscathed. It might just be workable.

Keith and Dean emerged from the engine room and lifted their masks off, faces covered with sweat. The fresh air inside the net store was cool, sweet relief after the humid confinement of the breathing apparatus masks.

Two recently serviced fire hoses had just failed on them, so brand-new fire hoses were pressure tested on the trawl deck before being pressed into service in the engine room. The teams switched over, and Jon and Scott took one of the working hoses into the engine room. They doused the area around the V12, cooling it down. Shortly after, the teams switched over again. Keith and his offsider began meticulously checking the engine room for other hotspots.

They slowly wound their way from the engine room bottom plates up toward the engine control room level, and had almost completed their inspection when something caught Keith's eye. Just outside the engine control room, a thin tendril of smoke was rising from a small bin. He peered into the bin; it was full of smouldering rags and was a possible ignition source for further fire. Keith grabbed a nearby fire extinguisher and let it loose on the smoking pile, but the dry powder had no effect on the embers, which still glowed sullenly. A crackling radio message from the team waiting outside reminded them their air would soon run out, and they needed to leave the engine room.

After Keith stepped out of the engine room and explained the situation with the smouldering bin, the second team plucked water extinguishers from the walls on D deck and carried them into the engine room. Jon and Scott tipped the bin upside down, spread the smouldering rags out with their booted feet and doused them, saturating the ashes and extinguishing the smoking threat.

The fire was out and there were no other hotspots. Finally, they would be able to vent the engine room, clearing it of smoke and halon.

But the *Aurora*'s cabling systems that had been so painstakingly repaired just months before had once again been decimated. The fire had destroyed essential power cables and electrical wiring required across the ship, including that of the engine room vent fan.

The only option for venting the engine room was natural draught. It would take hours, but they had no other choice.

Meanwhile, the engineers, still wearing their stifling BA gear, worked madly in the charred engine room to determine the extent of the damage and make a plan to restore the *Aurora*'s basic systems. They worked through the systems logically, beginning with the engine room generators, which would be needed when they were ready to start the main engine.

All engines such as generators require air to start, so the engineers first needed to supply air to the *Aurora*'s main generator. However, its starting air bottles were empty, so the engineers needed to fire up a compressor to refill the bottles. But when they switched the compressor on, the *Aurora*'s emergency generator cut out. The air compressor's power cables, damaged by the fire, were short-circuiting the entire emergency generator system. The engineers wound their way up through the ship to the emergency generator room to restart it, but found that the emergency generator's Automatic Voltage Regulator (AVR) had failed.

It was a lethal blow. Without the emergency generator, there was no start air; and without the start air, there was no main generator, which meant they could not start the main engine. Dick's hands were tied. He had no choice but to call for help. Dick rang P&O and asked them to arrange for a tug boat to come out to the *Aurora Australis* and tow her back to Fremantle.

Chief Engineer Keith was aghast. Following both of the disasters this season the *Aurora*'s other engineers had managed to patch up their ship and nurse her home. *They* hadn't needed a tow. This was personal. After everything the *Aurora* had overcome this season, there was no way she was going to take a humiliating tow back into port. Not on his watch.

So, even as P&O began to make arrangements, Keith and his engineers continued to work madly in the torchlight of the *Aurora*'s pitch-black engine room.

It was the emergency generator that was the problem. If they could just get that started, they could get a start air compressor going, then fire up a main generator, get some cooling water and other critical systems going, and then start the V16. The question was, how could they repair the emergency generator's AVR?

In a stroke of pure genius Keith decided to bypass the AVR entirely. Using all of his electrical nous, Keith rigged a series of two-volt batteries to use as starter excitation for the emergency generator. He sparked the generator to life, and, as the electrical load increased, Keith adjusted the system's output voltage by effectively applying a jumper lead at the appropriate battery along the series, giving the right level of output voltage for the system to hold up.

The next step was to tackle those air compressors. The wiring to all the compressors was blackened and charred, but the engineers did notice that the wiring to one compressor seemed slightly less damaged than the others. They gave it a go.

The bloody thing started.

They had start air! And with it they could try to start one of the ship's main generators. It was now 5.21 pm, and just sixteen minutes later, lights and basic electrical systems began to flicker to life across the *Aurora*.

Upstairs, the sixteen expeditioners still sat on the helideck, where they had been for almost twelve hours. As with the first fire, First Mate Les had watched over the expeditioners and was a reassuring presence throughout the crisis. Dick had regularly briefed them about the situation downstairs, but at each briefing he confirmed that the smoke and noxious fumes inside the ship were still too strong to allow them inside. As the sun made its weary descent to the west, the expeditioners continued to wait.

Finally, at 8 pm they were allowed back inside the ship. They filed down to the D deck rec-room, sombrely taking in the soot-covered, grimy walls along the way.

John Kitchener sat down on one of the few lounges lining the walls and examined his sunburnt arms, but a few minutes later looked up as the lights went off. The projector screen ahead lit up. Someone had prepared a slide presentation for that evening, and it sat waiting in the carousel. The captain and crew were still busy, and VL Warren Papworth and the expeditioners agreed they should give the talk, in an attempt to pass the time as much as distract themselves.

But the *Aurora* was still rolling heavily, and the lingering smell of smoke did nothing to help those who were feeling queasy. As the carousel loudly clicked and whirred from slide to slide, the *Aurora* wallowed in the swell. First one, then a number of expeditioners crept their way forward to a clear space in front of the screen. They lay uneasily on the floor, their pallid green faces and rigid body language obvious even in the flickering light.

The *Aurora* teetered alarmingly from side to side, and the expeditioners held on for dear life. The projector flew clean off its pedestal and onto the deck, narrowly missing one of the nauseated expeditioners laying nearby. Upstairs, cargo in the helihangar broke loose, then clattered across the deck with each roll.

Meanwhile, the oxygen levels in the engine room had returned to acceptable levels, and, finally free of their cumbersome breathing apparatus, the engineers worked with renewed, frantic energy in the murk of the cavernous engine room. While they worked on wiring, pipes, connections and pumps, bright blue sparks flared overhead and vanished like eerie blue fireflies as the exposed hanging wires arced randomly. The engineers worked on the *Aurora*'s cooling systems, lube oil, the gear box and CPP systems, which all needed to be checked and patched to the engine.

But Keith knew they couldn't sustain this frantic pace for long, so he sent Kenny and Rob to bed while he and Jon kept going, taking the first watch. The pair kept their heads down and went for broke. At about 11 pm, Keith and Jon crossed everything and held their breath while Keith pressed the start button to the V16 engine. It started with a triumphant roar.

The *Aurora* lurched forward, sending people flying across the ship. The *Aurora*'s clutch had immediately engaged, most likely due to damaged wiring. But Keith and Dick let her run, and the *Aurora* was officially making her way toward Fremantle.

Under her own steam.

But Keith and Jon were too exhausted to enjoy the exhilaration of this massive accomplishment. They also needed to keep working furiously to keep the *Aurora*'s fragile systems operating. The V16 was constantly on the cusp of overheating; in addition, there was no pitch control (or control of the *Aurora*'s speed) from the bridge: that wiring had also been decimated somewhere along the line. Instead, down in the dark, cool stern beneath the *Aurora*'s trawl deck, an engineer stood at the *Aurora*'s manual controls. He adjusted her speed according to the directions of the bridge officer, whose voice emanated from the black, art deco form of the rarely used, crank-operated emergency phone system.

Just after midnight, Keith sent Jon to bed while the other engineers took up the watch. Jon trudged wearily up the stairs to his cabin on B deck. But when he gratefully opened the door, his familiar little refuge was a scene of carnage. Jon later remarked, 'I know what that ship does in a sea, and I've been in plenty of big seas in it, but my cabin had never been in such a shit fight. The floor was just covered in shit: books and clothing, all my drawers were open, the cupboard doors were open. My overalls . . . were off the hooks and on the deck . . . the chair upside down – [the cabin was] just nailed.'

Focused only on the tasks at hand, Jon hadn't even felt the *Aurora* roll, despite the orange ship swinging over thirty white-knuckling degrees at times. Exhausted, he closed the drawers and latched the cupboard, trudged a path through his belongings to his bunk and collapsed onto his bed.

Just before 3 am, the tug boat *Wambiri* came into view on the *Aurora*'s radar. But she was not required for a tow, and instead had to content herself with running as an escort.

Ten hours later, with her engineers having waged successful battle against constantly overheating and failing systems, the *Aurora Australis* arrived safely at Fremantle harbour.

But the whole situation still felt surreal. 'I personally could not believe a second fire was possible and nor could anyone else, especially those who had been onboard for the first,' Dick Burgess wrote in his captain's report.

But how had the fire started? It was the second in just three voyages; had P&O, or the crew, failed in some way? It was a question that many were asking.

The subsequent MIIU fire investigation found that the fire was caused by fuel spraying from a failed flanged joint on the V12 engine. Two of the joint's screws had failed in fatigue, but the report couldn't definitively conclude whether these failures were due to vibration (a common problem on an icebreaker) or from overtightening, or a combination of both factors. This failed joint had a sheet metal cover over it, which had been constructed and installed by shoreside contractors two years earlier, but as bad luck would have it there was a very narrow gap at the aft end that aligned exactly with the failed flanged joint, allowing fuel to escape into the engine room's atmosphere. Every other cover on the *Aurora*'s engines was fitted perfectly.

The resulting spray of fuel had, once again, likely ignited on contact with the hot surfaces of the turbochargers or the exhaust system on the engine. The fire had burnt hot and fast, like a 'boiler burner', causing little smoke until the overhead wiring had begun to scorch, and then ignited. It was this wiring and cabling that caused the huge pall of noxious smoke inside the *Aurora*.

The report noted that in twelve months, the MIIU had investigated four engine room fires onboard ships in Australian waters, 'which were directly attributable to the failure of flanged joints secured by socket head cap screws'. It also noted that, following the previous fire, 'P&O had taken all reasonable measures to reduce the risk of another such engine room fire'. It praised the prompt and effective response of the crew to the fire.

Dick agreed, later writing, 'A fight with an intense fire of this type is won or lost very early into proceedings and this victory was achieved only by the team skills displayed by the whole crew.'

Keith and his engineers, and the entire crew, had used all their knowledge and skill to bring a ship with near-terminal damage back into operation. They did it within hours; once again with no injuries to the entire complement.

In fact the *Aurora* had, again, been lucky in that her predicament could have been much worse. If it hadn't been for the exhaust leak at departure requiring the V12 to be started, the fire would have occurred in Antarctica when the *Aurora* was put into icebreaking mode (when the V12 would have been first started alongside the main engine). The *Aurora* would have found herself adrift and without power either in the tempestuous Southern Ocean or in the harsh realm of the pack ice. There would have been no safe harbour nearby; no tug to easily come and rescue them. And the *Aurora*'s temporarily rigged systems may not have lasted the distance home: as it was, Keith and the engineers had to do all in their power to nurse the *Aurora* the relatively short 97 miles back to Fremantle.

But a third disaster, and the loss of yet more scientific programs, in one season still stung the crew's pride, as well as their beloved *Aurora*'s reputation. Dick wrote somewhat dejectedly that, 'The voyage south only lasted 9 hr 15 min, which must be some sort of record and which I am sure will never be challenged.'

VL Warren Papworth, however, was slightly more circumspect:

Although none of the objectives of the voyage were met, perhaps giving it the dubious distinction of being the most unsuccessful voyage conducted by ANARE, it was noteworthy for the fact that no-one was injured in the fire and for the exemplary conduct of expeditioners and crew in difficult circumstances.

PUEBLO BEZOAR – SENTINEL OF THE ENGINE CONTROL ROOM

If the engine room fires had taken place in 2004, there would have been one additional witness to the engineers' heroic actions: Pueblo Bezoar. This is an Aurora character that relatively few are familiar with. Since around 2004 this hairy orb has taken pride of place in the *Aurora*'s engine control room, but its presence and origin often go unnoticed by those simply passing by.

Discovered lurking in the dank depths of the *Aurora*'s grey-water tank, Pueblo is the result of more than a decade's worth of hair (and other unimaginable things) rolling around the tank as the *Aurora* dutifully undulated her way back and forth across the Southern Ocean. The softball-sized hairy 'monster' was eventually discovered and apprehended with repulsed glee by the *Aurora*'s engineers. It was caged and hung over the main desk in the *Aurora*'s engine control room as the engineers' unique pet; its purpose-built enclosure complete with a swing to keep their new companion happy.

Sarah Laverick

Pueblo Bezoar sitting on his perch, with 'Son of Pueblo' sitting on the bottom of the cage.

A subject of equal parts fascination and revulsion, Pueblo was soon 'officially' named by one of the *Aurora*'s doctors, its Latin classification loosely translated as 'village hairball' (a bezoar being an indigestible remnant found in the gastrointestinal tract of some animals). Catherine Di Murro, artist and wife of one of the *Aurora*'s engineers, was similarly transfixed by the unique by-product of years of shipboard communal living, and she exhibited Pueblo in two art exhibitions in 2005 and 2007.

A smaller 'Son of Pueblo' was, rather predictably, collected from the *Aurora*'s greywater tanks after a lesser number of years. The pair still happily perch together in the *Aurora*'s engine control room.

They say bad luck happens in threes. The *Aurora Australis* had managed to survive three catastrophic incidents in a single Antarctic season, but there were limits to even her fortitude and resilience. While each incident had been isolated, with each having nothing to do with the others occurring, the *Aurora* was understandably dubbed the 'jinx ship' by local media.

The AAD, P&O, crew and expeditioners, all exhausted and wary, prayed that the *Aurora*'s bad luck was over and done with.

Thankfully, it was. After seven weeks of engine room and system repairs, the *Aurora*'s fourth and final voyage of the 1998/99 season was an uneventful success. She visited all four of Australia's Antarctic stations (Mawson, Davis, Casey and Macquarie Island) in a single voyage – the third of only four times she did this in her lifetime – while also conducting marine science including deploying weather buoys and sea ice buoys, as well as trawling for krill. The six-week voyage was demanding and hectic; but the *Aurora* had finally thrown off the yoke of misfortune.

The *annus horribilis* was over – and good riddance to 1998/99.

Chapter Eight

A QUIET ACHIEVER

The year following the eventful *annus horribilis*, the curtailed science projects were attempted again, beginning with the polynya winter voyage. After calibrating the scientific equipment in the protection of Port Arthur, the *Aurora Australis* and her complement left the coast of Tasmania on 13 July 1999, arriving at a pancaked ice edge ten days later, just one month after the winter solstice. Antarctica's sea ice was rapidly expanding its frozen reach toward the north, and the *Aurora*'s scientists conducted their research in bleak conditions, working out on ice floes in the winter darkness, in bitter temperatures below minus twenty degrees Celsius, often in gale-force winds.

But the scientists persisted, and by the start of August the *Aurora* reached the Mertz Glacier polynya. The *Aurora* and her complement remained in the polynya 'ice factory' for four weeks, marking the first time a ship had worked in an active polynya in Antarctica during winter. Their research revealed that sea ice can form within this polynya at rates of about four to eight centimetres of thickness per day, and that the salt shed by the freezing water helps to form dense shelf water, which sinks, eventually forming Antarctic bottom water; a deep cold current that traverses whole ocean basins and is crucial to global oceanic circulation. Perhaps surprisingly, the voyage also showed there was very little biological activity in the Mertz Glacier polynya during winter – scotching the previous theory that the polynya was a winter oasis for Antarctic wildlife.

Later that same year, the five-year Antarctic Pack Ice Seals (APIS) program – the culmination of which had been hijacked by the CPP failure during the *annus horribilis* – was also successfully conducted. Colin Southwell and his team surveyed some 1.5 million square kilometres of East Antarctica (just under a quarter of the entire circumpolar region) between Mawson station and the French base Dumont d'Urville, with the *Aurora Australis* beating her way through more than three thousand kilometres of Antarctic pack ice, and the two helicopters on board flying more than six thousand kilometres of survey effort.

This survey, and the associated satellite tag deployments on seals over the five seasons before, resulted in the most robust estimates of crabeater seal abundance in East Antarctica in history. Crabeater seals are the most numerous of the pack ice seals in the Southern Ocean and make up over one-third of the total predator biomass in the Southern Ocean. The APIS survey's estimate of approximately 950,000 seals then provided the basis for estimating how much krill the seals would need to eat to survive, helping the conservation commission (CCAMLR) to manage the Antarctic krill fishery.

With the 1998/99 season's rescheduled science successfully achieved, and a further successful season now under her belt, the *Aurora* had truly left the bad luck of the *annus horribilis* behind her. And before long, she had a chance to play a new role, one that she would take up many times over her lifetime: the *Aurora Australis* would become a rescuer.

In the 2000/01 season the *Aurora* was conducting a marine science voyage called KACTAS (Krill Availability, Community Trophodynamics and AMISOR – Amery Ice Shelf Ocean Research – Surveys), and her complement were busily investigating the concept of 'krill flux': whether krill populations are resident to an area, or whether they simply passively drift from place to place carried by the Southern Ocean's currents. The *Aurora* was working in the waters off Béchervaise Island near Mawson station, which is home to a well-studied Adelie penguin colony, and during the KACTAS voyage penguins were being tracked in real time to see where they were going to find their food, Antarctic krill. Using that tracking information, the *Aurora* had been positioned in the feeding area to examine the changes in environmental parameters and krill distribution over time.

Just as the icebreaker was completing her first pass of the survey area, her crew received word that the *Polar Bird*, also under charter by the AAD, was stuck in pack ice off Casey station and would need assistance to break free. The *Aurora* immediately broke off her krill-flux experiment, and she and her exasperated complement made their way toward Casey station, some two thousand kilometres away, to liberate the *Polar Bird*.

It had already been an eventful season for the *Polar Bird*. Earlier in this same voyage, a helicopter had crashed on her helideck and rolled, sending rotor blades flying across the deck and flinging wreckage onto the ice next to the ship. Miraculously no-one had been seriously injured. This was also the second time in just two voyages that the beleaguered *Polar Bird* had been 'slowed' by the Antarctic sea ice, frustrating scientists and expeditioners across the Australian Antarctic Program whose projects were being hampered by the delays caused by the besetments; on the *Polar Bird* herself, and now on the *Aurora* as she detoured to lend assistance. Thankfully, the *Polar Bird* had managed to make her way to a band of open water off Casey; but thick pack ice to the north still blocked her way to freedom.

Five days after leaving the Mawson area, the *Aurora* effortlessly broke through the pack ice into the band of open water just off Casey. VL Graham Hosie, on the bridge at the time, saw the *Polar Bird* come into view in the distance. But as the *Aurora* drew closer to the ship Graham heard the chief mate, Peter Dunbar, chuckle mischievously at the helm. Dunbar promptly walked over to the bridge stereo, queued up a track, connected the ship's PA, and hit play.

Orchestral string flourishes erupted stirringly around the ship, quickly joined by a deafening brass trumpeting. Across the ship, while the *Aurora*'s personnel looked to each other in bewilderment and off-shift crew were grumpily wrenched from their slumber, the melodic strains of 'Ride of the Valkyries' boiled triumphantly from the *Aurora*'s external speakers, filling the frozen expanse between the two ships.

On the *Aurora*'s bridge, Dunbar cackled his boisterous machine-gun laugh as the full effect of the *Aurora*'s heroic arrival landed squarely where it had been aimed: at the ears of the vexed crew of the *Polar Bird*.

The *Aurora* circled around the ship heroically before she led the way north toward the ice, then cut a path for the *Polar Bird* to follow. Thirty nautical miles and five and a half hours later, the two ships parted, with one crew gleefully triumphant and the other's pride decidedly dented.

The *Aurora* then raced back to the west to conduct more research before the voyage was scheduled to return to Hobart. Her scientists managed to conduct some glaciological research at the edge of the Amery Ice Shelf, but the damage had been done to the voyage's krill program. There was simply not enough time left to conduct it. The krill flux project was rescheduled to the 2002/03 season – two summers later – on a voyage that would become informally known as KAOS (Krill Acoustics and Oceanography Survey).

Just eleven months after the *Polar Bird*'s rescue, the Norwegian ship again became stuck in the ice; this time southwest of Davis while trying to restock the Sansom Island fuel depot (the very same region where the *Aurora* had become crippled when her CPP failed in heavy pack ice). The *Polar Bird* had just ridden out a sizable blizzard and, despite taking refuge some sixty nautical miles from Sansom Island, she was now surrounded by thick dense pack ice pushed in from the north, and unable to move. Encircled by rafted ice made up of 'contorted blocks of floe upon floe' over two metres thick in places, and with weather again deteriorating, the master reported to the VL on 13 December that 'there was now pressure against the [*Polar Bird*'s] hull and that further movement was impossible'.

The *Aurora Australis*, having only just left Hobart for a Casey resupply and winter changeover, was put on notice. By 28 December she had completed the Casey resupply and changeover, and the *Polar Bird* was still stuck. Once again, the *Aurora Australis* was diverted to assist.

The *Aurora* quickly navigated the fourteen hundred kilometres to the region of Davis station; however, even the mighty icebreaker struggled to make her way through the thick uneven pack that had piled up in Prydz Bay. Her progress eventually ground to a halt some 45 miles from the stricken ship.

But the weather was fine and clear, and instead of continuing a futile fight with the ice, four helicopters – two from the *Polar Bird*, two from Davis station – were used to transfer the Mawson-bound people and cargo off the *Polar Bird* and onto the *Aurora Australis*, in a blade-churning frenzy of 42 flights. The *Aurora* would deliver the *Polar Bird*'s cargo and personnel to Mawson, then return to Prydz Bay; by which time it was hoped that the ice conditions might have improved around the *Polar Bird*.

With perfect weather on their arrival at Mawson, the cargo and personnel transfer was completed in a blistering time of just six hours. By the time the *Aurora* returned to Prydz Bay on 11 January, the pressures of the ice had just begun to ease slightly. The helicopters droned constantly overhead, both guiding the *Polar Bird* out through some intricate leads and leading the *Aurora* in toward the *Polar Bird*. But while the ice had loosened its grip slightly, it was not easy going for either ship.

'Finding a way though the ice was like doing a giant maze with thousands of optional routes,' the *Aurora*'s VL Greg Hodge later reported to the AAD. 'If we had not had use of helicopters to sort the leads from the dead ends, we would still be in the ice.'

The *Aurora* was just three miles from the *Polar Bird* when the pack suddenly closed in around her. It took another eight hours of determined ramming to reach the *Polar Bird*. Finally, hefty tow lines were cast between the two ships, who faced each other at right angles, bow to bow. The *Aurora* tugged back at the *Polar Bird*, but almost immediately one of the huge lines parted with a cracking snap.

After some quick discussions, the *Aurora* awkwardly turned around and her massive tow lines were transferred aft. She began to heave the *Polar Bird* forward; but just like the *Aurora* had done three years before, the *Polar Bird* began to zigzag on the end of the tow line. One of her massive tow lines broke, promptly followed by the other.

The *Aurora* was abruptly slowed by the ice, but the *Polar Bird* was less impeded by the relatively clear trail behind the *Aurora*. She bore down on the *Aurora*'s stern with horrifying speed.

'Then all of a sudden, the two ships moved closer together than anticipated, the tow rope snapped, and it all looked like it might turn to . . . ah, into an epic!' *Polar Bird* VL Joe Johnson later reported to the AAD.

With both captains' pulses racing, Tony Hansen threw the *Aurora*'s full power into the ice ahead, and the *Polar Bird*'s captain yanked his ship into full astern. Somehow, the two ships narrowly avoided the seemingly inevitable, but only just: they reportedly came within ten or fifteen metres of colliding.

In the end, the tow was abandoned, and instead the *Aurora* led the *Polar Bird* to safety by breaking into the ice out in front, reversing back toward the *Polar Bird*, and then leading her ship-length by painful shiplength toward the open water. After three days of stop-start back and forth, the two ships eventually cleared the ice.

But as the polar vessels parted ways, the *Aurora*'s crew could not help themselves: they bid a cheeky farewell to the *Polar Bird* by again broadcasting 'Ride of the Valkyries' irreverently over the *Aurora*'s PA system. The powerful anthem hung in the air as she steamed away from the *Polar Bird* and off into the distance.

But in a twist of fate, the seemingly calamity-prone *Polar Bird* would soon herself become a saviour of sorts.

Three weeks into the *Aurora*'s eleven-week KAOS marine science and resupply voyage of 2002/03, when the 'krill flux' experiment was finally underway, Captain Les Morrow anxiously approached VL Steve Nicol. There had been a stuff-up, he informed Steve; somehow, the *Aurora*'s fuel tanks had not been fully filled in port and the *Aurora* was running low on fuel. With no convenient petrol station to pull into, and the stations all in need of their own fuel, the atmosphere on board quickly turned tense. But a solution was soon provided in the form of the *Polar Bird*: she would transfer fuel to the *Aurora Australis* from inside Horseshoe Harbour at Mawson station.

By the time the *Aurora* arrived at Mawson station, Steve was in a state of nervous anticipation. The stress of trying to manage a voyage on a dwindling fuel supply was compounded by the concept of undertaking a hitherto untested manoeuvre. For the first time in history, two vessels would be moored together inside Horseshoe Harbour, which is usually a snug fit for one vessel.

Both vessels finally took up their positions side by side within the Harbour, with just a few large rubber fenders separating the two ships. When the vessels were safely secured to their moorings – and to each other – the nerve-racking process of the fuel transfer began. The bridges of both ships, just metres apart, constantly bustled with restless activity; the captains and crew on both vessels kept a sharp, weather eye on conditions, as well as the inherently risky transfer of fuel from ship to ship.

By one o'clock the next morning, the *Polar Bird* had successfully transferred a grand total of 220,000 litres of fuel to the *Aurora Australis*. But any sense of relief was short-lived; almost as soon as the transfer was complete a sixty knot squall roared down the hill and across Horseshoe Harbour. Long foam streaks whipped across the harbour's slate-grey surface, and the narrow gulf between the two vessels sloshed angrily. Miraculously both ships, still rafted side by side, held fast on their lines, and the *Aurora* gratefully left Mawson on 6 February with boosted fuel supplies, ready to complete her marine science program.

As well as unexpected blizzards, sudden squalls, or abrupt changes in ice conditions, the A factor has also been known to materialise in the form of medical or maritime emergencies. And while the *Aurora*'s icebreaking capabilities had twice freed a stricken ship from the ensnarement of the Antarctic sea ice, her medical facilities had seen her become a source of salvation to expeditioners working in the isolated extremities of the Antarctic wilderness.

The *Aurora*'s surgery had been put to use on her very first voyage, to conduct a skin graft on the vet who had sustained an injury from an elephant seal bite at Heard Island. And just one year later, her surgery was used by the doctor on board to conduct several operations on the hand of a crew member who had crushed the tips of two of his fingers in an incident while respooling a particularly uncooperative wire onto a winch drum.

The *Aurora*'s medical facilities, as well as the medical knowledge and generosity of the blood donors, had saved Ross McCallum's life during his emergency on the WOES voyage in 1994, sustaining him long enough to reach the safety of the Royal Hobart Hospital. In addition, the *Aurora*'s surgical capability has arguably saved the lives of an expeditioner who required an appendicectomy in 2005. Impressively, the *Aurora*'s doctor was ably assisted by expeditioners who had been trained for just two weeks in anaesthetic and surgery support at the Royal Hobart Hospital, and this team was supported remotely by the Polar Medicine Unit and specialists back in Australia.

The *Aurora* also had a central role in responding to medical emergencies that occurred on the Antarctic continent, during which international programs, logisticians and medical staff combined forces to evacuate critically injured or sick continental personnel to the safety of Australian medical facilities.

In 1994 the *Aurora* successfully repatriated two expeditioners back to Hobart. One had suffered a heart attack at Davis station over winter, and the other had broken her leg in a field training incident at Casey. In 1999, after an expeditioner had fallen down a crevasse during a field training exercise, the *Aurora* once again diverted from her scheduled duties and came to the rescue, successfully nursing her home a month later.

In 2008, an expeditioner at Davis station was seriously injured in a quad bike accident, sustaining multiple fractures to his ankles and pelvis. The *Aurora*, at Casey at the time, was immediately diverted to Davis, but was slowed by bad weather and heavy ice. Ten days after the *Aurora* left Casey, she was within fly-off range, and a break in the weather allowed her doctor and some expeditioners with medical training to finally be helicoptered to the station to assist with the medical care of the patient. By that time, the *Aurora* was one part of an international, multi-option rescue effort, and in the end, in a first for both the United States and Australian programs, a massive US Hercules aircraft landed on a 1.8-metre-thick sea ice runway at Davis. This runway had been painstakingly prepared by the station personnel over the previous week, and the patient was transported to Hobart by the National Science Foundation of the US, rather than enduring weeks of a rough ocean passage.

Davis station would later be the location of another dramatic rescue. In March 2015, the *Aurora* was turned back to Davis station to retrieve a winterer who had become seriously ill just days after the *Aurora* had resupplied the station. The *Aurora* battled heavy ice to return to the station, then turned to fight her way through one hundred nautical miles of sea ice before reaching the dubious 'ease' of open water, which presented her with seven-metre swells and sixty-knot winds. The AAD doctor, supported by the expeditioners, crew and medical experts back home, carefully nursed the seriously ill patient across the tumultuous Southern Ocean to the safety of the Royal Hobart Hospital some two weeks later.

The *Aurora*'s medical and evacuation capabilities became widely known and appreciated. As Dr Jeff Ayton, Chief Medical Officer at the AAD, later mused, 'The *Aurora* was . . . arguably the best medical facility in the Southern Ocean. In any Antarctic Program. And [she] still has capabilities that are envied by some nations.'

In between the action-packed years of the 2000s, the *Aurora*'s long-term marine science campaigns had also been very successful.

Back in 1990/91, the WOCE voyage had been the *Aurora*'s first oceanographic voyage in the Southern Ocean. The *Aurora* conducted a flurry of measurements using CTDs, radio-transmitted instruments and the *Aurora*'s underway water sampling system, in her first venture along the SR3 transect. At that early stage, every piece of data from the region was new, and thus the WOCE voyage instantly provided a baseline along the SR3 transect from which further, long-term data gathering could examine change in the Southern Ocean.

By its nature, this type of long-term research requires commitment and patience, as CSIRO oceanographer and Research Team Leader Steve Rintoul points out: 'extracting these signals of change from the ocean is really hard work. It does require really precise measurements done over and over again.'

While it may have seemed laborious and painfully slow at times, the oceanographic work and repeated transects conducted onboard the *Aurora* paid off in spades. Over the 1990s and 2000s the research conducted by oceanographers at CSIRO and the AAD slowly unveiled the secrets of the enigmatic Southern Ocean.

The Antarctic Circumpolar Current (ACC) is the world's largest oceanic current, and it is also the only current on the planet that circulates around the globe unbroken by land. Through their work on the *Aurora*, scientists learned how strong the ACC really was, and how it could vary with time and location. In addition, they came to better understand how the 'overturning circulation' in Antarctica worked: that is, how water at depth moved from south to north and also mixed in the interior of the Southern Ocean. And importantly, the long-term studies on the *Aurora Australis* also showed how these two major components of the Southern Ocean circulation – the ACC and overturning circulation – were linked. Scientists began to examine how these currents could be affected by climate change, and how these changes in the Southern Ocean in turn further effect environmental change.

But the oceanographers weren't the only scientists enjoying the capabilities and possibilities that the *Aurora Australis* had brought to Australian Southern Ocean research. Like Southern Ocean oceanography, sea ice research was another field that had proved difficult to conduct effectively from Australia's earlier fleet of non-icebreaking vessels. In fact, up to the 1990s it had been assumed that Antarctic sea ice was similar to that of the Arctic, where research by national research programs and the military had been ongoing for decades. The introduction of icebreaking research vessels into the Southern Ocean in the 1980s and 1990s changed that perspective forever.

Unlike her predecessors, the *Aurora*'s icebreaking capability allowed her to travel in a (more or less) straight line transect in the Antarctic sea ice. When the *Aurora* broke into sea ice, chunks of the ice often tipped onto their sides as the hull of the *Aurora* rubbed past; this allowed researchers to estimate ice thickness by simply looking down at the ice from the ship. Then in 1995 the *Aurora* became the first ever Australian ship to conduct a true winter voyage in the midst of the Antarctic sea ice zone. In these early years, the *Aurora*'s glaciologists worked to standardise techniques for estimating ice thickness and cover, and they began to build up a long-term database of *Aurora*-based sea ice observations in East Antarctica.

As well as looking at ice thickness, the glaciologists began to examine the physical properties of the sea ice, down to the level of ice crystal formation. The structure of the sea ice would indicate how it had established: the ice crystals' structures would be either frazil – formed by rapid freezing in open water or leads – or columnar crystals formed by slow basal freezing on the base of an existing sheet of ice; alternatively, isotope analysis would reveal if the ice was created when floes had become laden with snow and sunk, causing an influx of cold seawater which then froze among the snow.

But the sea ice research methods on board the *Aurora* quickly moved on from the rudimentary techniques used in these early years, where, as glaciologist Tony Worby remembers, '[glaciologists] were sitting down in the bowels of the ship . . . keeping our ice cores frozen in a blast freezer . . . and to get our thin sections thin enough to actually determine something about the ice we were cutting them and then rubbing them back and forward along bits of wood to melt them and get them thin enough!'

Two major Sea Ice Physics and Ecosystem eXperiment research voyages, SIPEX and SIPEX II, were conducted in 2007 and 2012 respectively. The cutting-edge SIPEX voyage formed part of Australia's contribution to the International Polar Year (IPY), the largest international polar research effort in the last half century.

The SIPEX voyage examined both the physics and biology of the sea ice itself, as well as the links with under-ice algae and the Southern Ocean ecosystem, by visiting fifteen designated research stations deep within the Antarctic sea ice.

Each time the *Aurora* pulled up to an 'ice station', dozens of scientists would tramp down her gangways or be lifted over the side, and then haul their gear along the ice extending out from the ship. The scientists used cutting-edge technology such as sled-based and airborne radar to estimate snow thickness and sea ice freeboard (the part of the ice that is raised above the water); and deployed a Surface and Under Ice Trawl (SUIT) to collect krill under the ice. Others would cut a large hole in the ice and deploy a remotely operated vehicle (ROV) into the crystal-clear water underneath, to look for algae and krill hiding below.

Deploying the ROV in drill hole beside the ship during the SIPEX voyage.

This work on the sea ice was not without its challenges and dangers; on SIPEX II a large floe unexpectedly cracked with a deep, dull thud and quickly broke up, leaving some scientists looking helplessly at a freezing trench of water between themselves and the ice surrounding their ship. But this scenario had not been unanticipated, and the scientists were quickly rescued using equipment carried on the *Aurora*, brought especially for that purpose.

These large, multidisciplinary SIPEX projects comprised a number of collaborators within the Australian Antarctic Program – with oceanographers, biologists and glaciologists from the AAD, CSIRO and the Institute of Antarctic and Southern Ocean Studies (IASOS) working side by side – but it also opened up collaboration with international organisations and scientists from Japan, Norway, the Netherlands and Germany, among many others. These multidisciplinary, international teams worked together in the freezing conditions in unison and good humour. As *Aurora* bosun Joe McMenemy proudly put it, 'It's like a little United Nations when you do SIPEX.'

This collaborative vision continued, and the *Aurora* again contributed to the International Polar Year research effort in the 2007/08 summer season. The *Aurora Australis* had even undergone a minor facelift in mid-2007 in anticipation of her large role in the IPY – with cabins and onboard systems updated and a new laboratory fitted to the mezzanine area above her trawl deck.

During the IPY, Australia was one of four nations jointly conducting the Collaborative East Antarctic MARine Census (CEAMARC), and the *Aurora*'s mission was to focus on examining the biological communities on the sea bed in East Antarctica. During the *Aurora*'s CEAMARC voyage, high-resolution cameras were deployed on massive sled trawls that collected samples from the ocean floor. These were identified, photographed and

Margot Foster/Australian Antarctic Division

Australian and French researchers sort a trawl catch during the CEAMARC voyage.

genetically sampled by a team of French experts also working onboard alongside Australian researchers.

The results of these trawls were beyond expectation, with species pulled up that had never before been documented; many with the characteristic Antarctic feature of gigantism, with sea insects that would normally be less than a centimetre long in Australian waters appearing in the *Aurora*'s nets at over five times their usual size. As the voyage continued, the images coming back from the trawls constantly enthralled the international team of scientists and technicians on board, with many large creatures enthusiastically dubbed the 'big' something as they were retrieved from the trawl. But the surprises didn't end there. As VL Martin Riddle wrote in one sitrep:

> We all expected the Big Polychaete to be the undisputed high-light of the voyage; however, the Southern Ocean continues to turn up surprises. Yesterday, while sampling the transect from 400 m to 2100 m down the shelf, we blew out the trawl net as we tried to bring it on deck after sampling the 800 m site. The video footage from the trawl-mounted camera explained why. Almost the entire day shift crammed into the elec-tronics cupboard to see the footage and, after the first gasps of 'incroyable!', watched in hushed awe as a scene rivalling the best parts of the Great Barrier Reef was revealed. The sea bed was 100% covered with living material – colourful branching coralline species and gorgonians forming the major lower-storey structure and large branching sponges the upper storey. Amongst this were numerous sea-stars, sea-cucumbers, crustacea and fish of types as yet unseen. After repairing the trawl nets we returned to resample the site, this time being very cautious with the time allowed for the trawl to be on the bottom, and were rewarded with a relatively small catch, but with many species not previously collected . . . The deck crew must be congratulated for their skill and persistence in suc-cessfully sampling these very difficult environments, without which the scientists would have nothing.

This voyage, in concert with voyages conducted by the Japanese onboard the *Umitaka Maru* and French and Belgians on *L'Astrolabe* that concentrated on the open ocean areas of East Antarctica, led to two areas of the Southern Ocean being declared Vulnerable Marine Ecosystems by CCAMLR, meaning they are protected from damaging fishing activities. They also contributed to the wider Census of Antarctic Marine Life (CAML) project of the International Polar Year, which involved a total of eighteen marine science voyages in Antarctica and the Southern Ocean.

But large science programs weren't the only way the *Aurora Australis* contributed to other international Antarctic programs. The *Aurora* was a welcome visitor at many of East Antarctica's international stations – particularly the Chinese station Zhongshan, which she visited nine times in her lifetime, transporting cargo and personnel to and from the station. The *Aurora* delivered aviation fuel to the Russian Progress station, visited the French Dumont d'Urville station to take on trawl equipment, and successfully delivered fuel to the Russian Mirny station, located between Davis and Casey. She was also chartered to resupply the Japanese station, Syowa, for the Japanese Antarctic Research Expedition (JARE) while their new replacement icebreaker was being constructed.

All the while, whether conducting large scientific campaigns or operationally focused voyages, biological researchers would be found lurking in the *Aurora*'s wet laboratories, bustling around sinks and pumps and hunched over microscopes, collecting and examining underway samples of the cold pure waters of the Southern Ocean.

While this crystal-clear water may seem devoid of life, it is in fact teeming with microscopic organisms. These microscopic organisms, or microbes, include phytoplankton, which are the minute 'plants' of the sea. Like terrestrial plants, they take energy from the sun and carbon dioxide (CO_2) from the atmosphere, but use nutrients from the ocean rather than the soil to sustain themselves. Microscopic animals, or zooplankton, feed on these plant cells, and are themselves a potential food source for larger animals such as krill, which are in turn an important food source for higher predators such as penguins, seals and whales.

As such, marine microbes are the base of the entire Southern Ocean food web.

Underway studies on board the *Aurora* concentrated on examining the microbial communities of the Southern Ocean surrounding Antarctica, and how they are affected by changes in the atmosphere and ocean. Over the years, the scientists amassed a considerable volume of data on species composition and distribution, and these huge databases will help inform if and how these are changing.

Another long-running program on the *Aurora* was the Southern Ocean Continuous Plankton Recorder (or SO–CPR) survey. The program used a Continuous Plankton Recorder: a one-metre long, steel fish-like sampling unit with a small aperture in its pointy nose. The CPR collected and trapped plankton in its rolling sampling silks, as it was towed across hundreds of miles of open ocean, behind the orange ship.

This equipment, which was developed in the 1930s, has remained virtually unchanged over the thirty years of the *Aurora*'s life, and the samples are still analysed by simple microscopy techniques in the lab back in Australia. But they have yielded a wealth of information. Scientists have shown which tiny (and not-so-tiny) zooplankton live in the Southern Ocean, and the long-running program has also given scientists an invaluable baseline from which to monitor changes in the microscopic communities in the Southern Ocean.

While the SO–CPR program is not unique to the *Aurora Australis* (other ships also contribute to the collection of plankton data in the Southern Ocean using CPRs), the *Aurora Australis* is responsible for a whopping 65 per cent of all samples collected for the program to date. Between her first CPR tow in 1990 and the end of the 2017/18 Antarctic season, the *Aurora Australis* conducted approximately 485 CPR tows, with the CPRs travelling some 163,400 nautical miles and generating more than

32,600 samples. At the end of the 2016/17 season, all SO–CPR partners – including Australia – had generated approximately 50,000 samples in total.

KRILL FISHERY – THE *AURORA'S* VITAL CONTRIBUTION

One of the *Aurora's* greatest contributions was toward the management of the krill fishery.

During the 1980s and 1990s the Antarctic krill fishery had operated without any regulation off East Antarctica. Krill catch limits are vital to ensure the sustainability of the industry in the long term so, in 1996, the *Aurora* set sail on the first scientific krill survey specifically designed for CCAMLR, to an area which at the time had no catch limits. The voyage was given the tongue-in-cheek voyage acronym BROKE (later translated into Baseline Research on Oceanography, Krill and the Environment) when the gearbox failed the day before the *Aurora's* planned departure, delaying the voyage by three weeks. But, contrary to its name, BROKE was a triumph. Pairing biological survey work with innovative oceanographic research (and, for the first time, integrating information on the distribution of whales and seabirds into the overall dataset), the team managed to obtain, analyse and submit the data to CCAMLR with such efficiency that a catch limit of 775,000 was set just seven months after the *Aurora's* return home: a remarkable feat of scientific planning and execution.

But the protection of the ecosystem off East Antarctica still had a weak link: the krill catch limit for the region to the west of that surveyed by BROKE in 1996 was based on old data. In 1991 CCAMLR had set a precautionary catch limit of 450,000 tonnes, but this was based on old data, collected in 1981 with fairly primitive technology. So, ten years after the BROKE survey, in 2006, the *Aurora* set sail again on a second krill survey voyage, unimaginatively named BROKE West.

The BROKE West voyage allowed scientists to observe how the ecosystem is structured across the region, looking at how biological production (the amount of krill, fish and predators) is linked to oceanographic processes such as currents, salinity and temperature. The new dataset provided a comprehensive picture of the ecosystems along one-third of the Antarctic coastline. The krill biomass results were used by CCAMLR to set an updated catch limit of 2.645 million tonnes, far higher than the old one, but reflective of the improved accuracy of the new survey. In 2016 the krill fishery reentered this region for the first time in more than twenty years, but because of the research carried out on the *Aurora* in 2006, the catch was well regulated.

As the years went by and the *Aurora Australis* and her complement steamed dutifully back and forth between Antarctica and Australia, a few things on board gradually changed. Communications improved, allowing the crew and expeditioners to keep in regular contact with their offices – and, of course, loved ones – back home; and the advent of laptops and wireless networks meant this could be done from the comfort of their cabins rather than using communal PCs in the conference rooms.

A gradual social shift also occurred over time, arguably as a result of a change in the AAD's alcohol policy. As the policy went from a fairly liberal one – various forms of alcohol were available at the bar and could be consumed in cabins – to a restricted version where limited alcohol was confined to the Husky Bar, and finally to one of almost total prohibition, save for one or two 'special occasions' on each voyage (where the number of beverages was strictly calculated on a per person basis); the Husky Bar became a shadow of its former self. Its familiar bar was eventually removed, and the image-clad space was relegated to use as a games room or exercise studio. Initially, the formalised alcohol policy caused a noticeable and negative social change on board, as instead of socialising in groups in times of idleness or boredom, people retreated to their own cabins and watched DVDs on their laptops. But eventually, thanks to the persistent efforts of a number of voyages' social committees, people realised 'life after alcohol' wasn't quite so bad: parties were replaced with nightly science talks and movies, 'mocktail' parties or trivia nights, encouraging people to socialise. And people still formed the close bonds that had become such a cherished part of Antarctic life.

In between all the rescues, research and station resupplies of the 2000s, the *Aurora Australis* found time while off-charter from the AAD to expand her repertoire. The icebreaker worked on seven different charters for the offshore oil and gas industry between 2001 and 2006, operating as a platform for drilling work and for pipeline maintenance and installation, as well as being an accommodation vessel.

The *Aurora Australis* at the Malampaya gas platform.

During this latter role as a 'floating hotel' the *Aurora* became home to an eclectic international mix of offshore personnel, whose rough-and-ready approach and complete disregard for mealtime queues came as a rude awakening to the *Aurora*'s crew, who had become accustomed to the relatively genteel demeanour of scientists and Antarctic tradies.

The *Aurora Australis* also became a subantarctic patrol ship in the early 2000s, when Customs and Australian Fisheries Management Authority (AFMA) personnel conducted two patrols of the Heard Island and McDonald Islands regions for illegal Patagonian toothfish poachers. In 2003, on the first of these trips, the *Aurora* and her complement battled heaving seas and terrifying Southern Ocean storms – a casualty of which was the *Aurora*'s beloved orca windvane, which was wrenched from its post on the foredeck and whipped into oblivion by the screaming winds of the Southern Ocean (the killer whale was replaced in this instance, but has been revamped a number of times over the *Aurora*'s life). The complement sighted and identified one vessel in international waters, then left the subantarctic quietly in an effort to keep potential illegal vessels guessing about their whereabouts.

But on the second trip, the *Aurora Australis* brought out the big guns – literally.

The *Aurora*'s killer whale/orca windvane visible on the foremast, while looking across the pack ice toward the *Xue Long*.

Two huge .50 calibre machine guns were intimidatingly strapped to the *Aurora*'s sides, and in July and August 2004 she strutted her stuff around Heard and McDonald islands, sending 'a very clear message to those illegal fishing cartels their presence in Australian waters illegally will not be tolerated', as Senator Ian Macdonald told the *Mercury* newspaper. During this voyage, the *Aurora Australis* carried about forty highly trained and well-armed customs officers on board; but they did not find any illegal fishing vessels.

The 1990s and 2000s had clearly been a busy and eventful period in the *Aurora*'s scientific life. But by the conclusion of her second decade, something had begun to change. Over the three decades of her life, her focus would slowly shift away from marine science.*

The *Aurora* had initially been intended to be part of what was termed a 'two-ship solution': meaning another ship would continue to conduct station resupply voyages while the *Aurora* primarily conducted marine science voyages and then second-arily contributed to resupply and changeovers. As planned, in the *Aurora*'s first few years the *Icebird* continued to support ANARE, freeing the *Aurora* to conduct marine science as well as operational voyages.

Then, in 1994, the Federal government slashed $4.2 million, or 11.3 per cent (in real terms), from the AAD's budget. Similar cuts were to follow over the ensuing years. Facing the necessity of fiscal efficiency, the AAD was forced to consider radical options for cost-cutting, such as closing one of Australia's Antarctic bases. Instead, the government chose what seemed at

---

* In her first decade, science voyages had accounted for over half of all the voyages the *Aurora* conducted; these included both dedicated marine science voyages, along with logistics voyages with a significant marine science component to them. In her second decade, the number of science voyages had reduced to one-third of all voyages. But during her last decade, science voyages only accounted for less than one-fifth of voyages the *Aurora* conducted. Similarly, the average number of marine science days per season went from approximately 67 days in the first decade, to 43 between 2000 and 2010, down to 20 between 2010 and 2019.

Polar ship packing heat for fish poachers

The Mercury, Wednesday 30 June 2004.

the time a less extreme measure; to transition from utilising two ships in their Antarctic operations to one: the *Aurora Australis*. This option was not celebrated at AAD headquarters, but with limited options available to them, the director had little choice.

The *Aurora Australis* would now be tasked with resupplying each of Australia's four Antarctic stations, as well as conducting science voyages if and when time allowed.

Incredibly, while there was no dedicated marine science voyage in the 1994/95 season, the *Aurora* still managed to conduct 74 days of marine science, spread over three voyages that were also changeovers or resupplies. And in 1996/97 and 1997/98, the *Aurora* continued to conduct stand-alone, dedicated marine science voyages, despite being the only ship operating for ANARE.

Then, throughout the 2000s, the government once again began to charter larger cargo vessels on an *ad hoc* basis each year. They utilised the *Polar Bird*, the French Antarctic vessel *L'Astrolabe* and occasionally the Russian cargo vessels the *Vasiliy Golovnin* and *Kapitan Khlebnikov* – and even later, the mammoth *MV Amderma*. Australian Antarctic marine science thrived during this period of the *Aurora*'s life; it was the period of krill and fish surveys, the expansion of the glaci- ology program, the era of large ecosystem studies and the International Polar Year. It was also the period of increasing awareness and concern about climate change, and Antarctica's role in this global process.

But come 2010, the *ad hoc* vessel charters all but evaporated. The recent advent of the ice runway at Wilkins was a great success that allowed summer aviation in Antarctica, but it came at the cost of the AAD being financially able to charter a second ship. In addition, during the late 2000s, the AAD's budget had in effect become fixed as part of government budget efficiency measures. Meanwhile, fuel and running costs began to rise steeply. With both new and established Antarctic infrastructure to support, and costs of transport and logistics rising, the *Aurora* once again became Australia's only Antarctic maritime resource.* As her logistic responsibilities increased, the *Aurora* became less and less used for research.

But while her role in Australia's Antarctic science program may have been on the decline, she still had a central role to play in Australian Antarctic operations. In fact, the start of the *Aurora*'s third decade would begin much like her second: with the *Aurora Australis* once again becoming a heroine.

In mid-2011, in the Antarctic off-season just before her 22nd birthday, the *Aurora Australis* was chartered by the Royal Australian Navy as a training vessel for a series of three voyages. During the first and second of these voyages, the iconic orange icebreaker sailed gracefully between Hobart, Jervis Bay, Brisbane and Sydney while groups of RAN trainees busily completed coastal navigation exercises, man overboard drills and small boat training. The *Aurora*'s P&O crew proudly coached the trainees in the nuances of their ship and their own roles onboard, and cheerily imparted their collective wisdom to a new generation of seafarers.

During the last of these three training voyages, the *Aurora* was also simultaneously tasked to conduct a resupply at Macquarie Island for the Macquarie Island Pest Eradication Project (MIPEP). Just months earlier, the *Aurora* had transported a quantity of logistic equipment and baiting stations to multiple locations around the island, plus delivered eleven rabbit-detection dogs – labradors and spaniels (and their handlers) – to the station. Now, the *Aurora* would be conducting another resupply and would deliver more MIPEP personnel, giving the lucky RAN trainees on board this voyage a scenic trip to the subantarctic. But the trainees were subsequently inducted to the typical 'Macca' experience on arrival, enduring days of heaving seas and gale-force winds complete with subzero wind chill, driving hail and snow storms.

---

* The French *L'Astrolabe* continued to assist the AAP for short periods in relatively ice-free areas, but while her assistance certainly helped, especially in the subantarctic, the small ship could not ease the *Aurora*'s Antarctic operational burden.

In true Macca form, after several days the weather unexpectedly eased, revealing the island in all its snow-dusted, vibrant glory. The *Aurora* took up position in Buckles Bay and the helicopters were set loose to revolve between the *Aurora*'s steel helideck and the dark shore at the station, ferrying cargo from ship to shore. As darkness fell, the helicopters were secured on station and the *Aurora* retreated from the island's rocky shore to the safety of the sea, steaming up and down the east coast of the island, seeing out the night hours in the shelter of the island's lee.

At about one o'clock the next morning, the *Aurora* received an alert from the Rescue Coordination Centre (RCC) in Australia. The RCC provided all search and rescue alerts in Australia's search and rescue region. A fishing vessel southeast of the island, the *Janas*, had engine difficulties and was drifting, but at this stage no assistance was required. The *Aurora*'s officers quickly made radio contact with the *Janas*, whose crew reported they were currently trying to repair the engine and did not yet require assistance.

But six hours later, the seas were once again rising and the *Janas* crew still hadn't been successful. They called the *Aurora* and officially made a request for assistance, giving details of their location, drift rate and the number of people on board.

But a storm was bearing down on the area, and the *Aurora*'s captain, Scott Laughlin, knew that if the *Aurora* and her complement were going to be able to tow the *Janas* and her 21 crew to safety, they needed to get going as soon as humanly possible. As Scott turned the *Aurora* south and steamed toward the *Janas*, the rest of the crew put their heads together to work out how best to arrange the tow. The RAN trainees were pressed into service, and they eagerly manhandled a hefty green tow line from the forward end of the *Aurora* down to her stern. The *Aurora*'s skilled crew sat uncomfortably on her cold trawl deck and worked on the huge rope, rapidly splicing its thick strands to a bulky shackle that would later be attached to a tow bridle on the *Janas*.

The *Janas* appeared on the *Aurora*'s radar just before 9 am.

RAN trainees transferring the tow line down aft just prior to the *Janas* rescue.

But official approval to conduct the tow had not been given to the *Aurora*, so instead she slowly steamed around the area while the crew of each ship waited for permission from each of the vessels' managers to conduct the tow. Scott glanced regularly at the bridge's meteorological screen. The atmospheric pressure was rapidly falling, the swell was coming up and the wind outside was starting to bite; if they didn't take up the tow soon, they wouldn't be able to. Finally, the necessary approvals were given, late in the afternoon. Almost immediately the *Janas*'s crew tossed a small buoyed messenger line into the grey water toward the *Aurora*. The *Aurora*'s crew grappled the line, tied their huge tow rope to it and the *Janas* crew hauled it back over the water. Within 45 minutes, the two crews were ready.

The storm was almost upon them, and the *Aurora* slowly turned under the heavy skies and increased speed, carefully towing the *Janas* toward the protective lee of Macquarie Island. Scott compulsively checked on the ship from the aft bridge windows. The *Janas* was yawing back and forth on its line as she was dragged through the spray-tossed swell behind the *Aurora*, and he was worried the line might part under these pressures. If the line snapped, the *Janas* would swing beam-on, and in this wild weather she would be tossed violently by the Southern Ocean. Reattaching the tow line would be almost impossible.

Snow began to fall, and it was whipped into confused clouds by the fierce winds. Soon, the only sign the *Janas* was still with them was a dim swaying light that valiantly glimmered through the thick grey fog and snow behind the *Aurora Australis*.

After ten tense hours, the ships reached the lee of Macquarie Island, where the seas began to ease. But it was still too rough to anchor the incapacitated vessel at Macquarie Island: the risk of it dragging anchor and going aground was just too high. Instead, the *Aurora* slowly towed the *Janas* up and down the island's coast while her crew continued their efforts to repair their engine.

The gusts and snow squalls continued, but they began to be interrupted by short lulls that slowly increased in length. Taking advantage of one such break in the weather, the *Aurora*'s helicopters, which had been stranded on base when the *Aurora* hastily departed, returned to the ship, and the *Aurora*'s Fast Rescue Craft was launched and sent to the *Janas* to retrieve the broken engine component. The *Aurora*'s engineers expertly conducted a quick but effective repair using the icebreaker's well-equipped workshops, and just two hours later the repaired part was returned to the *Janas*.

But there was no way to be sure the repair would hold, so, after much discussion between the captains, VL and RAN leaders, it was agreed the safest option was to tow the *Janas* to the safety of the nearest harbour: the Auckland Islands, roughly 450 kilometres south of New Zealand's South Island. The weather forecast for the next few days was unusually good, which would make the tow relatively low risk.

So that afternoon, the *Aurora* altered course for the Auckland Islands, with the *Janas* trailing along behind, hauled by the green towing line. But meanwhile, a RAN trainee who had become ill on their arrival at Macquarie Island was suspected to have appendicitis and needed to be evacuated, instigating yet another rescue coordination effort, this time with RCC New Zealand.

Two and a half days later, as the *Aurora* and *Janas* slowly approached the Auckland Islands, the *Janas* clutched in her engine and kept it running. The following morning, her crew were able to gently urge her forward. As the weight slowly came off their tow line, they released their tow bridle, and slowly motored away from the *Aurora* to conduct four hours of engine trials.

Shortly afterwards, the *Aurora* entered Port Ross, and was unexpectedly greeted with about three hundred right whales bobbing around the harbour, their glistening backs like stepping stones across the water.

'What a spectacle!' VL Rob Bryson wrote in his daily sitrep. 'This place was as busy as the MCG on a Collingwood vs Essendon game day! Whales were everywhere! We had a crew up on the bow, whale spotting and feeding info back to the bridge.'

Captain Scott carefully picked the *Aurora*'s way through to the anchorage, where she was finally able to drop anchor. Just two hours later, two long-range rescue helicopters settled side by side on the *Aurora*'s helideck; for just over an hour the *Aurora* had more helicopters on board than she'd ever had in her life, with four in the hangar and two on deck. The ill trainee was stretchered onto the helideck and carefully manoeuvred into one of the craft, and the helicopters were off again. Shortly after, the *Janas* made her way into the anchorage and also anchored within the safety of the harbour.

Finally, two days after they arrived, the *Janas*'s crew announced that their engine repairs had been completed. Released from her duty of care, the *Aurora* began to make her way to Dunedin to unload her passengers, before she would head back home to Hobart.

Once again, thanks to the capabilities and skill of the *Aurora* and her crew, a vessel in distress had been rescued from a precarious situation. The *Aurora Australis* had safeguarded the lives and livelihood of the 21 members of the *Janas*'s crew, and her protective spirit no doubt touched the lives of their families back at home.

According to the International Convention for the Safety of Life at Sea, 'The master of a ship at sea which is in a position to be able to provide assistance on receiving a signal from any source that persons are in distress at sea, is bound to proceed with all speed to their assistance . . .' The duty to assist those in distress is a rule of maritime law that transcends the usual divides of nationality and politics. But for many professional mariners it is also a moral compulsion, and the urge to uphold the time-honoured tradition to assist fellow mariners in distress is often stronger than the obligation to do so.

Mariners sailing in the empty wilds of Antarctica are particularly bound by this unspoken camaraderie, sharing a special connection that only extreme isolation can bring. But as the *Aurora*'s complement would soon find, in Antarctica, the closest help can be hundreds – or even thousands – of nautical miles away.

Chapter Nine

HEROICS ON THE HIGH SEAS

In mid-December 2013, nearly two years after the *Janas* rescue, a scuffed grey amphibious craft charged across the undulating grey water of Buckles Bay toward the pebbly coastline of Macquarie Island. A low stern wave boiled from the rear of the LARC (Lighter, Amphibious, Resupply, Cargo vehicle), drawing a diminishing frothy streak between the *Aurora Australis* and the island. As it neared the shallows, the vessel rumbled past slippery, writhing masses of kelp, then revved its engine and found purchase, its submerged rubber tyres bouncing the craft easily up the smooth rocks of the beach. With a satisfied puff of smoke, the dripping wet amphibious vehicle trundled down the muddy track that snaked along the tussock-covered isthmus, carrying its load toward the weathered buildings at Macquarie Island station.

The *Aurora* was performing a relatively straightforward voyage involving a light summer changeover of Macquarie Island and a full resupply and refuelling of Casey station. Unlike most, this voyage had been blessed with a gentle start, with kind rolling seas on the way to Macca that even the most seasickness-prone expeditioners could easily endure.

VL Leanne Millhouse and Captain Murray 'Muz' Doyle chatted easily on the bridge, discussing the cargo operations for the day while the two LARCs busily puttered back and forth between the ship and the station. They would later lose the afternoon to deteriorating wind conditions, but in one day they managed to transfer 5.5 tonnes of cargo, delivered thirteen incoming expeditioners to the island and welcomed four outgoing expeditioners aboard.

It was Leanne's first Antarctic voyage as VL, and she watched from the bridge as the *Aurora* weighed anchor then turned to steam offshore along the island for the night. 'That's Day One done and dusted,' she thought with satisfaction, mentally planning the next day. But an excited cry immediately distracted her from her planning; a pod of killer whales was swimming north across Buckles Bay, their shiny black backs and tall wedge-shaped dorsal fins stark against the surrounding grey. As word of the whale sighting spread through the ship, expeditioners poured into the *Aurora*'s bridge, and some excitedly reported that the whales had been visiting Buckles Bay daily. Leanne couldn't help but smile at all the sudden, animated activity. It was a good gang on board, she thought, and everything boded well for the rest of the voyage.

By the close of the following day the *Aurora*'s crew and expeditioners had completed the Macquarie Island operations – with all 41 tonnes of cargo delivered and personnel changed over – one day earlier than scheduled.

When the *Aurora* turned away from Macquarie that evening, the setting sun cast a warm glow over the rugged slopes of the island, prompting Leanne to write appreciatively:

The setting sun provided a beautiful backdrop to Macquarie Island and will leave lasting memories for us all of how spectacular the island is. Unfortunately for all those with cameras in hand waiting for a glimpse of the orcas that were rumoured to appear – it did not happen.

The transit to Casey was also relatively calm, and the *Aurora* bustled with preparations for the Casey resupply. Preparatory briefings for the many aspects of resupply were held, including refuelling, watercraft operations, and embarkation and disembarkation of vessels, and expeditioners conducted frenzied cleaning of gear, equipment and clothing before their arrival at the pristine continent.

The onboard social committee was also busy; Christmas was fast approaching, and the ship's tree was dusted off and erected and tinsel was hung around the mess like bunting. Actually, Christmas would be celebrated five days early, as the Casey resupply would be in full swing on Christmas Day. And so, on 19 December, or 'Christmas Eve', carols once again cheerily resounded around the *Aurora*'s mess, followed by a well-contested trivia night. Breaking slightly with tradition, King Neptune made his visit to the ship on 'Christmas morning', performing his customary goop-dolloping anointment of those who were travelling beyond sixty degrees south for the first time.

After the ceremony, the resulting mess was soon cleared away and the restaurant was prepared for Christmas lunch. Tables were set and laden with roast meats, oysters, prawns and crayfish and, of course, delectable desserts, and lunch was served to cheers and toasts. Many expeditioners sampled more than they should have, and retired with overindulged contentment that evening, their centres of gravity having shifted ever so slightly.

By now the *Aurora* had crossed the ice edge and was sailing through vast patches of ice floes that hosted an array of charismatic wildlife. Sinuous, lithe leopard seals angrily mouthed their displeasure as the *Aurora* sailed past their patches of ice; their gaping jaws a conspicuous patch of pink in an otherwise cool-toned landscape. Pudgy crabeater seals lounged on the ice until, suddenly startled, they rolled and lolloped across floes and slid into the water with a plop. Humpback whales and a few of their smaller cousins, the torpedo-like minke whales, gracefully surfaced between scattered patches of ice.

The *Aurora* and her complement arrived at Newcomb Bay, Casey station, on 22 December. Their good fortune with the weather continued, and thanks to the unbroken daylight hours of the Antarctic summer, the resupply began almost immediately (after the obligatory inductions, toolbox meetings and safety briefings). The barge puttered loads of cargo across to the uneven snow-blanketed shore, and rubber boats buzzed across the water, carrying incoming passengers to the base. The expeditioners trudged up the road from the wharf, past the station's cylindrical fuel tanks and the geometric form of the satellite dome, up to the colourful buildings sitting atop the low hill.

Leanne watched on from the bridge, occasionally lifting her radio to her cheek to relay information or direct resources, but for the most part she was able to leave her capable staff to get on with the job, content with keeping an eye on activities from on high.

The station's refuelling was supposed to begin the next day, but overnight a large ice floe had broken free in Brown Bay and was threatening to move between the *Aurora* and the shore, exactly where the fuel line was supposed to be set across the water. They could do little but watch and wait. The following day, the real Christmas Eve, arrived clear and calm and Leanne was pleased to see that the offending floe had moved to a more convenient location away from the ship. With the good weather forecast to continue for the next few days, Leanne, Captain Murray Doyle, DVL Mark Skinner and Station Leader Anthony 'Hully' Hull all agreed that the station refuelling could commence.

Refuelling supervisor Brad Collins and his team swung into action, and soon a small fleet of rubber boats buzzed around the ship, conducting the painstaking task of laying out the hose, deploying the anchors and connections and pressure testing the line. That afternoon they finally began to pump fuel to the upper fuel farm at Casey, all the while keeping a close watch on the fuel line.

After dinner that evening, the *Aurora*'s complement happily welcomed five French and Italian expeditioners from the

French–Italian base Concordia research station, 1100 kilometres inland from Casey station. They had flown from Concordia to Casey and would be transported back to Hobart by the Australian Antarctic Program, onboard the *Aurora Australis*.

In the bright Antarctic light of five o'clock Christmas morning, Brad and the second mate Naomi Petersen stood quietly on the *Aurora*'s bridge, watching over the continuing refuelling. The rubber boats slowly chugged along the floating line, keeping an eye out for leaks and nudging the occasional piece of wayward ice away from the hose. Naomi glanced regularly at the plateau to the east for any hints of angry snow flurries on the skyline – always a telltale sign at Casey station that a sudden, fierce Antarctic change was on its way. Every fifteen minutes, Brad's radio clicked and sparked to life as the diesos at the station's fuel farm reported the current fuel reading.

Brad jotted down the latest figures in his notebook. Volume and flow were all looking good, he thought with satisfaction, putting down his pencil. As the lanky man picked up his binoculars, the calm quiet of the bridge was interrupted again, this time by the peal of the bridge's international phone.

'Don't answer it,' dared Brad, his eyes twinkling mischievously as Naomi turned toward the chart table. The international phone only rings occasionally, and Brad was convinced that, during a refuelling operation, it only ever brought bad news.

'I have to,' Naomi replied, with her own friendly grin. She picked up the phone.

'Good morning,' said Naomi in her gentle Kiwi tones. 'This is the *Aurora Australis* bridge.' She waited while the satellite connection struggled.

'Good morning bridge, this is RCC Australia, RCC Australia, over.' Naomi immediately straightened her back.

'Yes RCC Australia; copy, over.'

'Would the master be available please; the master be available.'

'Shit! He's asleep,' thought Naomi.

'I will have to call him. Can you . . .'

'I will stand by on the phone,' the RCC confirmed before she even asked the question, cutting her off. Naomi stepped over to the *Aurora*'s internal phone and dialled Murray's cabin, then quickly told him that the RCC was on the line. On the international phone, the gentle hubbub of people talking with professional intensity could be heard in the background.

Naomi returned to the international phone. 'Yes Sir; he's on his way.'

'Roger that, thank you. What's your current position, please?'

'Current position: we are at Casey station, Casey station. I can give you the lat–long if you wish.' Lat–long is the latitude and longitude coordinates of the ship.

'Yes please.'

'It's 66 degrees . . .' Naomi began, but she trailed off as Murray threw open the bridge door, arriving at her side an instant later. She handed the captain the receiver with a quick word.

'Morning,' Murray greeted the RCC pleasantly, not quite knowing what to expect.

'Yes good morning Sir . . . this is . . . RCC Australia . . . Who am I speaking with, Sir?'

'The Master, Murray Doyle.'

'We have just received an Inmarsat C distress alert,' began the RCC officer, his tone immediately changing to one of urgent formality. (Inmarsat C is a satellite communications system often used for emergencies by ships.) 'We have received it for the passenger vessel *Akademik Shokalskiy*.'

Murray picked up a pad of paper and started writing frantic notes as the officer continued in his clear, urgently precise radio manner: 'The vessel is in position 66 degrees 52 minutes south, 144 degrees nineteen minutes east. The vessel is carrying 74 persons on board. The vessel is stuck in ice. The vessel has two icebergs closing. The first iceberg is 1.2 kilometres off, and will be in an approximate position of three cables to the vessel. The second iceberg is closing at three knots, and will be two cables off the vessel. And this will occur during the day today.'

Murray furiously took down the details and then answered more questions about the *Aurora*'s current location and capability. Brad, all trace of cheekiness gone, gravely looked on. It was pretty clear just from this side of the conversation that a vessel somewhere was in distress.

Murray answered another question. Then another.

'We are at the moment pumping fuel,' said Murray, at the end of the conversation, 'so it may take me a bit of time to stop the fuel line and things, and make as best pace I can to get going.'

After another minute or so, Murray hung up the phone. He stared down at his notes for a moment, then looked out at the fuel line crossing the water to the station. The VL needed to know they'd just been tasked to a rescue, and she needed to know right now – before the proverbial hit the fan. Murray turned to Naomi and asked her to hold the fort, then went out the bridge door and padded quickly down the stairs.

Leanne, roused by the sharp rap at her door, was surprised to find it was the captain who'd come knocking. Muz began to tell Leanne about the RCC tasking, and that they needed to assist a ship called the *Akademik Shokalskiy*.

The MV *Akademik Shokalskiy* was a Russian-flagged vessel currently under charter to conduct the Australasian Antarctic Expedition (AAE). This privately funded voyage aimed to visit a small number of subantarctic and Antarctic locations to conduct some scientific research, with a focus on public communication. It also ran under the banner the 'Spirit of Mawson', with both voyage titles attempting to link the voyage with that conducted by the famous explorer of the heroic age. The *Shokalskiy*'s complement comprised 22 Russian crew and 52 passengers, who were an eclectic mix of scientists, students, journalists, three members of the Mawson's Hut Foundation (funded by the Australian government), a large contingent of paying citizen scientists and two children. The AAE had already conducted one leg of the voyage to the subantarctic Auckland and Campbell Islands, and during their Antarctic leg, had deposited the conservationists for a brief visit to Mawson's Hut. It was after this visit, when the expedition had moved on to visit the Hodgeman Islands, that their ship ran into trouble.

The stage had already been set by loose pack ice that lay north of the region in which the ice-strengthened *Akademik Shokalskiy* was operating. The ship was waiting at the edge of the solid fast ice while a number of the complement had crossed the ice and were undertaking a field trip on shore. Stories of how the vessel came to be beset varied depending on the source reporting them; but whether it was a simple breakdown in communication between the ship and the field party or wilful defiance of the captain's desperate orders as he saw pack ice closing in behind them, it caused a delay in the *Shokalskiy*'s departure from the region. The *Shokalskiy* was ice-strengthened, but she did not have a large icebreaking capacity, and just as the *Polar Bird* and *Nella Dan* had found so many times under such conditions, she had little to no chance of making her way through the pack ice that had closed in around her. In the *Shokalskiy*'s frantic attempt to escape the icy ensnarement, a hole was torn in her hull above the waterline. By Christmas morning she was stuck – and two icebergs were rapidly bearing down on her.

Captain Igor, concerned for the safety of his ship and the lives of his passengers, issued a distress alert. Greg Mortimer, a well-known mountaineer and adventurer who was one of the expedition's co-leaders and the head of logistics on the *Akademik Shokalskiy*, was asked to act as point of contact for the ship.

As Leanne listened to Murray's earnest words about the RCC tasking and the situation with the *Shokalskiy*, the bleary curiosity written across her face was immediately replaced by earnest concentration. When Murray finished briefing her and returned to the bridge, she hurriedly changed and followed him, noting as she shouldered through the heavy bridge door that its sign had already been turned over to a firm 'BRIDGE CLOSED' to everyone except crew and voyage management.

It was an RCC tasking, so Leanne knew that Murray, as captain, now had absolute authority over the *Aurora*'s movements and all her onboard assets. But before the icebreaker could go anywhere, the AAD resupply personnel and the *Aurora*'s crew needed to work together to prepare the ship for departure. Standing together on the bridge, Muz, Leanne, Naomi and Brad agreed that the refuelling would need to be stopped immediately, despite only delivering just under half of the fuel required for the station for winter. Cargo operations had also not been completed yet: about seventy per cent of the inbound cargo had gone ashore, but there was still land-based project cargo on board and none of the return-to-Australia cargo had been loaded.

But there was little else they could do; they had to up stumps, fast.

Brad radioed his refuelling team to advise that the pumping would be shut down shortly, threw on his heavy blue jacket, beanie and gloves, then bustled down to take position at the main valve out on the *Aurora*'s forecastle. The refuelling team would need to pig the line (cleaning the inside of the fuel line with a foam 'pig', using compressed air) before they could disconnect each end, and then they'd have to retrieve the cumbersome hose by boat. He gripped the pages of his Standard Operating Procedure in one hand and spoke intermittently into the radio handset at his shoulder, earnestly confirming and cross-checking each step with the ship's engineers, station diesos and the watercraft officers. The last thing they needed to deal with right now was a fuel spill.

Meanwhile, Leanne and Station Leader Hully began to mobilise the expeditioners. Incoming expeditioners still on board the ship needed to go ashore ASAP, and, given they had no idea whether the *Aurora* would even be returning to Casey this voyage, all outgoing expeditioners still at the station were ordered to board the ship immediately, regardless of whether or not they had completed their summer projects.

Soon, Murray received word from the RCC that the Chinese icebreaker the *Xue Long* and the French vessel *L'Astrolabe* had both been contacted by the RCC and had immediately abandoned their programs to make their way toward the *Akademik Shokalskiy*. Air evacuation options were also being examined by the RCC, and they reported to Murray that they had spoken with the French Antarctic station Dumont d'Urville, which was the closest station to the beset ship.

The *Aurora*'s helideck was swiftly cleared of cargo. Forty drums of aviation fuel were lifted on board just in case helicopters from the *Xue Long* or Dumont d'Urville station might need reserves, and after seven hours of frantic activity, the *Aurora* weighed anchor. She steamed north, cleared the heavy pack ice and then turned east, steaming in the relatively clear but swell-dampened region of the loose pack. For two days the *Aurora* raced under heavy skies across the ice-dappled water, a speck of vivid orange streaking across an expanse of mirror-calm grey.

Meanwhile, hurried discussions between the French, Chinese and Australian vessels established the cumulative assets of the three ships, and the captains began to form a rough plan. The *Xue Long* had a large helicopter onboard; however, the Chinese ship didn't have enough room to accommodate more than nineteen expeditioners. If, at some point, all 52 passengers from the *Akademik Shokalskiy* required evacuation, many would be sleeping on the floor. The *Aurora Australis* had just delivered personnel to Casey station and easily had enough accommodation available for 52 evacuees, but the *Aurora* didn't have any aircraft to transport the passengers on board. The French *L'Astrolabe*, fresh from a resupply of Dumont d'Urville, could act in a support capacity, but the vessel was limited in its area of operation by her lower icebreaking capacity. She could, however, stand by to take some persons on board if required.

Adding to the complications, an intense low-pressure system passing through the *Shokalskiy*'s area on Christmas Day and Boxing Day had pushed a massive band of pack ice in behind the vessel. The *Shokalskiy* was now some twenty nautical miles from the ice edge, and the thick band of ice had become consolidated under the pressure of the foul weather system.

The Antarctic flagships of three different national Antarctic programs would need to work closely together. It was clear that each of the rescue vessels had limited resources, but united, the two larger icebreakers could try to break the *Shokalskiy* free, or evacuate the passengers if needed and transport them safely back to Australia.

On 27 December, the *Xue Long* and *L'Astrolabe* both arrived at the region north of the *Shokalskiy*. Being less than eight times the volume of the *Xue Long*, *L'Astrolabe* was dwarfed by the impressive Chinese icebreaker, and the red, white and blue French vessel hung back near the ice edge to act as standby support if an emergency evacuation was required. The mighty *Xue Long*, however, pointed her red bow toward the ice and charged.

At a gargantuan size of 167 metres, the *Xue Long* had slightly less icebreaking capability than her Australian counterpart and ally, the *Aurora Australis*. Initially the *Xue Long* made good headway into the pack, but as she advanced her progress slowed against the compacted, frozen mass that had formed in the region. The thin, squiggly grey lines of water that had snaked between ice floes all but disappeared, until the seascape around them resembled a violent wasteland of smashed meringue that was periodically interrupted by towering pressure ridges jutting angrily into the air.

At a point about 6.1 nautical miles away from the *Shokalskiy*, the *Xue Long* stopped moving altogether. Off in the distance, separated by an immense, rutted field of ice, was the blue and white form of the *Akademik Shokalskiy*. Captain Jianzhong Wang reported on their status to the RCC and the other ships by email (in English, the standard language for rescue requests):

In the past 11 hours our ship moved ahead only 2nm [nautical miles], the pack ice around here almost 10 tenth, with some floes about three to four metres thickness with ice-ridge, which is far more exceeding to MV *Xue Long*'s ice-break capability. If we keep moving on in the same way, I am afraid we would get stuck too . . .

So we propose a more powerful icebreaker could come to support this situation and help MV *Akademik Shokalskiy* to get out of stuck. We will stay here and standby in case of any unexpected situation until MV *Akademik Shokalskiy* get out of stuck, we have got plans ready for this rescue, although there is no helicopter deck on the MV *Akademik Shokalskiy*, we have found a floe that large enough near MV *Akademik Shokalskiy* for our helicopter landing in case of emergency evacuation.

The *Aurora* continued to race toward the *Shokalskiy*, with Captain Murray not quite certain if the *Xue Long* was also stuck in the ice, or was simply standing by until further help arrived.

With the *Xue Long* already on site, and the *Aurora Australis* en route, the RCC released *L'Astrolabe* from the emergency tasking. Meanwhile, Captain Igor had advised the RCC that the main danger had passed for the *Shokalskiy*; the two menacing icebergs had drifted past his beset ship without incident. Nevertheless, they were still firmly stuck in the expanse of sea ice, and Captain Igor decided that if the *Xue Long* and *Aurora Australis* couldn't get through the ice to free his vessel, he would request the evacuation of all 52 passengers.

Captain Wang and Captain Murray immediately began working on an evacuation plan. They agreed that, if evacuation was required, the *Xue Long*'s helicopters would evacuate the passengers from an ice helipad next to the *Shokalskiy*, and take them to the Chinese icebreaker, where they would then be transferred by barge over water to the *Aurora Australis*.

But the *Aurora* had to get there first.

The *Aurora* reached a point north of the *Shokalskiy* on 29 December, after almost four days steaming, and turned toward the stricken ship. But as she motored southward, the grey gloom above her began to contract, eventually enveloping the *Aurora* in a cloud of soft, horizontal snow that reduced visibility to about a ship length. Lumpy floes ghosted out of the mist only shortly before they met the *Aurora*'s hull with a sharp clang or juddering thud. Up on the snow-crusted bow the *Aurora*'s killer whale weathervane stood sentinel, the black and white talisman valiantly leading the way into the miasma.

The *Aurora* began to ride and judder over large chunks of sea ice, sometimes pushing whole floes along in front of her; driving the huge wedge-shaped pieces through the water like battering rams before they eventually broke apart and disappeared down the *Aurora*'s side. Adelie penguins, the only defined objects within the dimensionless gloom, skipped and hopped across nearby floes, hurriedly squawking their way away from the approaching ship before clumsily bellyflopping into the frozen ocean. They rocketed away with surprising agility, leaving only a stream of bubbles in their watery wake.

The *Aurora* continued to race south, and broke into the open water of the Mertz Glacier polynya overnight. On the morning of the 30th she made her first push into the dense pack ice surrounding the *Akademik Shokalskiy*.

But the consolidated pack ice soon brought the mighty orange ship to a standstill, and Muz began the painstaking icebreaking process; repeatedly reversing the *Aurora* back, then determinedly ramming her forward. Down in the *Aurora*'s belly her engines roared, and her propeller shaft spun and rumbled with effort as she exerted her monumental force against the ice. The sea behind the *Aurora*'s stern raged like whitewater, and chunks of ice tossed and churned within the boiling chaos. Slowly – painfully – she inched her way forward.

Then the wind began to pick up.

Muz sighed at the A factor's impeccable timing. They were still 9.7 nautical miles from the *Akademik Shokalskiy*, but they now had thirty knots of tailwind which could pack more ice up behind them. The *Aurora Australis* could quite easily end up another victim of the horrendous ice conditions and become stuck herself.

Murray had been beset in the ice before, once so badly that the *Aurora*'s hardy reinforced hull had even been dented. While the physical traces of that sticky situation had long since been repaired, Muz didn't want to put the *Aurora* through that again. As much as they all wanted to break the *Shokalskiy* free, the safety of the *Aurora* and her complement was paramount. It was time to retreat back to the safety of the Mertz polynya and its open water.

Murray quickly sent an email to the RCC, relaying the current situation and his decision to move back to open water. He also recommended that the *Xue Long* likewise move out of the ice and wait for better conditions from the safety of open water. 'That's if they're not already stuck tight,' he thought. They certainly looked it, despite their recent assurances they were not beset.

The next day, the *Aurora* gave the ice surrounding the *Shokalskiy* one last try, but it was no use. The sea ice was an impenetrable confusion of thick, jumbled floes and pressure ridges. Murray informed the captain of the *Akademik Shokalskiy* that he did not consider it feasible to break into their position, and the two captains agreed that a helicopter evacuation of the *Akademik Shokalskiy*'s passengers was now the best option.

Now, having committed to the passenger evacuation, the three ships simply waited until conditions were calm enough to begin the air evacuation of the *Shokalskiy*.

But on 1 January, the situation changed again. Captain Wang contacted the *Aurora*, asking for assistance to break his ship out of the heavy pack: they had large floes both in front and behind the ship, and they could not move, he reported. The *Xue Long* was officially stuck.

'Bloody hell,' thought Muz. They'd all been suspicious that something was up with the *Xue Long*, so it wasn't exactly a surprise, but it was still another massive problem. The *Aurora* now had two beset vessels on her hands. The *Aurora Australis* would try to assist, Muz responded to Captain Wang reassuringly.

Despite his own assurances, Murray was nervous. The *Aurora* didn't have all that much more icebreaking capacity than the *Xue Long*; would she be able to handle the ice out there without becoming stuck herself? She had struggled in her earlier attempts . . .

But the *Xue Long* had asked for help, so Murray and the engineers prepared the *Aurora* for another incursion into the ice. Half an hour later the icebreaker re-entered the pack.

Meanwhile, VL Leanne had called a meeting with the AAD expeditioners on board. It was now a question of when, not if, they would be housing the *Shokalskiy*'s passengers, and she wanted to ensure that the AAD made their arrival as easy as possible for them, and as simple as possible for the *Aurora*'s crew. She began to task every expeditioner with a role in the evacuation process. Later, Leanne called Greg Mortimer on the satellite phone to discuss some of the inevitable last-minute details. Her rapport with the expedition co-leader had built, and a friendly camaraderie of sorts had formed between the two logisticians. When Greg mentioned that the Australian Antarctic Program's beloved guide-dog donation box mascot Stay was currently on board the *Shokalskiy*, Leanne's playful sense of humour kicked in.

STAY: A TREASURED ANTARCTIC CHARACTER

Legend has it that Stay, a former guide-dog donation box, was stolen from the dark streets of Hobart by some inebriated expeditioners after a night on the town in 1991 (another version of this story has the culprits being a rowdy group of IRs). In both versions, the group's plan was to take a dog to Davis station via the *Aurora Australis* in protest to the recent news that the beloved husky dogs would soon be removed from Antarctica.

Yet another version of Stay's origin story has her embarking on her Antarctic adventures by being borrowed entirely with permission from the Guide Dog Association, partly as a fun way to raise money, but also partly as a pointed political protest to the removal of the huskies.

Whichever story people believe, it is universally agreed that Stay has become an icon within the Australian Antarctic Program. The dog's presence is considered an honour by every station, voyage or Antarctic field team she graces, and she is often dog-napped by wily personnel eager to take her on a new adventure.

Over more than 25 years of adventuring, Stay has visited every Australian Antarctic station, several international stations, Mawson's Hut, Heard Island and Béchervaise Island. She has journeyed to the Arctic Circle, visited Europe and travelled Tasmania (and these lists are by no means exhaustive). She has voyaged on board the *Polar Bird*, *Aurora Australis* and the *Akademik Shokalskiy*, as well as traversed parts of Antarctica in Hägglunds and helicopters, and she has been diving under the Antarctic ice. Stay has even had a children's book published about her by author Jesse Blackadder.

Stay meeting some local king penguins at Macquarie Island in 2017.

'You realise,' Leanne said to Greg cheekily, 'that if Stay is not on the first helicopter, none of you are coming on board?'

There was a momentary pause on the line.

'Ah,' Greg countered, 'I was actually going to leave Stay until the last load, because that way I'd know you'd be taking all of us!'

Leanne laughed. Greg could give as well as he got, which was great.

All the while, the *Aurora* continued to lunge into the ice, each monotonous rumble and juddering crunch taking her ever so slightly toward the *Xue Long*. Her progress was slow, but the *Aurora* managed to ram her way more than eleven nautical miles into the frozen jungle, and by midnight she had managed to reach a distance just 2.3 miles from the *Xue Long*.

But when Murray checked the charts again on the morning of 2 January his heart sank. Despite all their efforts, and five more hours of slow but seemingly steady progress in the small hours of the morning, the *Aurora* had actually moved away from the *Xue Long*. The colossal force of the drifting pack ice had pushed the *Aurora* away from the Chinese icebreaker faster than her valiant icebreaking attempts could keep up with.

It was senseless to keep burning fuel in a futile attempt to get closer to the Chinese icebreaker, and Murray went to the radio to break the news to the Chinese captain.

Captain Wang's disappointment was short lived: the weather was clear and fine, he pointed out to Murray. The crisp Antarctic air was now the calmest it had been since the *Xue Long* had arrived some six days earlier, and the conditions were, at long last, perfect for flying. If the evacuation was going to happen, the Chinese captain told Murray, it should happen today.

But the *Xue Long* was well and truly stuck in the ice. And with her besetment, the plan to move passengers from the Chinese ship to the *Aurora* via barge in open water was scuttled. They needed another strategy to transfer the passengers onto the *Aurora* – and fast.

They considered three options:

The first option – landing the *Xue Long*'s helicopter on the *Aurora* – was simply not possible, the Chinese assured them. The *Aurora*'s helideck was too small for their massive Kamov aircraft; there was not enough clearance between the helipad and the *Aurora*'s superstructure to land the large helicopter safely. In addition, the near-catastrophic crash of a Kamov helicopter on a South Korean vessel in Antarctica just weeks before was still fresh in the collective Antarctic memory, and it acted as a harsh reminder of the potential for disastrous results if they tried to push the envelope too far.

The second option was to fly the *Shokalskiy*'s passengers to the *Xue Long* and keep them there. It was certainly doable, but, as they had already established, the *Xue Long* only had nineteen spare berths, so 33 people would be sleeping on the floor. With many of the *Shokalskiy*'s complement being tourist seniors, this option, with its cramped, basic quarters, was not ideal; especially as they had no idea how long the *Xue Long* might also remain stuck.

The third option was to try to find an ice floe in the *Aurora*'s vicinity that was large and thick enough on which to land a Kamov helicopter, and position the *Aurora* next to it, mirroring the unloading situation at the *Shokalskiy*. That was the preferred option.

A large floe on the starboard side of the *Aurora* stood alone in a conglomerated mess of jumbled, fractured floes and ice ridges. The floe was uneven and lumpy, but there seemed to be a small, relatively flat section in the middle. But there was a slight problem with its current location: the *Aurora*'s gangway and bunker door – the two entry points to the ship – were both on the *Aurora*'s port side. But Muz didn't want to try to turn the *Aurora* around: with the ice being so consolidated, any movement by the ship as she manoeuvred might crack the only floe in the vicinity that seemed large and stable enough to be used as a landing pad.

The answer was elegant in its simplicity: the *Aurora*'s Fast Rescue Craft (FRC) would be repurposed as a glorified lift. It was located on the *Aurora*'s starboard side, and could be lowered from its mounting davits over the side of the ship and down onto the ice floe on that side.

With that, the *Xue Long* dispatched its huge Kamov helicopter to assess the ice floe next to the *Aurora*.

At the same time, two of the *Aurora*'s expeditioners – Marty Benavente, an experienced field training officer (FTO) and Paul Steyne, a water craft operator (who, rather handily, happened to be an experienced Police Search and Rescue officer) – were quickly lowered onto the ice to check the floe before the chopper landed.

Leanne nervously watched on as the pair, fully kitted up wearing drysuits, lifejackets and bright hard hats, carefully trod their way across the floe, poking their ice picks and probes into the snow before them as they went. The carabiners and ropes slung on their harnesses swung and clinked around their hips and legs as they cautiously made their way to the flat section in the centre of the floe. They trod around the even space, poking and prodding through the snow at regular intervals, always finding the comforting solidity of rock-hard ice below.

Marty and Paul test the ice floe for landing prior to the passenger air evacuation of the *Akademik Shokalskiy*.

Finally, Marty lifted his radio to his face. The floe seemed pretty good, he reported back to Murray and Leanne, with the team agreeing over the radio that the pair should quickly try and clear a landing area for the approaching Chinese helicopter.

The pair tramped back and forth, flattening the snow in a square a few metres wide for a landing pad. Marty, having prepared Antarctic helipads once or twice in his time as an FTO, had thought to procure some red food dye from the galley before leaving the ship. He pulled the small bottle from one of his pockets and poured a square around the peripheries of the patch. The thin, crimson dribbles quickly stained the white snow, conspicuously marking out the landing site.

Within minutes, the hunched form of the *Xue Long*'s red, white and yellow helicopter appeared and quickly grew larger in the sky behind the *Aurora*. Much like a bumblebee, the Kamov seemed impossibly large and heavy to be flying, but it was held aloft by two coaxial rotor blades that spun powerfully in opposite directions. Marty and Paul knelt on the ice on one side of the landing pad while the impressive aircraft circled the floe and then hovered above the landing site. Ice crystals whipped like shards of glass against their exposed noses and cheeks, and they raised their arms to shield their faces against the thrumming downforce. The aircraft slowly descended, then gently touched its four wheels down on the ice. With its blades still whirling powerfully, the pilot looked down at the kneeling pair and gave an enthusiastic thumbs up, before expertly lifting his craft back off the ice and banking it away into the sky.

The airwaves between the three ships were immediately filled with urgent chatter between the Chinese and Australian captains, and Greg Mortimer on the Russian vessel. The evacuation was 'go'. The Kamov would return to the *Aurora* with Chinese National Antarctic Research Expedition (CHINARE) personnel who would triple-check the ice with a ground-penetrating radar before constructing a timber helipad, and do the same at the *Shokalskiy*'s landing area.

Down on the ice, two more watercraft operators, Doug and James, joined Marty and Paul to help with the evacuation.

Moments later, the huge CHINARE helicopter swooped past the *Aurora*'s bow and carefully landed on the ice. This time its fuselage door slid open, and nine Chinese personnel leapt out, pulling large, flat planks of wood behind them, and dropped them onto the ice. The group moved away from the helipad, signalled to the pilot, and the chopper lifted back into the sky with a roar.

One of the Chinese personnel turned to Marty. He could speak English, he said, and would act as a translator.

'Okay, so you want to put a new pad, a new landing site?' Marty asked the CHINARE translator.

'Yeah. This area is okay for a helideck. Okay?' the CHINARE spokesperson said, gesturing to the landing site.

'Yes, great,' Marty answered. 'So, the snow is a bit deeper this high side, so we can dig and flatten if you want, or just pack it down . . .'

With the aid of the CHINARE expeditioner busily translating for the teams, they quickly formed a plan for the site, and moved into action. The Chinese team walked up and down the landing area, checking the site and its surrounds with their ground-penetrating radar. They were soon satisfied, explaining to their Australian colleagues that the landing area was crack-free and safe to use. The team busily arranged the timber planks into three flat pads on top of the flattened snow.

While their Chinese counterparts finished their preparations, the four Australians dragged two black sleds along the ice, each piled high with white plastic pails and cardboard boxes containing some of the *Aurora*'s emergency food supplies. The emergency rations were being provided at the *Shokalskiy*'s request and would be backloaded to the *Shokalskiy* to supplement their food supplies. As the two teams busily worked together on the ice floe, a lone Adelie penguin inquisitively waddled over to the landing site and stood watching the bustling activity with brazen curiosity.

A lone Adelie penguin comes to investigate all the activity.

The huge Kamov helicopter noisily approached the ice floe and descended onto the timber pads. The landing teams retreated from the airborne needles of ice whipped up by the rotor blades, and were quickly joined by the penguin, who stood uncertainly alongside the human huddle.

As soon as the helicopter's door slid open, suitcases, bags and backpacks were passed one after the other out of the craft and placed on the snow, quickly forming a pile. Up on the *Aurora*'s bridge Leanne involuntarily shrugged and gave a resigned chuckle. The luggage wasn't supposed to come until everyone was safely evacuated: the RCC had been adamant that it was all supposed to come with the cargo loads.

But one piece of welcome cargo suddenly turned Leanne's rueful smile into a broad grin. There was Stay, looking ever-unfazed, being carefully unloaded from the aircraft. The precious icon was lowered gently onto the snow alongside the pile of bags, where she sat expectantly, calmly waiting for the next move.

Finally, passengers began to emerge from the aircraft. Each awkwardly stepped down the two rungs and then made the final hop onto the ice, and the four Australians greeted them with a smile and pointed them along the compacted path leading over to the *Aurora Australis*.

'Thank you!' some of the new arrivals cried, smiling as they trudged carefully along the trail.

'No worries!' answered Marty with a grin. 'It was a long wait, but we got there!'

'Thank you so much!' added another happily as she tramped by.

The penguin, who had hopped onto a raised chunk of ice set back from the footprinted track, calmly watched as the line of people marched past.

Meanwhile, the pails and boxes of emergency food were loaded into the chopper and some of the Chinese landing team climbed aboard. The door was slammed safely shut behind them and the Kamov lifted into the air, soaring in a graceful arc back toward the *Akademik Shokalskiy*.

The *Shokalskiy* passengers arrived at the *Aurora*'s orange rescue craft and looked up at the huge icebreaker looming above them. They boarded the craft in small groups, then were winched up to the *Aurora*'s helideck.

Leanne had tasked every single AAD expeditioner on board with a job, and the first of her helpers welcomed the new passengers with wide smiles, directing them to the nearby door. The new arrivals pushed open the door, trod down the stairs and were greeted by another chirpy expeditioner on the landing, who guided them down another flight. On and on they descended through the maze of the *Aurora*, and at each landing and every corner they were met with beaming expeditioners showing them the way. Eventually the evacuees arrived into the *Aurora*'s warmly lit mess, where their names were checked off the arrivals list by DVL Mark Skinner. More friendly AAD expeditioners showed the *Shokalskiy* passengers around the restaurant, pointing out where mugs were stowed and giving them a quick tour around the ever-important 'calorie corner' where they could grab a restorative cuppa and a bickie or two.

In fact, their greeting was so warm it actually struck a nerve with some.

'We thought you were going to hate us!' one new arrival said tearfully, the relief of their neighbourly welcome temporarily overcoming her.

Outside, the flights had continued, carrying about a dozen evacuees each trip. Finally, on the final trip, expedition leader Chris Turney and co-leader Greg Mortimer arrived along with a load of cargo. As Chris carefully climbed down the steps and onto the ice, Greg went forward to the cockpit and gratefully thanked the pilots. Then the tall, lanky man wearily stepped out of the aircraft and made his way across the ice to the *Aurora*, the relief on his careworn face plain.

The two remaining CHINARE personnel began packing their shovels and gear into the helicopter, helped by the Australians. Then with warm handshakes and a triumphant thumbs up, the Chinese landing crew jumped into their helicopter. The pilot also waved a warm farewell from the curved window at the front of the aircraft, and a moment later they were in the air, soaring away from their new Australian friends and back to the *Xue Long*.

Murray felt a massive weight lift from his shoulders as the helicopter took off for the last time. He turned away from his control station and went to the phone to let the RCC know that the evacuation was complete.

Meanwhile, there was still work to be done on the ice floe, and Leanne watched as Marty, Paul, Doug and James dragged and then manhandled sledload after sledload of the AAE's bags and cargo across the ice to the *Aurora*, then began to pack up the heavy timber boards of the helipads. Heart swelling with pride, she picked up her radio.

'Can you please thank all of your guys down there,' she called to Marty, 'that's a huge effort today and it's been much appreciated.'

The team down on the ice floe gave her four wide smiles and a simple thumbs up.

Stay arriving onto the *Aurora Australis* safe and sound, into the arms of Voyage Leader Leanne Millhouse.

When the packing up was finally complete, Murray manoeuvred the *Aurora* carefully away from the floe, then alternated between picking, pushing and ramming the icebreaker back out through the pack.

But that evening, the RCC received an email from Captain Wang.

'*Xue Long* is now stuck by the surrounding sea ice and there is an iceberg before my head, about 0.3 mile. I cannot ahead again and change course is very difficult, I wished *Aurora Australis* may come closer to *Xue Long* and get us out of this area, but [she] failed' the Captain wrote urgently going on to describe the ice conditions and onboard provisions. 'The current and ice information change very fast and complex in this area, there is danger all time for [our ship].'

With an iceberg now threatening the *Xue Long*, the RCC immediately put the *Aurora* on standby, asking Murray to keep the *Aurora Australis* in the area in case assistance was required. But after having to abandon the earlier rescue attempts, Murray knew there was little the *Aurora* could do to assist the *Xue Long*, except evacuate and take on more passengers if the iceberg threatened to hit the Chinese icebreaker.

The next evening, Captain Wang radioed the *Aurora*'s bridge. The *Xue Long* was still firmly stuck, but the iceberg that had threatened the ship was now moving away from them. The danger had passed, the captain relayed with relief.

With no other icebergs currently threatening either ship, and both having enough provisions to see their complements through an extended wait, the RCC officially released the *Aurora* from the emergency tasking. She was free to resume the Casey resupply, before making the journey back to Hobart.

Over the next few days the evacuees settled in to the routine of life on board Australia's icebreaker. There was a small adjustment period as the passengers became used to the relatively basic accommodation and self-sufficient housekeeping practices on board the *Aurora*, transitioning from having the run of a full-service charter vessel to being guests on a working ship.

By now Leanne had become known as having a friendly, sympathetic ear and the VL's office was frequently visited by both Spirit of Mawson and Antarctic Division personnel. Some had been traumatised by their experiences on the beset ship; others were frustrated with the interruptions and delays to their AAD programs. Leanne good-naturedly plied such visitors with steaming mugs of coffee and generous helpings of sweets and chocolate, and simply listened as they talked. Her sense of humour helped too, and she always felt she'd done her job well when the previously irritated visitors walked away with smiles on their faces.

But not everyone was unhappy. Shortly after the evacuation, Leanne was working in her cabin writing the daily sitrep when the sound of her fingers tapping at the keyboard was joined by something else. Her hands paused above the keys for a moment and she turned toward the door.

Someone was singing in Italian! Her face broke into a delighted smile and she leapt up from her chair, poking her head out into the corridor. There was Giuseppie from Concordia station, merrily cleaning the corridor walls as he sang in his glorious dulcet tones. He'd volunteered to help the ship's stewards while they were busy with their additional workload. 'That's what it's all about,' Leanne thought with pride. 'We all muck in where we can once the A factor strikes.'

Meanwhile, the media interest in the rescue was intense. Reporters had been regularly calling the ship, but Murray and Leanne had done their best to deflect requests for interviews or information, pointing the outlets instead to the AAD, P&O or the Australian Maritime Safety Authority (AMSA). One morning, as the *Aurora* continued on her course back to Casey, Leanne went up to the bridge and greeted Murray with her usual cheerful enthusiasm.

'I wonder what we've said today?' Murray replied jokingly to Leanne, nodding his head toward a pile of printed news reports on the top of the chart table.

'Hmmm,' mused Leanne, her eyes sparkling cheekily. 'I'm not too sure.'

Leanne went over to the chart table and began to rifle through the pile of papers. Some articles had quoted her most recent sitrep, she noticed, but as she flicked through the articles, her eyes widened slightly. Opinion-piece headlines they'd received over the last few days, such as 'Ship Stuck in Antarctica Raises Questions About Worth of Re-enacting Expeditions' and 'Rescue Efforts for Trapped Antarctic Voyage Disrupt Serious Science', had now been joined by '*Aurora Australis* Bill Looms After Antarctic Rescue of Russian Research Ship' and, more ominously, even scathing pieces such as 'The Moral of the Antarctic Ship of Fools: never treat a scientific debate as if it is closed.'

The rescue operation appeared to have reignited a debate over the validity of climate change, with some commentators gleefully guffawing at the irony of a ship studying climate change becoming stuck in the ice; misconstruing a weather event that had pushed pack ice south behind the *Shokalskiy* with an assumption that the ship had been 'frozen in' by new ice.

Questions were also raised about the scientific validity of the Spirit of Mawson expedition, and why it had been in the region in the first place. Prior to departure, the expedition had published a number of research aims on their website. Days after the rescue these aims were questioned by the French Polar Institute's Director Yves Frenot, and later also the AAD Chief Scientist Nick Gales, who both doubted how such broad aims could be addressed in just a few weeks of routine sample collection by a handful of students, scientists and tourists, when myriad international Antarctic programs, thousands of scientists and decades of study and analysis had still had not been able to answer the very questions posed by the AAE for its relatively short stint in Antarctica.

Leanne quietly placed the papers back down on the chart table and walked over to the bridge wing. 'Yikes,' she thought as she looked out at the floes and scraps of ice streaming by. 'Thank goodness only the crew have internet access on board the *Aurora Australis*.'

Meanwhile, back toward Commonwealth Bay, the *Shokalskiy* and *Xue Long* were still trapped in the stubborn clutches of the ice. The day after the passenger rescue, with the ice showing no signs of loosening its determined grip on the two ships, the RCC officially requested that the US-run icebreaker the *Polar Star* help break the two ships free. Operated by the US Coastguard, the *Polar Star* was 122 metres long, and, while she was shorter in length than the *Xue Long*, was capable of breaking ice 1.8 metres thick while cruising at a respectable three knots, and breaking ice up to a colossal six metres when using the ramming technique.

However, three days after the *Polar Star* set a course for the two ships, Captain Igor of the *Shokalskiy* reported to the RCC that the ice around his ship suddenly appeared to be breaking up.

Shortly after, the captain started the *Shokalskiy*'s engines and was finally able to extricate his ship from the troublesome ice.

'I confirm that we have no further requirement for attendance of the USCG *Polar Star*,' Captain Igor wrote to the RCC on 7 January. 'We are especially grateful for the help rendered to us in this difficult situation and readiness of all to help us to leave it.'

Not long after, the captain of the *Xue Long* also reported to the RCC that he no longer required assistance. He added touchingly, 'Thank you so much for your kindly and long-lasting assistance in the past few days, it would be the best memories in the CHINARE 30th.'

The two ships were finally free, and the *Shokalskiy* slowly made her way north toward Bluff in New Zealand, while the *Xue Long* resumed her survey operations in Antarctica.

The *Aurora Australis* turned in to Newcomb Bay that night, and with a general lightening of the spirits onboard, the *Aurora*'s crew and expeditioners turned to the task at hand at Casey. Once again, refuelling and cargo operations worked around weather windows, but eventually the refuelling and resupply was completed.

Finally, still running two weeks late, the *Aurora* began the transit north to Hobart. The Continuous Plankton Recorder was deployed off the trawl deck and trailed faithfully behind the ship, catching plankton in its metallic maw as the *Aurora* steamed north across the Southern Ocean.

As the *Aurora* motored north, the *Shokalskiy* passengers, grateful for the rescue, wanted to show their appreciation to the heroic crews of the three ships. They created a mosaic of individual thoughts and drawings, which was scanned and sent to the gallant crews of the *Xue Long* and *Akademik Shokalskiy*. They made cards and handcrafted other items for the *Aurora*'s crew and hung them on a wall in the *Aurora*'s mess.

Spirit of Mawson leader Chris Turney was also busy. As Murray and Leanne had already discovered, during the besetment the world's media had been watching the continuous updates from the expedition and many outlets and scientists had started to judge. When word of the increasingly frosty public reception got back to the expedition leader, Professor Turney went on the defensive.

In a piece published in the *Guardian* two days after he boarded the *Aurora Australis*, Chris defended the scientific merits of the voyage, writing, '[w]e worked on our research programme with the Australian Antarctic Division and other bodies and the expedition was considered significant enough to be given the official stamp of approval'.

And again, in another article for *Nature* on 9 January while the *Aurora* was conducting the resupply at Casey, he declared, 'The science case took two years to develop, and was approved by the New Zealand Department of Conservation, the Tasmanian Parks and Wildlife Service and the Australian Antarctic Division.'

But the Australian Antarctic Division never approved the science on this voyage. Like all voyages conducted in Australia's Antarctic jurisdiction – including tourist voyages with no scientific programs – the AAD had a responsibility under the Antarctic Treaty system to evaluate the voyage's environmental impacts in Antarctica, such as risk of oil spill or effects on wildlife. The environmental impacts of the *Shokalskiy*'s visit to Antarctica were assessed by the AAD, and the *Akademik Shokalskiy* was approved to operate in the Antarctic for the duration of its voyage. Despite the claims of AAE Leader Chris Turney, the AAD had no hand in planning or approving the science of the AAE voyage.

By 21 January the *Aurora* was approaching the coast of Tasmania, and the earthy, wooded scent that hung on the sea breeze told her complement that they didn't have long to go until they sighted land. It was just as well they were almost home, thought Leanne – the shelves of the *Aurora*'s huge dry store were almost completely bare. But not once had the *Aurora*'s galley crew needed to break into the emergency rations.

CATERING FOR THE UNEXPECTED

The detour and rescue operation delayed the voyage by two weeks, which meant two unplanned weeks in which the forty AAD expeditioners and 24 P&O crew on board needed to be fed three meals a day. In addition, they had 52 extra mouths to feed for the three weeks still remaining before the *Aurora* was due to arrive back at Hobart.

Morale on vessels at sea is closely linked to food, and the *Aurora*'s Chief Cook Rebecca and Chief Steward Darcy wanted to keep everyone content for as long as they possibly could. Together they made a detailed inventory of the *Aurora*'s food supplies. Generally, the *Aurora*'s huge dry store and freezers are stocked with food supplies catering for about two weeks longer than the voyage scheduled, in case of delays caused by difficult ice conditions, weather, or emergency taskings. In addition, the *Aurora* also carried a container stocked with emergency rations: enough rice, beans, pasta and dried meats to last one hundred passengers for sixty days if required, although some of these had recently gone over to the *Shokalskiy*.

When the extra passengers first arrived, Darcy and Rebecca pored over their lists and made some calculations. To stretch their supplies as far as they could, they would bake fresh bread, make hearty soups and cook more 'wet' dishes such as pasta bakes and curries to replace the usual 'main with vegetables' options. They made simple changes where they could: scrambled eggs were taken off the breakfast menu and were replaced with poached or fried eggs, stretching their stocks. They even took pains to ensure that people with dietary requirements continued to be well looked after.

'The galley staff need the biggest pat on the back,' Leanne said later. 'We were on the ship for an additional fortnight [longer] than was planned . . . plus three weeks of another 52 people. They did a magnificent job of making sure we still ate well. I think if we were another three or four days we [would have been] struggling. They deserve massive credit for what they did; that was just a phenomenal job.'

The next morning the *Aurora Australis* arrived at the mouth of the Derwent River under an overcast sky glowing golden with dawn. As the icebreaker made her way up the river, expeditioners and crew lined the *Aurora*'s rails, some chatting happily under the painted sky, others deep in their own thoughts. Murray, Leanne and DVL Mark had all been forewarned that the *Aurora*'s arrival would be met by a large media contingent eager for information about the rescue and so, in order to protect the wary evacuees from the media's gaze, a plan had been formed to disembark the Spirit of Mawson passengers first, and put them straight onto a bus which would immediately take them to their hotel.

As the *Aurora* turned in to Sullivans Cove, the group of journalists crowding behind the barricades of Macquarie Wharf all

Media waiting on the wharf for the arrival of *Akademik Shokalskiy* expeditioners.

focused their lenses on the approaching ship. When the *Aurora* finally pulled alongside the wharf and was made secure, she lowered her gangway and a white bus rumbled up to the foot of the stairs.

At the top of the gangway, Leanne stood facing the *Shokalskiy* passengers, who had formed a line along the companionway. Once Murray gave the okay for the passengers to disembark, they began to file forward, and Leanne gave each of them a broad smile and a reassuring, warm hug before they carefully made the descent onto solid land.

It was finally over.

The rescue had been emotionally and physically draining for all of them, and it had been a baptism of fire as her first voyage as VL, but Leanne knew that she and the *Aurora*'s crew would do it all again in a heartbeat. The *Aurora Australis*, led by Murray and his crew and assisted by the Australian expeditioners, had worked in harmony with the other national Antarctic programs, saving 52 people from a precarious situation and even completing the Casey resupply to boot.

'It is worthy of note,' AMSA wrote in one of its last sitreps during the incident, 'that throughout such a prolonged incident in the harshest of marine environments no lives were lost, for which all participants should be commended'.

The rescue of this private expedition came at a cost of $2.17 million to the Australian government and taxpayer, plus almost $500,000 in transfer costs to get the AAE passengers back to Hobart. These costs do not include the substantial losses borne by the Chinese, French and US programs, nor the original costs of the voyage itself; all of which would run into the millions, or come at a cost to their Antarctic operations.

At the time, both the AAD Director Tony Fleming and Environment Minister Greg Hunt stated that the Australian Government would try to recover Australia's out-of-pocket costs from the various insurers or parties involved in the incident.

However, the Department later concluded that further action to pursue cost recovery was not warranted. But the experience did lead to a rethink of the way that Australia handles permission for privately funded expeditions to Antarctica.

As AAD Chief Scientist Nick Gales wrote at the time, 'No nation hesitates to aid a vessel in distress.' Even with doubts over the scientific value of the voyage and questions over how the *Shokalskiy* got stuck in the first place, not one of the four polar programs involved in the search-and-rescue response had hesitated to come to the aid of the distressed ship.

The Russian Federation wrote gratefully in their report to the Antarctic Treaty Consultative Meeting in 2014:

> The Russian Federation expresses its deep gratitude and appreciation to the national Antarctic programs of Australia, France, China and the USA for their readiness to provide support to the Russian ship beset in ice and for the financial costs they had to bear during the rescue operation. On its part, Russia assures that it is always prepared to provide assistance to our foreign colleagues in difficult situations in full compliance with the letter and spirit of the Antarctic Treaty.

The spirit of the Antarctic Treaty was alive and well, and the Australian, Chinese, French and Americans had pulled together without question. They put politics aside to rescue 52 people in a truly international effort, in one of the most remote and inhospitable wildernesses on the planet.

In Antarctica, assistance will always be given to those in need. And you never know when you might need it yourself.

Chapter Ten

ON THE ROCKS

On Valentine's Day 2016, Andrew Constable, chief investigator of the science component of the 'K-Axis voyage', walked onto the bridge of the *Aurora Australis*. He'd just watched a trawl land on the *Aurora*'s cavernous trawl deck, and it still felt like the Antarctic breeze was biting at his cheeks, despite the unnaturally warm confines of the bridge. As Andrew's face slowly thawed, he expectantly watched the crew deftly prepare the *Aurora* for a CTD cast.

For five weeks the *Aurora* and her complement had busily worked in the inhospitable region of the Kerguelen Axis, or 'K-Axis', of East Antarctica (a straight line that runs from the South Pole up the middle of the Indian Ocean between Heard Island and the Kerguelen Islands). They'd deployed countless scientific instruments over dozens of stations; they'd caught, sampled, and measured all sorts of curious creatures from the deep, collected and filtered a multitude of seawater samples, and captured hundreds of live krill for growth experiments in the *Aurora*'s krill laboratories. They had worked in the scenic realm of pack ice and in open-water polynyas, but these easygoing vistas had been regularly interspersed by forays further north into the windswept, lumpy wilds of the Southern Ocean. The voyage's attention would soon be turned to resupplying and refuelling Mawson station and a visit to Davis, but already – thanks to the dedication of the scientists and crew, led by VL Lloyd Symons and Captain Benoit Hebert – the K-axis voyage had achieved far beyond what Andrew could have ever hoped it would. The data had absolutely streamed in, and it felt fantastic.

WHY STUDY THE K-AXIS?

The K-axis spans thousands of kilometres and is one of only three such lines of longitude where cold Antarctic water currents flow across the continental shelf and deep abysses of the Southern Ocean, all the way to the windswept coastlines of Southern Ocean islands. The K-axis also crosses strikingly different marine ecosystems along its length. In the northern reaches of the subantarctic, fish are the dominant prey for predators such as birds, seals and whales, but in the icy waters of the south, Antarctic krill form the basis of the food web.

Scientists believed that there was a rapid transition between the fish-based food web in the north and the krill-based food web in the south along the K-axis, but what drove this transition was yet to be determined. The scientific component of this voyage would examine the physical, biological and chemical conditions in both ecosystem types along the K-axis, which would help explain why these food webs occurred where they did.

Hours later, the CTD finally emerged and the gear was safely stowed. First Mate Gerry O'Doherty* (or 'Gerry O') switched the *Aurora*'s controls from the bridge wing to the main helm,

---

* With a full schedule of logistic and scientific tasks, the K-axis voyage was deemed so busy that two first mates had been stationed on board, to help manage the multitude of operations.

slowly moving the *Aurora* off at a steady, chugging pace, heading for the waypoint of the next research station.

Suddenly, an excited shriek rang around the bridge and Andrew looked over to see one of the expeditioners pointing beyond the *Aurora*'s bow. He followed the line out from the extended finger to see two or three fuzzy blows suspended in the air about half a mile in front of the ship. Whales! Almost immediately, a small knot of expeditioners standing on the opposite side of the bridge gleefully pointed out more puffs of salty air erupting in front of them. In the distance ahead, there was some kind of line on the water. Andrew squinted, trying to make it out.

As the *Aurora* slowly approached, the line in the water actually seemed to be a margin where the Southern Ocean inexplicably transformed from deep blue in colour to pea green. The *Aurora* sailed on, and as soon as she hit the 'green' water the echosounder instantly showed what many had already guessed: it was a krill super-swarm. The teeming mass of orange crustaceans completely transformed the ocean's colour and extended as far as the eye could see. But the *Aurora* was hundreds of nautical miles north of where Antarctic krill – let alone a super-swarm of krill – should usually be found, and the scientists quickly asked for the RMT to be deployed, to sample some of the unlikely swarm.

The *Aurora* was also surrounded by whales in every direction, extending out to the horizon. There were more than one hundred of the foraging leviathans, including some slender, greyhound-esque fin whales as well as the more muscular humpbacks. Closer to the ship, huge lithe bodies broke above and then slipped under the water. Dark gaping mouths broke the surface, displaying strips of bristling baleen that cascaded from the whales' upper jaws. The vast open mouths implacably closed, gulping huge mouthfuls of krill-filled water. The whales' bulging throats contracted as they forced the sea water out of their mouths, trapping the hapless krill against their baleen plates.

VL Lloyd Symons, who was on the trawl deck for the RMT trawl, peered out a large window-like opening on the side of the ship. One of the whales was coming so close to the *Aurora* that he could see its dark form emerging from the deep, its light underside glowing ever brighter and larger as the whale ascended toward the surface. Just before it broke the surface, it extended its long, knobbly pectoral fins out to the side. There was a soft, quick 'pfffft' as the whale's blowholes cleared the water, followed by a sharp intake of breath as it gracefully arched its back, then clamped its blowholes shut before disappearing into the depths again.

On the *Aurora*'s trawl deck behind Lloyd, the crew's pulses had quickened. The RMT was being hauled in and one whale was now gliding between the ship and the net; rolling, slapping and diving with gleeful abandon. At a painfully steady pace, the net was carefully hauled in – the catch was later estimated at around 30,000 krill, a mammoth haul – and a number of brows were wiped in relief when it was successfully landed. Lloyd smiled to himself. He couldn't help but wonder what paperwork would have been involved had the *Aurora* unexpectedly turned into a whaling vessel.

Lloyd was characteristically dry when he described the remarkable event, noting in his daily sitrep:

All parties were enjoying the krill fishing; except perhaps the krill, some of whom foolishly took refuge in our net. Whereupon they were delivered into the clutches of another group of voracious seagoing mammals more commonly known as marine scientists. Just like the whales, the scientists were pretty excited to be catching large numbers of *Euphausia superba* this far north where in theory they should not be. Construction work on a new theory will commence as soon as the rubble from the old theory has been cleared away.

Over the next week the weather held uncharacteristically clear and fine, and instruments and trawl nets were deployed from the *Aurora*'s beam and stern with uninterrupted vigour.

By the time the marine science leg came to a close, Andrew, Lloyd and even the reserved Captain Benoit were elated with their scientific accomplishments. As Watercraft Officer Andrew Cawthorn quite aptly summed up, they had achieved the science 'need to do' and the 'want to dos' and had even made a huge dent in their 'wish list'.

Thankfully, the majority of the marine science team would now have a chance to take a break for a couple of days before the Mawson resupply would begin.

The *Aurora* arrived at the entrance between the rocky arms of Horseshoe Harbour on 20 February. A moderate breeze rippled the water in Kista Strait, and the station's colourful buildings nestled snugly on the bank of East Arm with the smooth ice sheet of the Antarctic plateau rising gracefully behind.

The breeze was rapidly dropping, but not quite enough for the *Aurora* to safely enter the confines of Horseshoe Harbour. Instead, Benoit brought the *Aurora* to a standstill just outside the harbour, and an inflatable rubber boat was launched to string a guest line down the side of the ship, preparing the *Aurora* for her entry later in the day. But shortly after the boat was launched, a loud bang reverberated through the ship.

Lloyd winced.

The rope had been sucked into the *Aurora*'s forward thruster, which had seized and was now completely out of action. And the icebreaker relied heavily on her bow thruster for manoeuvring in close quarters.

The Mawson refuelling was a major objective of the K-axis voyage, and if they couldn't get the *Aurora* into the harbour, it simply couldn't happen.

While the *Aurora*'s crew checked the damage to the thruster, the breeze dropped off to next to nothing and the harbour glittered merrily. As Lloyd put it, 'It was turning into one of those glorious days which is not to be wasted.' Desperate not to squander good weather when it was on offer to them, Lloyd and Benoit agreed that the resupply operations would begin from outside harbour; they could ferry the cargo on barges from ship to shore through the entrance and across the increasingly smooth surface of Horseshoe Harbour.

But while the resupply started, Lloyd stood on the bridge with a posture of dejected deflation. After the success of the marine science program it was such a shame that the refuelling would not be done. The expectations of the AAD, the station and his gang on board weighed heavily on his shoulders.

Captain Benoit, ever the problem solver, quietly approached Lloyd with a plan. He suggested they could use the *AA2* as a proxy bow thruster; the *Aurora*'s small orange workboat could push and pull the *Aurora*'s bow around as needed, to get her safely moored in the harbour. Lloyd jumped at the idea.

The *AA2* was swiftly lowered into the water and Lloyd was relieved when, just three hours later, the *Aurora* was holding position at her mooring location in the middle of the harbour. The VHF radio on the *Aurora*'s bridge blared with an assortment of clipped voices while the crew down below, working in concert with the watercraft officers and station personnel, began the complex process of mooring their ship. One by one, the boats dragged two steel wires out from the *Aurora*'s bow to bollards on the shore, followed by a series of large braided 'poly' ropes that strung out from large openings (called 'leads') in the *Aurora*'s hull.

When the wires and ropes that radiated out from the *Aurora*'s bow were secure, they ran two of the *Aurora*'s trawl wires and another rope out to West Arm behind her. By the time the complex operation was complete, the *Aurora* was surrounded by a series of lines like the strong radials of a spider's web, with her bow facing toward the station to the southeast of East Arm, and her stern pointing toward the end of West Arm. Once the crew declared all the mooring lines were fast and secure, the *Aurora*'s engines were shut down. After the nonstop action of the mooring operation, the *Aurora* suddenly seemed eerily quiet.

With the Aurora now located much more conveniently in the Harbour thanks to Benoit's clever brainwave, cargo operations could re-start. Standing in the depths of the cargo hold, the bosun, Joe McMenemy, squinted up at the hook descending from the long orange arm of the *Aurora*'s forward crane. He held his radio to his bearded cheek, giving constant direction to his crane driver, who, from his elevated perch, was operating completely blind thanks to the raised hatch cover in front of his feet that blocked his view. The crew worked as a tightly knit team based on mutual trust; the crane driver relying on the crew below to be his eyes; the group below trusting the hand above, who controlled the hook and the weighty cargo rising and descending above them.

Two satisfyingly successful days of cargo operations were brought to an abrupt halt by increasing winds. The bureau forecasters also predicted some gnarly winds overnight, and so Lloyd, pleased with the progress they'd made, shut activities down until the weather subsided. By that evening, the wind whistled through the rails of the ship and roared around the cavernous trawl deck. Snow peppered the *Aurora*'s decks and coated the windows, blinding the ship to the outside world. The officers regularly checked their position on the electronic chart display instead, the navigational equipment now the ship's eyes.

This was a decent blizz, thought First Mate David Thomas on his watch later that night. The angry gales roared across Horseshoe Harbour, but up on the *Aurora*'s bridge, all was still and warm. Mellow music drifted from the bridge's stereo as David looked at the numbers on the weather screen; currently the wind was cycling between fifty and seventy knots. He looked at the frosted windows surrounding him. It was easy to forget the ferocity of the storm outside when the bridge was blinded like this. For David, a whiteout always made the bridge feel slightly claustrophobic, but he was also very thankful to be within the cosy confines of the protective sanctuary. He regularly checked the *Aurora*'s chart plotter: the outline of the ship was sitting perfectly on station.

The winds continued to slam against them the next day, and into the following morning when they finally began to ease. As soon as conditions fell to within workable limits, it was all hands on deck, and time to conduct the station refuelling.

At around 10.30 am, a red IRB puttered from the shore toward the ship, dragging the lay-flat hose across the water behind it. With help from the *Aurora*'s crew, refuelling supervisor Brad Collins winched the hose on board and coupled it to the complex connections on the *Aurora*'s foredeck. Fuel was soon pumping across the water into the station's eight cylindrical brown fuel tanks, each emblazoned with a white letter of 'M-A-W-S-O-N' between two painted, preening emperor penguins acting as bookends.

The station had received a lot of fuel the season before, so it took just seven hours to top up the tanks with some 350 tonnes.

Brad, who had just finished the refuelling log up on the bridge, looked out of the windows to appreciate the familiar landscape of Mawson station. He squinted, and then frowned. The usually sharp horizon of the white escarpment rising behind the station had turned fuzzy. He grabbed his binoculars and peered through the window. Up on the plateau snow was swirling to great heights, forming long, thin mares' tails that rose hundreds of metres into the air. 'That's the A factor for you,' Brad thought. Eyes twinkling, he lowered the binos and turned to Gerry O.

'If we were at Casey, this is when I'd tell everyone to pack up, and run and hide,' Brad said.

Gerry chuckled in agreement. The weather at Casey was notorious for turning foul in a terrifying instant. But they both knew this wasn't Casey, and they still had time to finish packing up before the katabatic winds ran down the slopes to meet them.

Or so they'd thought. By the time Brad had wound down to the foredeck, pigged the fuel line, and disconnected the now-clean hose, the freezing winds were biting painfully at the strip of exposed skin between his beanie, sunnies and balaclava. Snow began to swirl erratically onto the deck and settled in the recesses between the hull's frames.

The fuel line was hastily retrieved and operations were then abandoned. The weather forecasts indicated that these winds would blow for at least two days, and Lloyd was soon busy on the radio: some of the boat drivers were stranded on base, and a handful of Mawson summerers who had been helping with onboard operations were marooned on the *Aurora*.

As the evening wore on, the winds rose from a howl to an abusive scream. The thick horizontal snow solidified, and volleys of snow grains and ice pellets peppered the *Aurora*'s windows and decks, thickening the icy crust covering the ship. Up on the monkey deck the *Aurora*'s wind anemometer whirled and spun furiously, and the corresponding wind speed readings on the bridge monitors rose steadily above sixty knots. The *Aurora* shuddered and shook, the ship cringing slightly under the relentless barrage.

Inside the icebreaker, the howling of the wind was muted to a hum. The soft grey light filtering through the portholes simply meant one thing for the expeditioners: it was time to hunker down, settle in and get comfortable. Lloyd was among them:

> I retired with a smug sense of self-satisfaction concerning the progress we had made and was looking forward to a restful couple of days. I fully expected that my biggest issue was going to be finding toothbrushes for the Mawson personnel who didn't have their personal bags aboard.

That night, those on board slept soundly in the comfort of their bunks, warmed and protected by their faithful ship.

But outside the snug confines of the *Aurora*'s steel hull, the blizzard's fury continued to grow. New records for vessel-based wind readings at Mawson were shattered again and again as the winds gusted higher and higher: Eighty-five knots. Ninety knots. Ninety-five.

The *Aurora* began to sway back and forth on her mooring lines.

When Lloyd woke the following morning and parted the curtain at his porthole he was greeted by a solid-black nothingness. They were well past the summer solstice and sunrise should have been about 5 am, but today the blizzard had blotted out any trace of morning light.

He skipped lightly up the stairs, heading for his daily 7 am meeting with the captain. It was abundantly clear that no operations would be happening today, and Lloyd and Benoit had a relaxed meeting over their coffees. Lloyd was unfazed: they still had plenty of time up their sleeves, and after the weeks of nonstop activity, everyone on board had earned a chance to rest.

Plankton scientist Karen Westwood, however, didn't quite feel the same. Yes, she had spent the voyage working around the clock filtering and processing litre after litre of seawater, and downtime had been a scarce and valuable commodity; but she had also promised herself she would stay active this voyage, and so far she hadn't been to the gym once, she thought guiltily. So, while everyone else either slept, or slowly woke, breakfasted and put their feet up, Karen laced up her runners, grabbed a towel and strode down to the small confines of the *Aurora*'s windowless gym, keen for a good workout. She plugged her music into the sound system, cranked up the volume and stepped onto the treadmill, keen to lose herself in the rhythm and beat of music and footfalls.

An hour later, just as Karen was breathlessly stepping off the machine, the familiar voice of one of the mates came over the tinny PA in the gym. In fifteen minutes, at 9 am, there would be a crew-only emergency drill on the bridge, the voice announced.

'No problemo,' Karen thought to herself, wiping her face with her towel. 'Sunday is nearly always the crew's safety drill day – not something I need to worry about then.' Karen casually stretched her aching muscles, then unplugged her music and wound her way back up to her cabin, feeling satisfyingly knackered after her workout.

At the same time, Captain Benoit and mate David tramped up the stairs from their cabins on B deck, talking quietly as they made their way to the bridge for the safety drill. When the pair ambled through the bridge door, their years of watchkeeping experience at sea automatically compelled them to glance over at the ship's chart plotter.

Benoit's eyes widened in horror.

'This is bad! This is bad!' Benoit cried, dashing forward to the helm where the officer on watch was standing.

David, who had stopped in his tracks, felt like an icy hand had grasped his heart. It was an infinitesimal change on screen, perceptible only to a trained eye, but the *Aurora Australis* had unmistakably begun to stray from her mooring location.

Benoit reached the console and dialled the PA, broadcasting across every space in the ship: 'ALL ENGINEERS, ALL ENGINEERS, START ENGINES IMMEDIATELY!'

He stretched for the bridge's button to start the *Aurora*'s engines.

Across the ship, people stopped what they were doing and looked up in confusion. It was exactly fifteen minutes after the last announcement. Was it the drill? The broadcast had sounded a bit more urgent than that . . .

Chief Engineer Evan Peters, working on C deck, immediately recognised the alarm in his captain's voice. Without a second thought, Evan dropped his tools and sprinted for the central stairwell to the engine room, a small knot of fear in his stomach. He didn't know what the hell was going on, but whatever it was, it did not sound good.

In his cabin on B deck, Chief Mate Gerry O also recognised the sound of a critical command and raced up toward the bridge.

Lloyd, sitting at his desk in the VL's cabin, was typing the daily sitrep to send back to Kingston. He too recognised the tone of urgency in Benoit's voice. The *Aurora* shuddered slightly, and Lloyd turned in his chair, looking at the heading display screen on the wall in his room. The *Aurora* was rapidly changing direction.

It seemed impossible, yet was simultaneously obvious, that the *Aurora Australis* was loose.

Somehow, the *Aurora Australis* had broken loose from one – or all – of her nine mooring lines, and on all sides of Horseshoe Harbour there was nothing but unforgiving, frozen rock. While Benoit desperately attempted to start the engines, the blood drained from David's face as he watched the plotter. In this wind, at this speed, the result was surely inevitable.

Seconds later, a sharp bang ricocheted through the ship.

'That's it; she's gone aground,' David thought.

But on screen, the *Aurora*'s outline suddenly started drifting due west. The *Aurora* hadn't grounded, David realised; the last remaining forward mooring line, stretched to its absolute limit, had finally parted. Released from an impossible strain, the snapped line had whipped back, striking the hull with such colossal force the *Aurora* had rung like a bell. But David's realisation didn't bring him any sense of relief. Now, entirely at the mercy of the blizzard's frozen gales, the *Aurora* was being pushed straight across Horseshoe Harbour – away from Mawson station and toward the long, rocky bank of West Arm.

That moment, Gerry O arrived on the bridge, and he blinked as he took in the unthinkable situation on the plotter. With its iced-over windows the bridge felt helplessly, suffocatingly blind.

Benoit was in command at the helm and David was stationed at the plotter. Gerry set his shoulders, threw on his jacket and beanie and strode across the rear of the bridge, grabbing something off the shelf along the way. He shouldered through the starboard side door, into the blustering winds.

The wind tore at Gerry's clothes as he edged his way around the narrow, grated platform that skirted the outside of the bridge. Then he set his feet wide, braced his backside against the rail behind him and started scraping the ice off the starboard side windows. The blizzard, while slightly tempered on this side of the bridge, determinedly pushed him against the railing, and Gerry tried not to think about the precipitous drop to the invisible, freezing water below. He clenched his jaw and kept scraping, lost in a flurry of swirling ice and snow.

Downstairs, just as Evan leapt down the last flight of stairs to the engine room, he heard the *Aurora*'s engines rumble to life. He launched himself through the two heavy doors to the control room and flew toward the console. He clutched the *Aurora*'s engines in to the propeller and looked up, waiting.

As soon as the bridge indicator showed the engine was clutched in to the propeller, Benoit immediately threw the *Aurora* into full power astern.

David looked at the lonely figure of the captain standing at the helm. His hand clenched the pitch-control lever, pushing it hard back against the console, while his eyes were glued to the display showing the *Aurora*'s form drawing inextricably closer to the rocks.

David felt a kind of helpless dread descend through his body. It was a dark, overwhelming horror that he had not felt since he was a child.

'F#%k, this could be it.

'This could be how we all die.'

Engines blazing, the *Aurora*'s propeller churned frantically against the wind-lashed, freezing water of Horseshoe Harbour. The deck began to vibrate under David's feet as the icebreaker strained with all her might against the streaming air and water currents pushing her relentlessly downwind.

Downstairs, Karen stood in the middle of her cabin, her gym towel still clutched in her hand. She still wasn't convinced that the PA announcement was part of the safety drill. After hesitating a minute or two, there had been no further broadcast, so she opened her door and put her head out in the corridor to see what everyone else had made of the announcement. Her neighbour was doing exactly the same thing. Their eyes met.

'Do you think that was real or not?' her neighbour asked Karen in a slightly choked voice.

'I'm not sure . . .' Karen replied.

Suddenly, there was an ear-shattering bang, and their safe little world lurched slightly underneath them. Karen's eyes widened in horror.

Downstairs, the crunching impact reverberated like thunder around the steel-walled engine room.

'What the f#%k was that?' one of the engineers exclaimed behind Evan. There was a pause. Then the sickening screech of metal grinding against rock reverberated through the *Aurora*'s hull.

'We've just gone aground,' Evan said incredulously.

The *Aurora*, their beloved home, their refuge and protector, had unmistakably hit the rocks of West Arm.

Upstairs, the chart plotter showed the *Aurora* had hit the shore bow-first, and Benoit instantly knew what would inevitably follow. He slammed his hand down onto the red emergency stop button, cutting the *Aurora*'s engines.

In the silent seconds that followed he desperately hoped that her propeller would stop turning before the *Aurora* pivoted, and her stern followed her bow onto the rocks. Blind to the world outside, he fixed his eyes on the chart plotter and waited.

The silence was suddenly shattered by the *Aurora* squealing in agony. She juddered and groaned as her steel belly scraped against the hard teeth of West Arm.

David gripped the chart table, his knuckles white as the *Aurora* tilted alarmingly over to her port side. David knew that running aground here didn't protect them from the threat of sinking. Horseshoe Harbour is deep and incredibly steep at its periphery: if the *Aurora* flooded and rolled toward the harbour's freezing heart, she would slide down the rocky slope and sink into the deep water. Eighty people would die.

*

Down on D deck, Karen was feeling lightheaded with shock, in no small part thanks to having overdone things in the gym. 'Oh! We've hit the rocks,' she thought dreamily. 'That's no good at all. But I've just been to the gym . . . and I'm going to have to put all my survival clothing on,' she realised. 'There's no way I'm going to smell like this for however long, with all that lot on over the top!' With that disgusted thought, she spun on her heel, marched back into her cabin and hopped straight into the shower.

Meanwhile, having heard the solid, ghastly bang of the *Aurora*'s collision with the rocks, Lloyd had dashed straight into the stairwell. But he hesitated on the landing. Should he go to the bridge and find out what was happening? Surely his presence wouldn't be appreciated by the crew, who were no doubt in the throes of what Lloyd had already concluded was a catastrophic event. Or should he go down to D deck to check on the expeditioners, many of whom might still be in bed, exhausted? It was a no-brainer.

Lloyd streaked down the stairs to the expeditioner's cabins on D deck. He ran straight over to cabin D1, opening the door even as he knocked. The darkened cabin contained several sleeping bodies in their bunks. Shit! Lloyd roused the occupants, and moved swiftly from cabin to cabin, loudly banging on doors and telling everyone to get their emergency survival gear on and get down to their alternate muster station in the mess.

Karen didn't hear Lloyd's bang at her door. But after about a minute or two of standing under the steaming water, clear, horrifying comprehension finally came over her.

'Shit! We've hit the rocks!'

Visions of the *Titanic* movie came flooding into her mind and several sickening realisations washed over her. 'The ship could be taking on water . . . we could lose electricity . . . it could get dark . . . and I won't be able to see my way around . . . and I'm standing here IN THE SHOWER!'

Karen hurriedly twisted the tap, hastily threw on her thermals and sprinted toward the mess with her grab bag, her hair still dripping wet. She was the last person to arrive at the mess, and she saw mate David standing in front of the group, with Lloyd standing gravely beside him.

David clasped his clipboard, watching the last of the expeditioners hurriedly take their seats. They had about two more seconds before he would start the muster call. Just then, a pair of scientists casually walked past David.

'This is great! We'll have this human impact site we can study for years!' one commented, clearly more excited about the opportunity to study the future effects of whatever disturbances they were currently causing on the shore below.

David's eyes flatly followed the scientist as he found a seat. Most of the expos were calmly expectant, some were pale and distressed, but that one there had absolutely no idea how serious the situation was right now. David took a breath, put on his reading glasses and began calling out names from his list.

As he worked down the roll, he was acutely aware of the unnatural angle of the restaurant deck beneath the soles of his feet. As Chief Mate, he lived and breathed the *Aurora*'s stability: controlling it was one of his main duties. The discomfort of the *Aurora*'s unnatural position radiated like electricity through his entire body.

After each name had been met with a solemn reply David pulled off his glasses and looked at the group. There was total silence. Under the expectant, unbroken gaze of the crowd David's eyes began to burn slightly. 'Keep calm, David, keep calm,' he told himself. He took another breath.

'The *Aurora* has broken her moorings and gone aground on West Arm,' David told them simply. 'Try not to worry. I remind you that you are on an icebreaker, and one that's incredibly strong.'

The heat of emotion was rising at the back of his head and neck now, and David fought a lump growing in his throat.

'With the conditions as they are out there,' he steadily continued, 'this is the safest place to be right now. The *Aurora* is the best lifeboat we could possibly have: we have power, water, food and shelter, and we will stay here unless it becomes absolutely necessary to leave. The wind is holding us here, and we're not bouncing against the rocks or heaving up and down, so further damage is unlikely.'

It took all his energy to give the expeditioners a small, comforting smile. Then, after another glance around, David handed the meeting over to Lloyd and took his leave. He ducked into the stairwell and climbed up the stairs to the bridge, happy for the break from the anxious faces and the requirement to put on a brave face. It was easier to just get on with the job of damage control.

Downstairs, the restaurant erupted in a hubbub of tense chatter. Karen, for one, felt reassured. David had been nothing but calm, frank and comforting during the muster; if he wasn't too worried, she thought, then neither was she.

Lloyd suddenly realised he now stood alone in front of the group.

'Okay . . .' he said softly, gathering his thoughts.

Silence cut through the room like a knife. Lloyd, taken off guard by the sudden snap to attention, floundered momentarily for words. But the eyes of his charges were expectant, and just as quickly, his hesitation evaporated. Lloyd smoothly reiterated David's message of remaining indoors and the relative safety of staying on board the *Aurora*.

'Frankly, nobody needed to be told that they couldn't go outside,' Lloyd wrote later. 'The weather conditions were apparent and everybody could see that staying on the ship was the only option.'

The bridge was crowded with crew in their orange boiler suits, and David edged past them, looking for his captain. He hadn't felt the *Aurora*'s list worsen in a while; it seemed to be hovering at around five degrees. 'At least it doesn't look like she's going to roll over,' he thought with a wave of relief.

David's eyes fell on Benoit's ashen face, which showed the unmistakable strain he was under. Somehow, the mooring system that had worked unfailingly for 25 years at Mawson had failed under the strain of the enormous forces of this huge blizzard.

Benoit, the bridge officers, Chief Engineer Evan and the bosun, Joe, gathered together in the centre of the bridge to make a plan of action. The rest of the crew gathered in a grave semi-circle around them.

Now that the *Aurora* was aground, there were standard grounding procedures to follow. The *Aurora* had been pushed and shoved backward along the rocks by the wind, and she seemed to have finally slipped into a natural cradle in West Arm, where she lurched less and less frequently. Benoit had already begun to ballast the *Aurora* down onto the rocks by deliberately flooding her seawater tanks. Making her heavy would hold her more securely in place and lessen her movement against the rocks, which in turn would reduce further damage.

Next, he dispatched his officers to check the water ballast tanks between the *Aurora*'s double hull, the engineers to check the tanks in the engine room, and the bosun to find out what was going on with the mooring lines.

As the captain then turned to other tasks, Joe looked around at the grim, resolute faces of his IRs. The brutal winds outside would certainly knock them all off their feet; if he had to go out there, he was taking someone who had the fighting weight to hold their ground. He picked one of his more robust lads, Ben McLucas, and the two of them raced to their cabins. They threw on multiple layers under their boiler suits, pulled neck warmers, beanies and goggles over their heads and noses, zipped up their thick jackets, donned several layers of gloves and hurried down to the forward end of D deck. They met at the watertight door leading to the forward cargo deck.

After quickly checking that Ben was set, Joe turned the metal handwheel, unlocking the forward sea door with a clunk. As soon as he threw his shoulder against the door, wind and snow whistled through the narrow gap into the corridor; it took both of them to prise the door open long enough for them to climb through. They let the wind slam the door closed and latched it behind them.

Joe faced straight into the freezing wind and leaned against it, staggering slightly as he tried to keep his feet. Daylight had weakly begun to permeate the gloom, and the darkness of the morning was becoming a whiteout. But the snow lashing at his face was very nearly blinding, and he could barely make out the deck three metres in front of him. A huge chunk of ice fell heavily onto the deck near his right side and bounced away into oblivion. God knows where that'd come from, or whether there was more to come. His shouts to Ben were instantly whipped away by the wind, and he dropped to his hands and knees and motioned for Ben to do the same. Together, they crawled forward, grubbing a path through the ankle-deep snow. They slowly made their way around the cargo hatch toward the *Aurora*'s forecastle.

Ice-crusted winches, drums and coiled ropes loomed out of the blank white air as they neared the forecastle. Under its shelter they were protected somewhat from the wind, and Joe rose to his feet and lurched unevenly past the snowy shapes. He scanned the area between the leads and the winch drums, but there was nothing but air in the space where the mooring cables and poly ropes should normally be strung taught. Two feeble, frayed ends of steel wire lay at the feet of the drums. The remains of a poly line hung limply from one of the bollards. All the lines were gone.

The pair scrambled back around the port side of the hold, back into the forward door on D deck, and strode toward the *Aurora*'s stern, leaving a trail of melting ice flakes in their wake.

On the trawl deck, the blizzard's frozen cyclonic winds were cleaved in two by the helideck above, sending squally gusts swirling angrily around the space below. The blizzard's sharp white drift infiltrated every steel nook and every ropy cranny, turning the *Aurora*'s colourful trawl deck into a monochromatic moonscape.

Joe stepped and slid carefully over to the starboard rail and looked out. Horseshoe Harbour had been whipped into a frenzy and was a heaving, aerated grey–blue washing machine that raged around the *Aurora*'s hull furiously. And there, just metres across the water, was the ghostly shadow of West Arm. Its uneven, rocky surface was thickly blanketed by snow and ice, and the only visible part of the dark bank rising steeply out of the sea was where it had been stripped of snow by the churning water.

The *Aurora*'s turquoise stern rope was still attached, but instead of extending out behind her to the curved arm of West Arm as it usually should, it now trailed forward up the *Aurora*'s side and disappeared into the white in the direction of the bow, apparently still attached to the shore bollard. Two steel mooring lines hung slack from the trawl deck winch drums and davits; they were also still attached, but the shore points were invisible in the pall, no doubt somewhere much closer to the *Aurora*'s stern than they normally should have been. Joe and Ben beat their way through the gales and back inside the ship and strode quickly back up to the bridge to report their status to the captain.

'There's enough slack in the stern poly rope to be able to move it,' Joe advised Benoit after a quick explanation. They could possibly move the heavy line up to the bow and make it tight, giving the *Aurora* a bit more security on the rocks, and the stern wires should be able to be tightened on the winches easily enough. Benoit, his face careworn, looked at the dripping, snow-covered figures in front of him. He nodded. They needed to make the *Aurora* as secure as possible in this position to try and stop any further movement.

Joe gathered all his IRs, and together they made a plan. The concept of moving the unwieldy mooring rope was simple; first they needed to string a series of light messenger lines together from the *Aurora*'s bow, outside the ship, down to the stern (making one light rope running the length of the ship), attach the heavy mooring rope to it, and then pull the messenger and then the larger rope up to the bow. It was a simple concept; that is, if there wasn't a 197-kilometre-an-hour blizzard raging outside.

They split up, and Joe fought his way back down toward the bow with Ben. Their aim was to string the first of the messenger ropes from the forward winch, out of the *Aurora*'s shoreside lead and out around the curve of her bow, where the next line could be attached.

The wind and snow raged in a horizonal stream across the *Aurora*'s bow. Joe tied one end of the light rope around a green bollard under the forecastle, then staggered over to the lead. Clutching the coiled rope in one hand, and its monkey-fisted end hanging from the other, he knelt and leaned out of the lead, putting his all weight against its unnervingly thin safety rail. Looking back toward the stern, he couldn't see at all around the beamy curve of the *Aurora*'s bow, where he knew Ben must be waiting just beyond. He leaned out further, straining to stay upright as the wind drove against his back, trying to push him out of the window-like opening. He hooked the toes of his boots over the lip of the step under him, gripping it for dear life, while the snow and ice began to solidify on his clothes.

Ben had squeezed himself into a narrow gap between a container beside the cargo hatch and the *Aurora*'s rail. He leaned out, looking forward toward the bow while the wind loudly buffeted the container behind him. All he could see through the driving snow was the fuzzy outline of the *Aurora*'s orange hull. He leaned further over the rail, straining to either see his bosun or hear him over the wind thrumming in his ears. Finally, a tiny voice was just discernible against the roar.

'Put your arm out!' Joe was screaming down the side of the ship, again and again, at the top of his lungs.

Ben thrust his arm as far as he could over the rail and held it as steady as he could.

Finally, Joe spotted Ben's gloved hand protruding from the hull. Leaning his whole torso through the lead and outside the hull, he spun the end of the rope and hurled it down along the *Aurora*'s bow. By some miracle it flew straight over Ben's outstretched arm, trailing the rest of the line in its wake.

Ben immediately hooked his arm and seized the line before it was whipped away by the wind. He inched his way aft between the container and the *Aurora*'s solid bow rail, slowly making his way toward the *Aurora*'s superstructure.

Above him, three decks up and completely exposed to the blizzard's wrath, Doug Hawes and Keil Murphy crawled around the narrow grated ledge that skirted the bridge. They'd attached a grappling hook to the end of their messenger line for weight so that it didn't get snatched away by the wind, and they lowered it down to Ben, who hastily attached his section. The grappling hook was then hoisted back up to the bridge. The two quickly scrambled backwards along the precarious grill to the relative protection of the bridge wing, where IR Wendy Morice was waiting.

Together, the three IRs edged the rope outside the life rafts on the bridge wing and lowered it to the helideck level below. Ben and Doug then swapped positions, and Doug went below with Joe.

Wendy, Ben and Keil stood at the very edge of the hangar's protection and grimly stared into the full fury of the blizzard. The wind barrelled across the snow-crusted deck in a deafening wall of thunderous sound. Snow whipped by in a streaking blur; it formed an opaque white curtain that obscured everything beyond a stone's throw away. Just a few steps away from them, a lonely IRB sat mournfully on the helideck, strapped to the deck beside a twelve-foot container. Here the rushing blizzard had found some purchase; the boat's previously black pontoons were caked solid with ice, and its bow was piled high with thick snow.

They looked at each other. They needed to get that messenger line down to the trawl deck.

Then Keil resolutely looked into the white and stepped out from the protection of the hangar. The force of the gales immediately hit him, and he staggered and then dropped to his hands and knees. He tried to half-crawl, half-slide across the deck in the driving snow, but he was relentlessly pushed all the way to the hinged helideck railing downwind. He grunted, pulling himself upright using the chain link mesh of the railings, known as gates. The wind pressed Keil against the gates and he inched his way along them, disappearing into the white haze toward the rear of the helideck.

Wendy's eyes grew as wide as dinnerplates. The only thing keeping Keil from being blown from the deck and into the frigid, churning water three levels below was those flimsy helideck gates, which were secured by pins in their hinges and ratchet straps at their rail. They were now bearing the full brunt of the winds, with a hundred kilos or so of a man's weight pressed entirely against them. Wendy and Ben called out to Keil, but their voices were no match for the storm.

Wendy couldn't take it any longer; she needed to get over to Keil to tell him not to rely on those bloody gates. Wendy stepped out from behind the lee of the hangar and was instantly blown off her feet. She landed hard, her knees smacking the steel deck painfully, and slid along with the wind. She was now almost at the starboard rail herself. She brought herself to a kneeling position and inched her way toward the stern, but the wind constantly pushed her sideways. Wisps of her blond hair, whipped from beneath her beanie and neck warmer, swirled around her face. She yelled out to Keil's fuzzy form, already knowing she was wasting her breath.

Wendy turned and crawled back to the protective shadow of the *Aurora*'s helihangar. She grabbed a rope from the workshop, tied it to a lug on the deck just near the hangar door and gripped the coil tightly. Then she lowered herself to her knees and scooted toward the port side of the stern, into the wind. She let the rope go, hand over hand, as she inched her way across the deck, leaving her lifeline extending out taut behind her. As she knew it would, the wind pushed her sideways, and she made her way to her intended destination on the starboard side of the stern. Keil's shadowed form gradually became clearer. Wendy arrived at the aft end of the deck and secured the end of her blizz line to a lug. Keil inched over while Ben came along the rope behind Wendy, clutching the unfurling messenger line with its grappling hook.

But as Ben reached Wendy, he suddenly realised there was no way the remaining amount of the messenger line could make the distance all the way down to the trawl deck. He screamed into Wendy's ear, gesturing to the rope, trying to show her it wasn't long enough.

A howl somewhere between a curse and a cry of fear built in Wendy's throat. The pair hauled themselves back across the helideck and attached yet another length of rope onto the messenger line. They helped each other hurriedly crawl back along Wendy's blizz line, then passed the grappling hook to the waiting Keil, who lowered it down to Joe and Doug waiting on the trawl deck below.

Down on the trawl deck, Joe snatched the hook and tied the messenger line to the *Aurora*'s large turquoise mooring rope. The IRs then threw the assembly of ropes completely overboard. The messenger was carefully winched forward from its end at the bow and the IRs secured the heavy mooring line to one of the *Aurora*'s forward bollards. The stern wires were also tightened on their drums.

The IRs had secured the *Aurora* the best way possible under the circumstances. Now it was time to go help the others monitor the *Aurora*'s tanks, which were being sounded every hour to find out if any were taking on water. Meanwhile, Benoit and his officers and engineers began discussions with naval architects and P&O back in Australia about the possibility of refloating the *Aurora* once the blizzard finally abated.

Downstairs, the expeditioners waited in the restaurant, their red emergency bags by their sides. Despite the *Aurora* having been ballasted down onto the rocks, sharp bangs and metallic screeches punctuated the tense atmosphere like aftershocks, and the expeditioners flinched and murmured involuntarily at the unnatural noises.

At least now they had something to distract them. The AAD had already notified their families of their situation and had released a brief press statement about the grounding, but all the expeditioners were keen to speak to their families and tell them that they were safe. Lloyd granted each expeditioner a free three-minute phone call home on the satellite phone, and a queue quickly formed to the conference room next to the mess. It took hours to clear.

As the day dragged on, Lloyd noticed that the cringes and pauses in conversations became sparser as the expeditioners became more and more used to the sickening sounds of the *Aurora* grinding against the rock. He wasn't quite sure if that was a good thing or a bad thing.

By now, it seemed that the *Aurora* was relatively secure on the rocks, and Benoit lifted the expeditioners' muster status. They were permitted access to their cabins on D deck as long as they kept their emergency kit with them at all times.

Lloyd then met with the captain, and the pair discussed the plan of evacuation. The ideal option, Benoit told Lloyd, was for everyone to stay on the ship and be evacuated by barge when the weather improved.

'This sounded like an excellent plan to me,' Lloyd recounted in his VL report, 'but I was still concerned about what would happen were the ship to become flooded or unstable. We still had a raging blizzard outside and any discharge of people onto West Arm would have resulted in certain fatalities.'

It was obvious that if things did turn bad, if the *Aurora* sustained more damage and began to sink, they would need to get off in a hurry. The crew had told Lloyd that the inflatable life rafts would be useless in this weather, and even the tub-like lifeboats would be unnavigable in the gales. But Lloyd felt that they needed to plan for the worst-case scenario, and if an uncontrolled exit needed to happen, be armed with a plan of attack.

From his own experiences down south, Lloyd knew full well what eighty knot winds with zero visibility were like. It was bloody scary, and this blizz was gusting over one hundred knots. Conditions would be windy on West Arm, obviously, but that simplistic word played down the extreme forces of nature at work out there. People had already been knocked off their feet, and they might well be swept across the thin rocky isthmus in these howling gales. Visibility was at times so bad that Lloyd was certain they wouldn't be able to see their hands in front of their faces; the expos would undoubtedly struggle to remain together once on shore. If separated from the group, their odds of survival would be slim.

So while the crew were busy checking the *Aurora*'s tanks for damage, Lloyd formed a council of war with some of his more experienced expeditioners, refuelling supervisor Brad and senior gear officer Phil Boxall. The trio met in the VL's cabin to discuss their plan and make a list of their assets, and that evening Lloyd and his team spoke with Mawson station to fully develop an evacuation plan.

A major problem with an evacuation was that, while the *Aurora*'s belly may have been hard against the rocks underneath her, her flanks were still separated from the shore by metres of frigid, churning water. Should an exit to West Arm be required, it meant wading or swimming through the freezing water followed by a scramble up the rocks and ice. They would need to wear the ship's survival suits (large, one-size-fits-all red and black drysuits) to stay warm and dry on the risky crossing to shore. But there was a problem, as Lloyd wrote in his typically understated manner:

Survival suits provide great protection against wind and water but they are not much good for walking on ice, and West Arm is rather slippery territory at the moment especially in 60 to 80 knot winds.

In actuality, the feet of the drysuits had no grip at all, and would be a liability on the slick ice of West Arm. After the ship- and station-based teams debated whether the priority was to dress for protection or agility on the rocks, one of Mawson's field officers asked if the expeditioners' AAD-issued Baffin boots and chains could be made to fit over the chunky immersion suit boots.

Lloyd, Brad and Phil immediately set about experimenting. They grabbed several 'volunteers' and a pile of immersion suits and boots, and soon worked out that most of them could fit the Baffin boots over their immersion-suited feet by removing the boots' fluffy inner liners, but only those who had large enough feet would be able to do so. They quickly calculated that 25 out of the 38 expeditioners had feet big enough to be able to wear their boots.

Luckily, the Mawson personnel currently stuck on board were field trip leaders with excellent Antarctic survival skills. Because some of the smaller expeditioners would not be able to wear their boots over the chunky immersion suits, the expeditioners would be divided into small groups, each with a number of people with boots, and at least one with blizzard experience. 'The big boots and immersion suits' plan was soon drafted by Lloyd and approved by the station. But it made for sobering reading.

If the *Aurora* began to sink during the blizzard, and an 'abandon ship' call was made, the following evacuation plan was to be followed:

- The VL issues an emergency call on VHF channel 7 and notifies Mawson station that the West Arm Evacuation is happening (Mawson advises a ninety-minute response time to West Arm).
- We gather people in the Mess for the muster and get them to dress and put on survival suits. (The big-booted people put on their boots with chains – RETAIN BOOT LINERS IN SURVIVAL BAG.)
- We follow instructions from the crew to exit the vessel by whatever means are deemed appropriate to the situation.

- We get three experienced people to shore each with a fifty metre rope first [names redacted].
- As people come to shore they are clipped to the ropes . . . and sat down in a huddle (emperor penguin fashion: smaller people in the centre).
- The remaining big-booted should stay close to their designated team members as much as possible and help get them to the huddles (and get clipped on).
- Depending on the conditions, the groups could elect to move toward the station around West Arm OR if it is difficult and/or dangerous to move (far more likely) then wait for contact by the Mawson Response team. Radio contact will be maintained throughout on Channel 7 VHF.

The evacuation plan notes that at this point, the crew would also be likely to evacuate the *Aurora* and would become the responsibility of the shore party.

'In spite of all our preparations, the scenario seemed quite a grim one,' wrote Lloyd frankly. 'I was well aware that any such evacuation was unlikely to run smoothly.'

Most of the expeditioners, however, were unaware of the contingency plans that were quietly being made. The evening meal was served to its usual impressive quality, which helped keep a feeling of normalcy and routine to their surreal situation. But the *Aurora*'s awkward list to port was a constant and very real reminder of their precarious condition.

That night, the blizzard still raged outside, and Karen was one of the last people to walk wearily toward her cabin hoping to get some rest. She idly noticed that every single cabin door on D deck was open: everyone was too scared to sleep with their door closed.

As she stepped into her own cabin, a god-awful clanging rang repeatedly through the room, and continued as she got changed. Crap. She couldn't see anything through her iced-up porthole, but it was easy enough to work out what the source of the sound was. The *AA2*, the *Aurora*'s small service boat, was strung alongside its mothership right under Karen's porthole. The little orange craft was obviously being tossed about by the ice-laden gales and chaotic seas, and with every movement she desperately clanged and scraped into the *Aurora*'s hull.

Karen slipped into her sloping bunk and stared at the deck head above. The constant sound of metal striking metal made her increasingly uneasy, and she tossed and turned through the night as the racket continued. 'It'll probably be the *AA2* that puts a bloody great hole in us in the end,' she thought ironically, before finally slipping into an uneasy doze.

Just before seven o'clock the next morning, Lloyd hastily made his way to the bridge for his daily meeting with the captain. The view out of the windows was still predominately white, but today the *Aurora*'s orange bow loomed out of the streaming mist before them. To their starboard side, Lloyd could now make out the uneven, snow-topped rocks of West Arm unnervingly close to the ship.

Lloyd turned toward the waiting Benoit, who looked like he hadn't slept a wink. The quiet captain looked at Lloyd, then spoke plainly to the VL.

'The officers found a breach in the *Aurora*'s hull overnight,' he told Lloyd bluntly. 'The number one starboard double-bottom tank is taking on water.'

Benoit quickly went on, trying to reassure the VL. This tank was a ballast tank, so as far as hull breaches go, it was located in the best place possible because it could be isolated from the rest of the ship and wouldn't affect her stability. And so far, none of the other ballast tanks were taking on water. The engineers had examined their tanks in the engine room and found a small leak coming from somewhere between the bilge tank and the engine room cofferdam (a void between the various tanks beneath the engine room), but this was a small leak and not a threat to the *Aurora*'s stability.

'Okay,' Lloyd thought. A leak was a bit concerning, but something like this was bound to happen in a grounding. Frankly, the more he thought about it, it was incredible the *Aurora* hadn't sustained more damage.

Nevertheless, Lloyd waited until his expeditioners had eaten a good breakfast before telling them about the hull breach at their morning briefing. He took Benoit's lead and reassured them that a ballast tank was the best place to have a leak. 'Really,' he continued, 'it is just confirmation that the *Aurora* had sustained damage, which we already suspected she would, having all felt and heard her hit the rocks.'

He also explained the evacuation plan formulated the night before, pointing out that this would be absolute worse-case scenario and was unlikely to be needed. 'Ideally,' Lloyd told his expeditioners, 'not much should happen today, but we have to be ready to do a sudden evacuation at any time.'

He later reported, 'It should almost go without saying that nobody wanted to (or expected to have to) carry out this plan. It would have been a desperate undertaking in response to a desperate situation. Everybody was clear that the best option was to remain with the ship and get off via boat in a controlled fashion.'

But even the best-case controlled exit onto a barge was likely to be a wet and wild affair with the conditions as forecast over the next few days. Immersion suits would still need to be worn even for a controlled evacuation.

Thankfully, the expeditioners took the news of the leak and the evacuation plan in their stride. They formed small groups and busied themselves taking turns trying their boots on over a few immersion suits the crew had brought inside.

They then began packing up their cabins and labs as best they could. No-one knew how long they might be at Mawson, or how they might be getting home; but they did know they only had a fifteen kilogram baggage allowance they could take with them to the station. Nearly everyone had much more than this in their cabins, and they had to pick through their belongings and decide what to take with them, and what to leave behind.

After the expeditioners had tried on the immersion suits a few times, and their bags were packed and repacked, they simply waited. Either the blizzard that raged around their stricken ship would temper its anger, or all hell would break loose.

To distract themselves from a state of constant anxiety, some people set up a movie in the D deck rec room. Lloyd peeked in the door and raised his eyebrows to find the somewhat dubious choice of the survival movie *The Martian* flickering in the darkened space. Others helped out in the galley, eagerly getting up to their elbows in dirty dishes or potato peelings.

That night, with cabin doors once again left open, the expeditioners retired to their bunks with a sense of nervous anticipation. Karen slept worse than the night before. Not because of the noise – in fact, it sounded like the relentless clanging had abated slightly. But the tide had come up, and Karen was sure she could feel the *Aurora* starting to move. She winced at each and every infinitesimal shift. Sleep felt like a hopeless dream. 'Please don't let anything happen to the ship before we get off,' she begged the universe.

But sleep did eventually come, and when Karen opened her eyes the next morning, brilliant sunlight poured through her porthole, brightly illuminating her cabin. She blinked sleepily for a moment before realising its dazzling significance.

The blizzard was over.

Karen leapt out of bed, hastily threw on her thermals and hurried down to the restaurant. Smiling faces beamed around all the tables. 'It's funny what blue skies and sunshine can do,' Karen thought to herself, almost laughing in relief. 'We're still here on the rocks but somehow, the bright, gleaming light seems to have evaporated all sense of worry. We'll be fine,' Karen thought confidently, 'and so will the *Aurora*.'

Lloyd had already written instructions for the day on the whiteboard. His neat print explained that the expeditioner evacuation would commence at 9 am, and there would be a muster beforehand in the E deck conference room. NO IMMERSION SUITS REQUIRED, Karen read with a distinct sigh of relief.

Aurora Australis aground on West Arm after the blizzard.

At 9 am, the barge, adorned with an orange half-height shipping container, left the station and motored smoothly across the glinting waters of Horseshoe Harbour. The placid haven was the complete antithesis from the perilous trap it had become just days before.

The voyage expeditioners who had been stuck on the station during the blizzard climbed carefully up the rope ladder strung down the *Aurora*'s side. They greeted their colleagues with relief and wry gallows humour before rushing off to their cabins to throw their gear into bags. They had just half an hour to pack their things before they would be sent back to Mawson.

Lloyd went to the conference room to marshal his troops for the muster. They had come ready, wearing their yellow and black Gore-Tex survival clothing, and they were all passed lifejackets to put on over the top. Karen zipped hers up and joined the line at the forward end of the conference room. The space was suddenly silent and tense. Then, after the word was given, they began to filter through the door toward the bunker room.

IR Wendy had been stationed in the bunker room to help the expeditioners if needed, and to keep an eye on the barge while it was alongside. But as face after familiar face passed her and then disappeared out of the hatch, she began to choke up.

As Karen walked into the room she saw Wendy's eyes welling, and she instinctively stepped over to give her friend a hug. But as Karen put her arms around the IR, the reality of leaving the ship and its crew came crashing down on her. These were her colleagues – her friends – and it felt like she was abandoning them. Karen's face was stricken as she stepped back from the quick embrace.

With one look at Karen's expression, Wendy's eyes overflowed and she burst into tears. For a second, everyone in the small space froze while the two distressed friends looked at each other.

Wendy gruffly turned Karen toward the hatch, telling her to get going.

'Look after yourself,' she added as Karen reached the bright light of the bunker door. Karen turned and looked back at Wendy.

'See you soon,' she replied weakly. But the statement seemed more of a question than a promise.

With her back to the door and a lump in her throat, Karen gripped the ropes hanging down either side of the hatch and stepped backwards. She swung outwards slightly due to the lean of the ship, and she carefully felt her way down the wooden rungs of the rope ladder.

It took just three rungs. Three easy, wooden rungs to get to safety. Karen stepped back onto the barge and fleetingly looked up at the huge stranded ship looming above her, before she was quickly ushered into the safety of the waist-high container. The last of the group followed, and their bags were passed onto the craft.

Up on the bridge, a weight lifted from Lloyd's shoulders as he watched the final bargeload of waving expeditioners slowly putter away from the ship. They were safe and would be well cared for by the station. He was now the only expeditioner left

A load of expeditioners leaves the grounded *Aurora* for Mawson station.

on the ship, yet his typical dry humour never escaped him, and he later wrote in his daily sitrep:

> Well, I told the expeditioners that I would get them ashore at Mawson and I'm evidently a man of my word.
> . . . Thanks to Jenny and the team at Mawson for taking in our strays. But I'm afraid that I shall henceforth consider Mawson as a station best viewed from a distance.

The unexpectedly calm weather that allowed the passengers to evacuate also provided another opportunity for freedom. While the barge had motored back and forth across the harbour, the crew had been hastily making preparations to refloat the *Aurora Australis*.

In the first minutes of the crisis, the *Aurora* had been ballasted down onto the rocks to minimise her movement. Since then, Benoit and his engineers and officers had been in constant contact with P&O, Lloyds and several naval architects, discussing the ship's stability and damage control. They had all agreed that despite the hull breach, the *Aurora Australis* appeared to be sound. They would try to refloat the icebreaker and assess the damage from there.

The crew and experts back home had come up with an ingenious plan to refloat her. They would give the *Aurora* an 'official' list of five or six degrees, the same as the rocks were artificially forcing her into, by altering her ballast ratios. As the tide rose, it was hoped that she would slide off the rocks and into the deeper water on an angle; much like a delicate, slow-motion version of her launch almost 27 years earlier.

The *Aurora*'s fuel, usually held in secure, inboard tanks up the front of the ship, was pumped into the corresponding tanks down aft. The water in the ballast tanks on her shore side was pumped to the portside ballast tanks. Even the *Aurora*'s stabiliser tanks, the same ones that normally groan, whistle and wail, were also manually adjusted hard to port. The *AA2*, having been cleared of hundreds of kilos of thick, heavy ice that had actually threatened to sink her during the peak of the blizzard, was mobilised to help pull the *Aurora* off the rocks, along with the station's jet barge.

Then the *Aurora*'s crew waited for the peak of the high tide.

As the time of the high tide approached, the bridge was deathly silent except for the low rumbling of the *Aurora*'s idling engines. Eyes intent and standing at the helm, Benoit was the picture of determined concentration.

Lloyd, standing at the back of the bridge, bit his lip and fixed his eyes on a thin patch of brown–grey rock peeking out from the snow in front of the bow. The hairs on the back of Lloyd's neck stood on end.

The minutes dragged silently by, but there was no movement. Then suddenly, Lloyd realised the small patch of rock was almost imperceptibly moving across the front of the bow.

The *Aurora*'s aft end was gently swinging away from the rocks.

Off the *Aurora*'s portside bow, a puff of exhaust went up as the *AA2* heaved with all her might. Whitewater boiled from the orange tub's stern as she strained to keep her mothership's bow from grinding against the rocks while her stern pivoted away from the shore.

The angle between the *Aurora*'s stern and West Arm gradually increased, when, without warning, the *Aurora* began to glide smoothly backwards. Her bow slid off the rocks and she was suddenly afloat, free from the craggy grip of West Arm.

On station, the *Aurora*'s expeditioners cheered from their perch in the history-lined Dog Room in the Red Shed. Karen could have cried with relief. She had never quite realised how much the *Aurora* meant to her; she'd honestly never felt as happy in her life as she did right now, seeing the orange ship back in her proper place on the water.

But the *Aurora* was still floating with her ballast-induced list, and Benoit clutched her propeller in, and carefully manoeuvred her backwards into the centre of the harbour. Lloyd looked anxiously between the strained faces of the master and mate David, who stood looking out the portside window, watching the rocks of East Arm growing larger and calling distances to Benoit with increasing urgency. Then Benoit pushed the ship ahead, and with a helpful nudge from both the jet barge and the *AA2*, the *Aurora* turned to face the entrance of the harbour. Patches of hard, white ice still clung to her orange sides, but she gratefully limped out of the shimmering harbour.

A collective sigh of relief went up on the bridge and, for the first time in days, a peaceful calm descended on the space. It was now time to assess the *Aurora*'s wounds and patch her up as best they could, before getting her to the specialists back in Australia.

The immediate plan was to assess the *Aurora*'s external damage with underwater cameras mounted on long poles, repair her clutch (which was damaged by the sudden start in the emergency), make sure there were no major leaks and inspect the inside of her hull for damage. This final task meant emptying the ballast and bilge tanks and sending someone into the dank, cramped spaces to inspect them. Mates Gerry O and David were those unlucky souls.

The crew knew the *Aurora* had leaks at three locations. The main leak was in the starboard side double-bottomed ballast tank, which was a tricky tank to access at the best of times, with a large pipe that runs across the space that requires sliding under, on one's back, lying uncomfortably across the ribs of the ship. This difficult access also meant that there was no way to quickly escape if the tank was to rupture. It was just too risky, and the captain and mates agreed that the tank would be left isolated and full as the *Aurora* sailed north.

The other two leaks, however, while slow and relatively minor, required attention. One was in the engine room cofferdam, the oddly shaped, three-armed void between ballast tanks under the engine room deck; it was a small crack and would need a simple putty job. The other leak was somewhere in a bilge tank on the *Aurora*'s starboard side. The tank was emptied and degassed, and Gerry O, wearing a disposable white coverall over his orange boiler suit, and armed with a torch, a gas meter and a lumpy rucksack, climbed down from the engine room into the dingy chamber.

Gerry wrinkled his nose slightly at the rank smell of the pitch-black space. He was already getting goosebumps, despite the layers of thermals he was wearing under his boiler suit. He shivered and sighed as he swung the torch around – and was instantly blinded by a white fog of his own breath. It hung annoyingly in the frigid, motionless air inside the tank. He waved his hand through the mist and looked around. Almost immediately, his vision was impeded once again by the irritating vapour. He fanned it away and yanked his neck warmer up over his mouth and nose.

Finally, he could see that his torch shot a beam of light across to the browned steel on the other side of the tank. It illuminated the first lightening hole – a window-like access opening in the middle of the internal framing.

The *Aurora*'s sturdy steel frames, or ribs, ran in close parallel less than half a metre apart, giving the icebreaker her strength. Gerry carefully trod between them, his boots skating occasionally on the fetid, frozen film of greywater that remained in the tank. He crouched, and awkwardly climbed sideways through another oval gap. There, between the frames in the torchlight in front of him, the *Aurora*'s hull was warped and buckled inward, in a grotesque mirror-image of the *Aurora*'s familiar and shapely outward curve.

Gerry stared, astonished. An icebreaker is meant to be strong, but he'd never witnessed the reality of the *Aurora*'s impressive strength until now. Her hull plates were so violently bent inwards they should have cracked, but the close framing had supported the plating. It had held under the pressure, and there were no leaks in the external hull plating.

Where was this bloody leak then? The tank soundings had confirmed there was one. He turned toward the forward section of the tank, squeezed through another small lightening hole and awkwardly stepped over more frames. There, at the very front of the tank, a spray of water squirted upwards in a fine arc and fell onto an ever-growing frozen puddle on the deck. It was an internal leak! The external part of the *Aurora*'s hull was sound; this crack was at the join between the sea chest and the bilge tank. Like a beached whale, the *Aurora*'s weight had been unsupported while on the rocks, and the physical stress had led to some internal buckling between tanks.

Gerry opened his rucksack and pulled out an assortment of wooden chocks, a small piece of ply, some epoxy putty and a mallet. Half kneeling, half squatting between the framework, he got to work. But each strike of the mallet chimed piercingly around the plated space. Gerry remembers:

My biggest fear through that was really that I'd be in there and whatever it was that was holding all of that together finally just failed . . . you know – don't hit it too hard with the hammer or the wooden wedges and things like that or it might all just rip apart and flood the tank, with me in it.

He pulled his mind away from those grim thoughts and focused on the job at hand. He wasn't too far from the hatch, so if he did have to escape in a hurry he wouldn't have far to go. And there was the standby watchman, who was waiting at the tank entrance. It was fine, he told himself. Totally fine.

At the same time, David had wriggled his way through the low internal void beneath the engine room, through the engine room cofferdam, to the position where Gerry said the smaller leak was. David grunted. He was lying uncomfortably with his legs through one frame and his torso in another. The roof of the space was less than half a metre above him, and at full stretch his fingers could only just reach the problem spot to putty it up. It was like being in a dank steel mine tunnel. He hated confined spaces. He tried not to think of the steel pressing in on him and stretched again, huffing in exertion to plug the crack.

Like Gerry, his mind began to wander as he worked. How had this happened to them? The whole situation was beyond frustrating, he thought as he strained with the epoxy again. Things had been going so well this voyage; they had been 'kicking goals', as the VL had said. They'd worked so hard, achieved so much, especially for the science program; and then they'd gone from hero to zero in the space of just three terrifying minutes. He shook his head.

Three days later, having steamed up and down Kista Strait, the *Aurora*'s crew had completed the tank inspections, successfully repaired her clutch and made temporary tank repairs. After multiple phone calls and emails, the captain, crew, naval architects, insurer and P&O all agreed the *Aurora* was sound and able to limp her way home, with just the crew, VL and the doctor on board.

The *Aurora* made a brief visit to Mawson to pick up the ship's doctor, then pointed her bow north, making her way toward the safety of Fremantle.

Downstairs, Lloyd started to wander between the deserted cabins and laboratories, organising and packing gear that had been left behind by the expeditioners. As he rifled through books and turned over DVDs, checking if they were from the ship's library or the expeditioners' own property, it was hard to shake off a feeling of guilt at the invasion of privacy. Added to that, every discarded item, lying exactly where it had been left by its owner, gave the *Aurora* the atmosphere of a ghost town, with the expeditioners' presences lingering like phantoms.

Meanwhile, the Australian Antarctic Division back in Kingston had their hands full. The media unit were fielding a slew of enquiries from the global media, with reports of the incident being filed by CNN, BBC, Fox and NBC, as well as most of the Australian media outlets. At the same time, the AAD crisis response team were busy with the process of making arrangements to get their stranded expeditioners home. They had their work cut out for them. As well as the group at Mawson, the most distant of the Australian Antarctic stations, there were expeditioners stranded at Davis station who had been scheduled to be picked up by the *Aurora* after the Mawson resupply.

Once again, tested by a partner in crisis, the Treaty nations rallied. When news of the grounding broke, multiple offers of assistance were made to Australia to help transport their stranded personnel home. A plan quickly came together.

The Japanese icebreaker *Shirase* would divert from its scientific program to pick up the expeditioners stuck at Mawson, plus the contingent of outgoing Mawson winterers. She would then deliver the Australian personnel to Casey station, over two thousand kilometres away. From Casey, the expeditioners would travel seventy kilometres overland in Hägglunds to Australia's ice runway at Wilkins aerodrome, to be flown home by the Australian Antarctic Division's Airbus A319 plane.

Australian planes do not have the capability of landing at Davis, so the United States Antarctic program would come to the aid of the Australian expeditioners stranded at Davis, flying them in a ski-equipped Hercules aircraft to the US-operated McMurdo station, from where they would be transported home using the AAD's Airbus plane. Two expeditioners, left at Davis to look after field equipment and irreplaceable scientific samples collected over the summer season, would be transported back to Fremantle by the Chinese ship, the *Xue Long*, which had just finished helping the Australian program resupply Casey station, and was on its way to resupply Zhongshan station near Davis.

Minister for the Environment Greg Hunt would later publicly thank the Japanese, Chinese and US Antarctic programs and governments for their efforts, writing appreciatively:

> The assistance offered by all three Antarctic programmes is greatly appreciated as were the many other offers of support from other countries.
>
> The international Antarctic community has once again demonstrated its willingness to support one another in times of difficulty.
>
> Antarctica is a hostile, remote and inherently dangerous environment and international cooperation is vital for our dedicated Antarctic teams to be able to carry out their important work.

While it had been an amazing feat of determination to have refloated the *Aurora* without help and to make repairs so quickly, the mood on board the Aurora was solemn as the icebreaker journeyed north. After their frantic efforts during the crisis itself, and the feverish aftermath of refloating the ship and conducting checks and repairs, the quiet uninterrupted hours of the transit home suddenly gave the *Aurora*'s meagre complement time to think.

'The more I have thought about this incident,' Lloyd wrote sombrely in his VL's report, 'the more I have realised how lucky we were to be in a ship built as strongly as the *Aurora Australis*. Had the ship started to take on significant amounts of water then it may well have started to slip down the steep bank and settled into deep water. An uncontrolled exit from the vessel on Day 1 would have resulted in multiple fatalities due to the murderous conditions outside. Very few people would have found their way to the station from West Arm even if they had made it to shore. It's my opinion that the station would have been unable to do much beyond pick up the pieces.'

Lloyd had also been poring over the data from the ship's scientific GPS. It seemed that once the *Aurora* had hit the rocks, she'd been dragged down West Arm by the wind until she'd come to rest in a 'natural cradle with a steep drop off':

It is sobering to think that if this natural cradle did not exist, then it is possible that the ship may have been blown out of the harbour and across Kista Strait into the islands beyond. Or if the drop off was less steep then the damage to the ship might have been significantly greater.

While Lloyd was mulling over their narrow escape from disaster, the crew began to dwell on their own problems. There was no doubt P&O would conduct a full investigation into the incident, and the crew's own questions about how this had happened, how the system had failed and even wondering if they'd played some unknowing part in the incident, began to be replaced with fears for their jobs, and in turn concern for their homes and their family.

'You couldn't turn your head off,' David recalled later. 'You're [mentally] going up and down, up and down . . . And it was like, a week out of [Fremantle], that you're starting to sort of – just stop caring. You have to let go, otherwise you're just going to lose your mind . . . What will be will be.'

David also felt for his captain. Over the last few days, Benoit must have feared for his ship, for the lives of his crew and expeditioners; then later for his job and his reputation. But throughout, Benoit's quiet, stoic form had been unwavering. During the crisis he had ensured the expeditioners and crew were safe above all else, and after the incident he had triaged the *Aurora* as best he could.

The subsequent investigation by P&O found that the *Aurora* had experienced one of the worst blizzards that a ship moored in Horseshoe Harbour had faced in living history. The extreme forces of the blizzard exposed some weaknesses in the *Aurora*'s mooring arrangements that had previously been untested under such pressures. No individual was to blame for the event.

The *Aurora*'s mooring procedures were amended and updated to take such factors into account, and in the years following the event, the *Aurora* continued to be moored in Horseshoe Harbour during AAD resupplies, when weather (and the A factor) allowed her to safely enter the harbour.

After an uneventful transit, the *Aurora Australis* arrived in Fremantle ten days after leaving Mawson.

Lloyd looked out over the rail at the small group of P&O and AAD personnel waiting on the sundrenched wharf. Discounting the glaring exception that was the grounding, the voyage had actually been quite successful. While they hadn't been able to backload return-to-Australia cargo, or visit Davis for the cargo and personnel retrieval, the K-axis marine science program had been a huge success, and the Mawson refuelling and resupply had been completed. Lloyd sighed. He doubted anyone would remember this voyage for anything other than the stressful, near-disastrous event. Throughout the entire voyage the *Aurora*'s crew had been amazing, and what happened seemed incredibly unfair.

He wrote philosophically:

Even after the ship ran aground at Mawson and during the transit back to Fremantle, I always felt confident that we were in good hands. It would be a tragedy if [the crew's] considerable efforts before, during and after the event at Mawson will be overshadowed by the event itself. We should do our best to see that this does not happen . . .

The Master, officers and crew of the *Aurora Australis*
. . . knew better than anyone the full implications of what
was happening and they did everything they could to keep
us safe. I know that this probably sounds like it's the sort of
thing that one is obliged to say after such an affair but in this
case, it is simply true. We are all very grateful.

Many of the crew were compassionately sent home by P&O not
long after their arrival. A small number of crew, scarred by their
experience, would never return to the ship, but nearly all would
later rejoin their beloved *Aurora*, and return once more to the
beautiful frozen wilds of the south.

Once again, the resilient ship and her crew picked themselves
up, dusted themselves off and simply got on with the job. At dry
dock in Singapore, the damage to her hull was all too evident:
the *Aurora*'s hull plates were shockingly bent inward and her
sides rent with scars where her paint had been scraped away by
the Antarctic rock. Whole sections of her hull and pieces of her
framing were cut away and replaced with new steel members,
and after twelve days of painstaking metalworking surgery the
Aurora was lowered gently back into the water.

Despite the odds being stacked against them, the *Aurora* and
her crew had shown their grit, determination and strength of
character. Heads held high, she and her crew made their way
home, arriving in Hobart in early May 2016.

Over the next three Antarctic seasons, the *Aurora Australis*
and her crew would put the emotion and drama of the grounding behind them, going on to successfully conduct four resupply
voyages every season.

Chapter Eleven

ANTARCTIC ICON

The *Aurora Australis* celebrates her thirtieth birthday on 18 September 2019. And in the summer season following this milestone, she will sail to Antarctica for the last time for Australia's Antarctic Program. Her successful construction and decades of operation had proved that Australians had the knowledge, skill and confidence to build, operate and thrive on polar vessels, a realm previously dominated by Europeans.

Australia's current reputation as a world leader in Antarctic marine science is directly attributable to the *Aurora Australis*. Her icebreaking capability and state-of-the-art facilities expanded the reach of scientists and opened worlds never before explored in Antarctica and the Southern Ocean. Together, the *Aurora* and her scientists and crew surveyed vast swathes of Antarctica and, in the midst of the untempered Southern Ocean and the treacherous realm of sea ice, they discovered new species and communities and uncovered surprising oceanographic secrets of the deep. They contributed to the understanding and management of the fragile, pristine ecosystem and its role in the global climate process.

Over her thirty years, the *Aurora Australis* has completed more than 150 voyages, and is estimated to have carried more than ten thousand personnel to and from the frozen reaches of the Antarctic and subantarctic. She loaded and unloaded unmeasureable tonnes of fuel, equipment, food and consumables to keep Australia's Antarctic stations running year-round, and contributed to the success of multiple station-modernisation and pest-eradication programs. But above all, the stately ship cared for and safeguarded the lives of her charges on board, as well as those living in the isolated communities at the bottom of the world.

SMOOTH SAILING – THE *AURORA'S* FINAL YEARS

In the final few years of her working life, the *Aurora* performed all of her duties flawlessly, continuing to resupply stations and even occasionally doing some science along the way. In the 2016/17 summer, during a Casey resupply voyage, oceanographers busily took ice samples from a number of 'ice factory' polynyas and once again conducted the stop–start oceanographic sampling of the SR3 transect (and thanks to the *Aurora*, the SR3 transect had become one of the best temporal datasets of the Southern Ocean in the world). The *Aurora* also continued to deploy and retrieve the Continuous Plankton Recorder, conduct underway sampling and deploy and retrieve underwater acoustic recording devices on her transits. But, perhaps surprisingly, some of the last major science ventures she conducted were not in the field of marine science. Instead, in her late 20s the *Aurora's* gaze turned toward the heavens as her focus shifted to atmospheric research – unlocking the secrets of the supercooled clouds above Antarctica.

But whatever she was doing in her later years, the workhorse of the south simply got on with the job; quietly and efficiently resupplying and refuelling Australia's Antarctic stations, determinedly beating her way through Antarctic sea ice and raging blizzards in the process.

By safely navigating the highs and lows of her life, the *Aurora* has also come to embody the spirit of the Antarctic Treaty: of freedom of scientific investigation and unquestioning support to fellow Antarctic programs, regardless of politics. She has received her share of support during times of crisis, but she has also given support to other ships in distress such as the *Polar Bird*, *Janas* and *Akademik Shokalskiy*, as well as successfully conducted several emergency responses for sick or injured Antarctic expeditioners. She has helped other national Antarctic programs meet their scientific and logistic aims, transporting fuel, continental personnel and scientists to the far reaches of the Antarctic.

This spirit of the Antarctic treaty remains a positive and vital part of operations in Antarctica to this day, where transport, aid and rescue options are still limited in such a vast and inhospitable realm.

And while – thanks in part to her faithful service – the Australian Antarctic Program's science and infrastructure had expanded and diversified over the three decades of the *Aurora*'s life, they had also begun to outgrow their trusty icebreaker. In addition, maintaining aging ships (especially those constantly exposed to tough conditions and the vibrations associated with breaking ice), and keeping them in line with updated polar shipping codes, comes with an associated cost. Back in 2013, the government investigated options for replacing the *Aurora Australis*, and in 2014, when the government released the Twenty Year Australian Antarctic Strategic Plan, they announced they would fund the construction of a new icebreaker.

'This increased capability will help restore Australia's leadership in marine science and logistics in Antarctica and the Southern Ocean; it will also provide a platform from which to increase Australia's collaboration with other Antarctic nations,' Head Inquirer and former AAD Director Tony Press wrote in the Plan. 'But,' he went on to say, 'the capabilities of the new icebreaker must be matched with the capacity to conduct both scientific and logistic operations.'

In 2016 the contract to build a new icebreaker was announced, with the government investing $529 million to build the ship, and committing $1.38 billion to operations and maintenance over its thirty-year lifespan.

This new icebreaker would be developed by a Danish company, designed by a Dutch company and built in Romania. The keel of the new ship was laid at Galati, Romania on 24 August 2017; four coins, representing each of the four nations involved in her creation, were welded to her hull.

In an echo of the past, the AAD looked toward the school-children of Australia for the new ship's name, inviting the next generation to name the icebreaker in another nationally-run competition. On 29 September 2017, the name RSV *Nuyina* was proudly announced by then Minister for the Environment and Energy, Josh Frydenberg.

The word nuyina (pronounced 'noy-yee-nah'), in palawa kani – the native language spoken by Indigenous Tasmanians – means 'southern lights', and recognises the spiritual connection Tasmanian Indigenous people have with Antarctica. The apt name also links the *Nuyina* to both Sir Douglas Mawson's SY *Aurora* and the RSV *Aurora Australis*, in an unexpected custom that now connects many of Australia's iconic Antarctic vessels throughout modern history.

Nuyina, like her predecessor the *Aurora Australis*, was designed as a cutting-edge ship for her time. Having become familiar with the limitations of a one-ship solution, the AAD designed the *Nuyina* with multiple contingencies in mind: she will have two separate engine rooms and two propellers as well as multiple cranes, providing ample backup if problems, break-downs or disaster are to strike any of her major machinery. She will be able to break 1.65 metres of ice at a speed of three knots. The two icebreakers would have almost identical capacity for carrying expeditioners, but the *Nuyina* will be much longer than the *Aurora* at 160 metres in length, with almost three times the cargo hold capacity of the *Aurora Australis*. The *Nuyina*'s scientific resume is also impressive; as well as having standard scientific equipment such as state-of-the-art acoustic sensors in her hull and scientific winches, the *Nuyina* will have a moonpool, which will be used to deploy oceanographic equipment such as CTDs and ROVs from the safety of inside the ship – protecting crew and instruments from wind and swell. In a world first, the *Nuyina* will also be able to collect and process huge volumes of seawater for organisms such as krill via a purpose-built wet well and filter tables. The *Nuyina* has been designed with flexibility in mind, to carry her through the advancements of the next thirty years of polar exploration.

As for the *Aurora Australis*, her future is yet to be written. After she hands over the mantle of Australia's Antarctic flagship to the *Nuyina*, perhaps the *Aurora* will find use in another national Antarctic program, or be sold to a private owner. Thankfully, according to P&O it is unlikely, albeit not impossible, that she will be sent to the torches and grinders of a scrap yard.

Whatever the future holds for the *Aurora*, she will not sail into the sunset unrecognised, nor will she ever be forgotten. She has revolutionised Australian Antarctic shipping and research, and along the way she has changed the lives of many.

The symbiotic relationship that quickly developed between the *Aurora* and her complement allowed both to thrive in their polar pursuits. The skilled professionals of her complement are the icebreaker's lifeblood, but to them the *Aurora* is more than just an icebreaker. She has shown her expeditioners and crew the wonders of the Antarctic landscape and its countless vibrant moods, revealed the diverse life that abounds in the Southern Ocean's depths and displayed the intrepid wildlife that inhabits the fierce polar wilderness. She has been a home, laboratory and ferry, a heroine and a champion. But her reach also goes well beyond her designated role and functions. She has touched the lives of many in other major ways: some met their best friends or their partners on her well-trodden decks; others simply became part of a tightly knit community that has become an integral part of their lives, and even a large part of their sense of self.

Over the *Aurora*'s lifetime, three of her crew were awarded the Australian Antarctic Medal. This medal, part of the Australian honours system and awarded by the governor-general, honours those who have given 'outstanding service in scientific research or exploration, or in support of such work, in the course of, or in connection with, an Australian Antarctic Expedition', where 'the rigours of Antarctic climate and terrain prevail'. Captain Murray Doyle, Captain Scott Laughlin, and Bosun Per Larsen were honoured for their skill and dedication in carrying out their scientific and operational work for the Australian Antarctic program, while never compromising safety. In addition, scientists Steve Nicol, Steve Rintoul, Jono Reeve, Howard Burton and Dick Williams have all been honoured for their dedication and contribution to the success of the Antarctic marine science program in part, or wholly, due to their marine science work conducted on board the *Aurora Australis*.

The *Aurora Australis* is currently scheduled to sail away from the ice-laden waters of Antarctica for the last time in February/March 2020, ending her Antarctic service for the Australian Antarctic Program. Her story is one of triumph over adversity; the *Aurora Australis* has revealed herself to be a resilient, sometimes feisty character who persevered through whatever hardships and emergencies the A factor could throw at her.

The *Aurora*'s iconic orange form will soon be replaced, but her memory and legacy will persist. The arrival of a new ice-breaker and the departure of a beloved predecessor will again signal the end of one era and the beginning of another; but the *Aurora Australis* is, and will possibly always remain, the only Australian-built icebreaker. The European-built *Nuyina* will, in time, form her own beloved character. But the grit, determination, bravery, discovery and community of the distinctively Australian *Aurora Australis* will always be unique.

ACKNOWLEDGEMENTS

There are countless people to thank for the success of this project and book.

Firstly, I thank the Australian Antarctic Division (AAD) and P&O Maritime Services in Hobart, who gave their support to this concept from the very beginning. I thank the Australian Antarctic Division for enabling me to travel to Antarctica on a resupply voyage to assist with research for this book, and thank P&O for assisting with travel costs. I thank both the AAD and P&O for facilitating contact with interviewees, and for generously allowing me to access their image libraries. Thank you to all of the staff at the AAD and P&O for your enthusiasm and expertise, and for your assistance tracking down countless people, files, images and data. Sally, Jess, Tess, Rob B, David S, Andrew D and John E were particularly helpful, and I can't thank you enough.

Thanks go to the National Archives of Australia for allowing me to (carefully) scour box after box of design and tender files. Thanks also to the State Library of Tasmania, whose newspaper microfilms have been an invaluable source. To the authors of all media and scientific sources used in this book, thank you.

To the countless captains, crew, expeditioners, builders and experts and I've interviewed: I am so grateful for your time, your enthusiasm, your knowledge, and for trusting me implicitly with your precious memories. There are more than fifty of you, but every single one of you has my sincere and heartfelt thanks. You know who you are. Thank you to the captains and crew who have provided photographs and other valuable resources, and to the all the incredible photographers who have generously provided images. Kerry Dickson helped fill some name gaps, for which I am very thankful.

I am indebted to the captain, crew, voyage management and expeditioners of Voyage 1 2017/18, for their knowledge and passion, and for giving me wide access to the *Aurora*'s restricted areas and operations. This book has benefited greatly.

Thanks must go to Steve Nicol for his encouragement, advice, comments on early chapters – and his cheery forbearance along the way.

Many thanks to my family: my mum and dad, Colleen and Warwick, and my mother- and father-in-law Mareea and Bruce, for their love and unwavering support (and weeks of babysitting while Andrew and I were both at sea). To Grandad Don and Grandma Maureen, well, what can I say: you inspire me, quite literally. To my husband Andrew, for his unshakeable faith in me, his love, his constant encouragement – and his boundless patience when answering my many seafaring questions! And to our boys, for simply being who they are and bringing so much fun to our lives.

I thank my agent, Fran Moore, who instantly loved this concept and championed it from the start, as did Angus Fontaine. And thanks to Georgia, Ingrid and everyone at Pan Macmillan, who made this dream into a reality.

Me standing in front of the *Aurora Australis* at Davis station 2017.

SOURCES

Glossary: Nautical Terms

Australian Antarctic Division 'Brash Ice'. http://www.antarctica.gov.au/about-antarctica/environment/sea-ice/pack-ice/brash-ice

Australian Antarctic Division 'Development of sea ice'. http://www.antarctica.gov.au/about-antarctica/environment/sea-ice/development-of-sea-ice

Macquarie Dictionary Online 2019. https://www.macquariedictionary.com.au/

Introduction

AAD. 2002. History of ANARE shipping. May 2002. http://www.antarctica.gov.au/about-antarctica/history/transportation/shipping (accessed August 2015).

Anon. 1987. '$60m ship contract a boost for city'. *Newcastle Herald*, 24 December 1987.

Anon. 1987. 'Nella Dan "dies like a Viking"'. *Canberra Times*, 26 December 1987.

Anon. 1987. 'Carrington Confirmed'. *Daily Cargo News*, 29 December 1987.

Auditor-General, Department of the Arts, Sport, the Environment, Tourism and Territories (DASETT). 1990. Audit Report No. 9 1990–97. Antarctic Supply Vessel – Chartering arrangements, 10pp.

Bear, Ivan. 1988. '*Aurora Australis* construction gets under way'. *ANARE News*, December 1988: 3–4. Commonwealth of Australia.

Bowden, Tim. 1997. *The Silence Calling*. St Leonards: Allen & Unwin, 593pp.

Hawke, Hazel. 1989. 'Mrs Hawke launches *Aurora Australis* (text of Mrs Hawke's speech)'. *ANARE News*, September 1989:4. Commonwealth of Australia.

Interview with David Lyons, 25 February 2016.

Interviews with Don and Maureen Laverick, 9 March 2015 and 27 October 2015.

Lyons, David. 1988. 'The Last Voyage of the Nella Dan'. *ANARE News*, no. 53, March 1988. Commonwealth of Australia.

Lyons, David. n.d. Voyage Report. Voyage 4 1987–88, Nella Dan. Australian Antarctic Division, Department of the Arts, Sport, The Environment, Tourism and Territories.

McGhee, Karen. 1988. 'Carrington Slipways and the Antarctic Connection'. *The Newcastle Herald*, 8 September 1988.

Morgan, Anne. n.d. 'A True Viking Funeral! – Nella Dan 1987'. *The Shipwreck Watch – A journal of Macquarie Island Shipwreck Stories, 1987–88*. https://www.parks.tas.gov.au/fahan_mi_shipwrecks/journals/Shipwrecks/swnelladan15.pdf

Personal communication with David Lyons, 9 September 2015.

The Carrington Slipways Story. 2014. DVD. Produced by John & Margaret Laverick, Don & Maureen Laverick. Performed by John Church Advertising.

Wärtsilä. 'The History of Wärtsilä 1834–1990'. http://www.wartsila.com/about/history (accessed 10 August 2015).

Chapter One

Anon. 1990. '"*Aurora Australis*" exploits the Antarctic'. *Marine Engineers Review*, September 3pp.

Australian Antarctic Division. 1998. '"*Aurora Australis*" to be Australia's Antarctic flagship'. Media Release. Kingston, Tasmania, 88/382.

Bear, Ivan. 1988. '*Aurora Australis* construction gets under way'. *ANARE News*, December 1988: 3–4.

Bear, Ivan. 1989. 'A personal account of the launching of *Aurora Australis*'. *ANARE News*, September 1989: 5.

Bear, Ivan. 1989. '*Aurora Australis* – A progress report'. *ANARE News*, March 1989: 6–7.

Bowden, Tim. 1997. *The Silence Calling*. St Leonards: Allen & Unwin, 593pp.

Carrington Slipways. 1989. Order of Proceedings for *Aurora Australis* launch. Provided by Maureen Laverick.

Hawke, Hazel. 1989. 'Mrs Hawke launches *Aurora Australis* (text of Mrs Hawke's speech)'. *ANARE News*, September 1989: 4.

Interview with Alan Laverick, 17 July 2015.

Interview with Bruce Laverick, 2 August 2015.

Interviews with Don and Maureen Laverick, 9 March 2015 and 27 October 2015.

Longworth, Ken. 1988. 'Boy who named ship steals politicians' thunder'. *The Newcastle Herald*, 29 October 1988.

McGhee, Karen. 1988. 'Carrington Slipways and the Antarctic Connection'. *The Newcastle Herald*, 8 September 1988.

NBN News n.d. in The Carrington Slipways Story. 2014. DVD. Produced by John & Margaret Laverick, Don & Maureen Laverick. Performed by John Church Advertising.

PB. 1988. 'New Ship Named'. *ANARE News*, December 1988.

Pilgrim, Scott. 1989. 'Antarctic icebreaker work on schedule'. *The Newcastle Herald*, June/July 1989.

Richardson, Sen. Graham. 1989. 'Senator Richardson praises *Aurora Australis* (text of Senator Richardson's speech).' *ANARE News*, September 1989: 4.

The Carrington Slipways Story. 2014. DVD. Produced by John & Margaret Laverick, Don & Maureen Laverick. Performed by John Church Advertising.

Chapter Two

Anon. 1990. '"*Aurora Australis*" exploits the Antarctic'. *Marine Engineers Review*, September 1990, 3pp.

Bear, Ivan. 1989. 'A personal account of the launching of *Aurora Australis*'. *ANARE News*, September 1989:5.

Interview with Bruce Laverick, 2 August 2015.

Interviews with Don and Maureen Laverick, 9 March 2015 and 27 October 2015.

NBN News. n.d. in The Carrington Slipways story. DVD. Produced by John & Margaret Laverick, Don & Maureen Laverick. Performed by John Church Advertising. 2014.

Richardson, Sen. Graham. 1989. 'Senator Richardson congratulates Carrington's (text of Senator Richardson's speech at the reception)'. *ANARE News*, September 1989: 4.

The Carrington Slipways Story. 2014. DVD. Produced by John & Margaret Laverick, Don & Maureen Laverick. Performed by John Church Advertising. 2014.

Chapter Three

ABC & James, M. 1990. 'Icebreaker *Aurora Australis*'. TV report filed for *Quantum*. Retrieved from ABC Science, http://www.abc.net.au/science/articles/2015/03/25/4204494.htm (accessed 13 Ocrtober 2018).

Anon. 1990. 'Polar ship back after testing maiden voyage'. *Mercury*, 5 July 1990.

Betts, Martin. 1991. VL's Report Voyage 4 – 1990/91, Mawson and Davis Ice edges. Australian Antarctic Data Centre.

Department of Environment and Energy. 2005. 'Heard Island – Discovery'. http://hear disland.antarctica.gov.au/history/discovery, 28 February 2005 (accessed 13 August 2018).

Fyfe, Moya. 1990. 'New research ship broadens horizons.' *Mercury*, 5 April 1990.

Green, Ken (Ed). 1990. *Heard Island 1990 ANARE Report*. Australian Antarctic Data Centre, 77pp.

Interview with Andrew Tabor, 8 August 2018.

Interview with Jonathan Reeve, 20 April 2017.

Interview with Matthew Stewart, 4 April 2018.

Interview with Richard Williams, 18 February 2016.

Interview with Rick Burbury, 11 October 2017.

Interview with Roger Rusling, 19 April 2018.

Marchant, Ian. 1991. RSV Aurora Australis Voyage 2 – 1990–91 Report. Australian Antarctic Data Centre.

Rusling, R. 1990. Masters Voyage Report Season 1989–90 7.2. P&O Polar.

Rusling, R. 1991. Masters Voyage Report V2: 1990–91. P&O Polar.

Rusling, R. 1991. Masters Voyage Report, Voyage 4, 1990–/91. P&O Polar.

Sale, Penny. 1990. 'Ice Ship captures hearts of Hobart'. *Mercury*, 9 April 1990.

Sorenson, Bernie. ND. 'Breaking Ice for Antarctica' footage. Footage provided to author by Dion Dillon.

White, C. P. and Jewer, D. D. 2009. Seal Finger: A case report and review of the literature. Can J Plast Surg 17(4): 133–135.

Williams, Richard. 1990. VL's Report. Voyage 7.2. Australian Antarctic Data Centre.

Chapter Four

Anon. 1993. 'Torpedo lost below the Antarctic Ice'. *The Canberra Times*, 11 May 1993: 4.

Bain, Gordon. 2011. 'Husky's tale comes full circle'. *Australian Antarctic Magazine* 20:32–33. Commonwealth of Australia.

Bain, Peter. 1993. Voyage Report V9.1: 1992–93. P&O Polar.

Bain, Peter. 1993. Voyage Report V9: 1 1992–93. P&O Polar.

Betts, Martin. 1992. Voyage 1, 1992–93 Voyage Report. Australian Antarctic Data Centre.

Corby, Steven. 1993. 'Journey's end for huskies'. *The Canberra Times*, 28 December 1993, p. 4.

Hosie, Graham. Voyage 7, Marine Science Cruise 1992–93 KROCK, 5/1–7/3 1993, VL's Report. Australian Antarctic Data Centre.

Interview with Jono Reeve, 20 April 2017.

Interview with Ross McCallum, 26 February 2018.

Interviews with Steve Nicol, 21 February 2016 and 15 July 2017.

Nicol, Steve. 1993. Letters from Steve Nicol to his parents, 11 March 1993 & 19 May 1993.

Nicol, Steve. 1993. Voyage 9 Report (Marine Science). Australian Antarctic Data Centre.

Parliament of Australia. ESTIMATES COMMITTEE C 21/06/1994 DEPARTMENT OF THE ENVIRONMENT, SPORT AND TERRITORIES Program 2 – Antarctic Subprogram 2.2 – Expeditions. Senate estimates. Transcript accessed via Parlinfo.

Secretariat of the Antarctic Treaty. 'The Protocol on Environmental Protection to the Antarctic Treaty'. https://www.ats.aq/e/ep.htm (accessed 13 October 2018).

Chapter Five

Allison, Ian. 1998. RSV *Aurora Australis*, Voyage 1 1998–99 Report. Australian Antarctic Data Centre.

Associated Press. 1998. 'Fire halts ship's Antarctica trip'. AP 31 July 1998. AP News Archive.

Aurora Australis Rough deck log, 22 July 1998, 3pp.

Hansen, Tony. 1998. Report as taken from rough deck log records. (Further detail on deck log – Captain's recollections), 3pp.

Interview with Barbara Wienecke, 16 February 2016.

Interview with Jimmy Mackenzie, 29 June 2016.

Interview with Rob Cave, 19 May 2016.

Interview with Scott Laughlin, 25 May 2018.

Interview with Tony Hansen, 29 June 2016.

Marine Incident Investigation Unit. 1999. Investigation into the engine room fire on board the Australian Research Vessel at the Antarctic ice edge on 22 July 1998. Australian Transport Safety Bureau, 76pp.

Mercury, 'Deaths' – Classifieds section. Wednesday 5 August 1998, p. 64.

Personal Communications with Tony Hansen, 23 June 2016.

Personal Communications with Jimmy Mackenzie, July 2016.

Stevens, Jane. 1998. 'The Chilling Fields'. Reports for Discovery Channel Online. As appended to: Allison, Ian, 1998.

Chapter Six

Anon. 1998. 'Antarctic ship rescue mission underway'. *ABC News In Science*, 7 December 1998.

Anon. 1999. 'Mission Impossible'. MER (Marine Engineers Review), October 1999: 22–24.

Brooks, John. 1998. Voyage Report, Voyage 2, 1998–99 MV *Polar Bird*. Australian Antarctic Data Centre.

Doyle, M. 1999. 'International Cooperation in Antarctica'. Maritime Officer 4–6.

Interview with Murray Doyle, 26 August 2016.

Interview with Peter Pearson, 16 October 2016.

Interview with Steve Whiteside, 16 February 2016.

Interview with Tony Press, 25 February 2016.

Interviews with Colin Southwell, 2 August 2016 and 15 December 2016.

Interviews with John van Dam, 9 November 2016 and 24 April 2017.

Interviews with Suzanne Betts (nee Stallman), 13 April 2017 and 4 April 2017.

Lamb, Eve. 1998. 'Icebreaker stuck again: problem now propeller'. *Mercury*, 3 December 1998.

Pearson, Peter. 1998. V4 season 98/99 Davis Resupply (Captain's Report). P&O Polar.

van Dam, John. 2016. 'The RSV *Aurora Australis* propeller repair'. *On Watch*, April 2016: 8–9.

Personal communications with John van Dam re technical aspects of CPP September–October 2018.

Rogers, Matthew. 1998. 'Antarctic flagship breaks the ice after long lay-off'. *Mercury*, 30 October 1998, p. 5.

Secretariat of the Antarctic Treaty. 'The Antarctic Treaty'. https://www.ats.aq/e/ats.htm
(accessed 13 October 2018).

Stallman, Suzanne. 1998. Voyage 4 1998–99 Season, Voyage Report RSV *Aurora
Australis*. Australian Antarctic Data Centre.

Stallman, Suzanne. Sitrep: Thursday 5 November 1998. AAD. Provided by author.

Chapter Seven

Academy Gallery. 2005. 'Reflections 8 Aug–9 Sept 2005'. Exhibition pamphlet. School of
Visual and Performing Arts Launceston, University of Tasmania.

Burgess, Dick. 1999. Voyage Report – V5 Fremantle to Mawson 1999 (Captain's report).
P&O Polar.

Interview with Dick Burgess, 9 April 2018.

Interview with Jon Handicott, 8 May 2017.

Interview with John Kitchener, 6 December 2017.

Interview with Rob Cave, 12 January 2017.

Lamb, Eve. 1999. 'New fire blow for Antarctic vessel'. *Mercury*, January 15 1999.

Marine Incident Investigation Unit. 2000. Investigation into the engine room fire on
board the Australian Research and Supply Vessel Aurora Australis off the coast of
West Australia on 14 January 1999. Australian Transport Safety Bureau, 40pp.

Papworth, Warren. 1999. VL's Report, Voyage 5 – RSV *Aurora Australis*. Australian
Antarctic Data Centre.

Personal Communication with Catherine Di Murro, 8 March 2019.

Personal Communication with Jon Handicott, 7 March 2019.

Chapter Eight

Anon. 2002. '*Polar Bird* free of Antarctic ice after mammoth effort'. Australian Antarctic
Division (News Archive), 14 January 2002.

Anon. 2009. 'Australia's contribution to the International Polar Year'. *Australian
Antarctic Magazine* 16: 9–13. Commonwealth of Australia.

Anon. 2009. 'Sea Ice Physics and Ecosystem Experiment'. Australian Antarctic Division
(News Archive), 26 February 2009.

Anon. 2011. 'Stricken vessel towed to safety'. Australian Antarctic Division (News
Archives), 26 July 2011.

Anon. 2011. Voyage Report: Voyage 6 2011 RAN Charter. (Captain's report AA).

Anon. 2012. 'Antarctic scientists take high-tech approach to sea ice studies'. Australian
Antarctic Division (News Archive), 10 August 2012.

Commonwealth of Australia. 'Australia's future activities and responsibilities in the
Southern Ocean and Antarctic Waters.' ISBN 978–1–76010–104–6.

Bryson, Rob. Sitrep: Saturday 30 July 2011. Australian Antarctic Division. AAD voyage
sitreps: https://secure3.aad.gov.au/public/schedules/sitreps.cfm

Coats, Lucinda. 2002. Blog: 'ANARE Club Berth 2001–02'. http://anareclub.org/web/
club-berth/2001–02/lucv5.php (accessed 2017).

Constable, A.J., de la Mare, W.K., Agnew, D.J., Everson, I. and Miller, D. 2000. 'Managing
fisheries to conserve the Antarctic marine ecosystem: practical implementation of the
Convention of the Conservation of Antarctic Marine Living Resources (CCAMLR)'.
ICES Journal of Marine Science 57: 778–791.

Department of the Environment. Submission 15 (Chapter 5) in: 'Australia's future activities and responsibilities in the Southern Ocean and Antarctic Waters.' Commonwealth of Australia 2014. ISBN 978–1–76010–104–6.

Doyle, Murray. 2011. Voyage Report: Voyage – RAN Charter. (Captain's report). P&O Polar.

Hansen, Tony. Voyage Report V5. (Captain's report). P&O Polar.

Hodge, Greg. 2002. Initial Voyage Report. V5 *Aurora Australis*. Department of the Environment. Document 2, 170812 obtained under FOI.

Hosie, Graham. 2004. 'Plankton survey uses old technology to monitor the future'. *Australian Antarctic Magazine* 6: 15–16. Commonwealth of Australia.

Hosie, Graham. 2008. 'Underwater world gives up its secrets'. *Australian Antarctic Magazine* 14:2–3. Commonwealth of Australia.

International Convention for the Safety of Life at Sea (SOLAS), 1974, Chapter V, Regulation 33. International Maritime Organisation.

Interview with Andrew Constable, 6 December 2017.

Interview with Gerry O'Doherty, 7 June 2017.

Interview with Graham Hosie, 7 June 2017.

Interview with Jeff Ayton, 6 December 2017.

Interview with Nick Gales, 3 August 2018.

Interview with Robb Clifton, 10 November 2017.

Interview with Steve Nicol, 15 July 2017.

Interview with Steve Rintoul, 7 May 2018.

Interview with Tony Worby, 5 April 2018.

Johnson, Joe. 2002. 'Breaking out! *Polar Bird* free at last.' Australian Antarctic Division (News Archive), 18 January 2002.

Johnson, Joe. 2002. Voyage Report. V4 2001–02 (*Polar Bird*). Department of the Environment. Document 1, 170812 obtained under FOI.

Jones, Z. 2009. 'Australia's Antarctic research lags behind.' ABC News & AM, 3 March 2009.

Laughlin, Scott. 2011. Voyage Report Voyage VE1 2011 RSV *Aurora Australis* chartered to the RAN. P&O Polar.

Mapstone, Bruce. 2004. 'The Antarctic Climate and Ecosystems CRC: a truly collaborative partnership'. *Australian Antarctic Magazine* 6:12. Commonwealth of Australia.

Marchant, H.J., Lugg, D.J., and Quilty, P.G. (eds), 2002. Australian Antarctic Science: the first 50 years of ANARE. Australian Antarctic Division, 622pp.

McIntyre, Damian. 2004. 'Polar Ship packing heat for fish poachers'. *Mercury*, 30 June 2004, p. 3.

Nicol, Steve. 2003. 'Flux and KAOS: Voyage 4, 2003'. *Australian Antarctic Magazine*, Issue 5: 10–12. Commonwealth of Australia.

Nicol, Steve. 2010. 'BROKE West Breaks ground in marine research'. *Australian Antarctic Magazine* 18: 11–12. Commonwealth of Australia.

Nicol, S., Pauly, T., Bindoff, N.L., Wright, S., Thiele, D., Hosie, G.W., Strutton, P.G. and Woehler, E. 2000. 'Ocean circulation off east Antarctica affects ecosystem structure and sea-ice extent'. *Nature* 406: 504–507

Paterson, Tony. 2011. 'Sea Riding on *Aurora Australis*'. *Semaphore*: Issue 7, October 2011, 2pp.

Personal Communication with John Kitchener, 9 April 18.

Press, A.J. 2014. 20 year Australian Antarctic Strategic Plan, 72pp.

Priddle et al, (1998) in Southwell, C., Paxton, C.G.M., Borchers, D., Boveng, P. and de la Mare, W. 2008. 'Taking account of dependent species in management of the Southern Ocean krill fishery: estimating crabeater seal abundance off east Antarctica'. *Journal of Applied Ecology* 45:622–631.

Riddle, M. Sitrep: Sunday 6 January 2008. Australian Antarctic Division. AAD voyage sitreps: https://secure3.aad.gov.au/public/schedules/sitreps.cfm

Rintoul, S.R. 2000. 'Southern Ocean currents and climate'. In Banks, M.R. & Brown, M.J. (Eds): TASMANIA AND THE SOUTHERN OCEAN. Pap. Proc. R. Soc. Tasm. 133(3): 41–50.

Rintoul, S.R., Silvano, A., Pena-Molino, B., van Wijk, E., Rosenberg, M., Greenbaum J.S. and Blankenship, D.D. 2016. 'Ocean heat drives rapid basal melt of the Totten Ice Shelf'. Science Advances 2, e1601610.

Salleh, A. 2000. 'Major survey sets Antarctic krill catch limits'. *ABC Science Online*, 7 August 2000.

Senate Estimates Committee – Environment, recreation, communications and the arts legislation committee – 15/11/1994 – Dept. Of the Environment, Sports and Territories – Program 2 – Antarctic- Subprogram 2.1 – Policy and planning.

Senate Estimates Committee C – 21/06/1994 – Dept. Of the Environment, Sports and Territories – Program 2 – Antarctic- Subprogram 2.2 – Expeditions.

Southwell, Colin. 2001. 'Antarctic pack-ice seals count'. *Australian Antarctic Magazine* 1: 7–9. Commonwealth of Australia.

Southwell, C., Paxton, C.G.M., Borchers, D., Boveng, P. and de la Mare, W. 2008. 'Taking account of dependent species in management of the Southern Ocean krill fishery: estimating crabeater seal abundance off east Antarctica'. *Journal of Applied Ecology* 45:622–631.

van Wijk, E.M. and Rintoul, S.R. 2014. Freshening drives contraction of Antarctic Bottom Water in the Australian Antarctic Basin. Geophysical Research Letters 41: 1657–1664

Worby, A.P., Geiger, C.A., Paget, M.J., Van Woert, M.L, Ackley, S.F.,and DeLiberty, T.L. 2008. Thickness distribution of Antarctic sea ice. *Journal of Geophysical Research* 113, 14pp.

Worby, Tony. 2008. 'Sea Ice Physics and Ecosystem eXperiment'. *Australian Antarctic Magazine* 14:14–15. Commonwealth of Australia.

Chapter Nine

AFP. 2014. 'French polar chief derides Antarctic cruise as a jaunt'. 3 January 2014.

AMSA. 2014. US Coast Guard ice breaker to assist ships beset in ice in Antarctica. Australian Maritime Safety Authority. News and media releases, 5 January 2014.

AMSA. JRCC messages and audio files. Documents regarding *Akademik Shokalskiy*. Internal ref HPRM D17/260042 obtained under FOI.

AMSA. Various comms between the vessel and other entities. Documents regarding vessel *Akademik Shokalskiy*. Internal ref HPRM 2017/1707 obtained under FOI.

Anon. 2014. '*Aurora Australis* bill looms after Antarctic rescue of Russian research ship'. *ABC News Online*, 4 January 2014.

Australia. 2014. *Akademik Shokalskiy* incident. Item ATCM 10 Presented to the XXXVII Antarctic Treaty Consultative Meeting Brasilia 2014.

Author's correspondence with Department of Environment and Energy, 27 July 2018.

Benavente, Marty. 2016. Footage filmed and edited by M. Benavente: 'Antarctic Rescue Operation; from *Akademik Shokalskiy* to *Aurora Australis* via CHINARE helicopter, 2 January 2014'. Provided to author by Australian Antarctic Division.

Chandler, Jo. 2010. 'Plastic pooch still guarding Antarctic sub-cult'. *The Sydney Morning Herald*, 18 January 2010.

Clark, Ross. 2014. 'The moral of the Antarctic ship of fools: never treat a scientific debate as if it is closed'. *The Spectator*, 3 January 2014.

Cox, Lisa and Phillips, Nicky. 2014. 'Australian Antarctic Division stumps up $2.1 million after rescue of iced-in expedition'. *The Sydney Morning Herald*, 27 May 2014.

Day, Lauren. 2014. 'Australian Antarctic Division research behind schedule after *Aurora Australis* diverted to help ice-bound ship.' *ABC News Online*, 7 January 2014.

Department of the Environment and Energy. 2014. Talking points- *Akademik Shokalskiy* rescue. Document 2a, 170307 obtained under FOI.

Department of the Environment and Energy. Cost Recovery. Document 1, 170503 obtained under FOI.

Department of the Environment and Energy. Estimates Issues Brief: *Akademik Shokalskiy* Passenger Rescue: cost recovery. Department of the Environment and Energy. Documents 3–8, 170306 obtained under FOI.

Doyle, Murray. 2014. 'Rescue of Passengers from *Akademik Shokalskiy*'. Australian Maritime Officer, February 2014: 5–7.

Feldkamp, Lisa. 2014. 'The trapped Polar Expeditions: Spectacle or Serious Science?' Cool Green Science Blog, *The Nature Conservancy*, 9 January 2014. https://blog.nature.org/science/2014/01/09/trapped-polar-mawson-spectacle-science-shokalskiy/ (accessed 30 July 2018).

Frenoit, Yves, email published in Feldkamp, Lisa. 2014. 'The trapped Polar Expeditions: Spectacle or Serious Science?' Cool Green Science Blog, *The Nature Conservancy*, 9 January 2014. https://blog.nature.org/science/2014/01/09/trapped-polar-mawson-spectacle-science-shokalskiy/.

Gales, Nick. 2014. 'Polar rescue: Science not well served'. *Nature* 505: 291.

Hope, Emma. 2014. 'Home to an icy reception'. *Mercury*, 23 January 2014, p. 2.

Interview with Brad Collins, 24 November 2017.

Interview with Darcy Chalker, 2 December 2017.

Interview with Murray Doyle, 19 June 2018.

Interview with Tony Foy, 16 May 2018.

Interviews with Leanne Millhouse, 16 February 2016, 3 August 2016 and 27 June 2018.

Killick, David. 2014. 'Antarctic Icon "Stay" ready to chase new adventures'. *Mercury*, 3 January 2014.

Killick, David. 2014. 'Mawson voyage scrutiny explorers hit back'. *Mercury*, 7 January 2014, p. 12.

Letter from Tony Fleming, Director AAD to Professor Chris Turney, 8 January 2014. Department of the Environment. Document 1, 170307 obtained under FOI.

Millhouse, Leanne. Sitrep: Monday 16th December 2013. Australian Antarctic Division. AAD voyage sitreps: https://secure3.aad.gov.au/public/schedules/sitreps.cfm

Millhouse, Leanne. 2014. VL Report. Voyage 2/3–2013 – 14. Department of the Environment and Energy. Document 3, 170812 obtained under FOI.

Personal Communication with Jeremy Smith, 11 March 2019.

Phillips, Nicky. 2014. 'Passengers from ship trapped in ice safe on *Aurora Australis*'. *The Sydney Morning Herald*, 4 January 2014.

Phillips, Nicky. and Cosier, Colin. 2014. 'Stuck In The Ice'. *The Sydney Morning Herald*. Interactive https://www.smh.com.au/interactive/2014/stuck-in-the-ice/ (accessed 19 June 2016).

Question Time Brief: Antarctica: Rescue of *Akademik Shokalskiy*. Department of the Environment and Energy. Document 1, 170306 obtained under FOI.

Robinson, Michael. 2013. 'Opinion: Ship Stuck in Antarctica Raises Questions About Worth of Reenacting Expeditions'. *National Geographic*, 30 December 2013. https://news.nationalgeographic.com/news/2013/12/131230-antarctica-ship-ice-rescue-expedition-reenactment-opinions-mawson/ (accessed 26 September 2016).

Russian Federation. 2014. 'Ice incident with the Russian vessel 'Akademik Shokalsky'[sic] in the season 2013–2014'. Item ATCM 10 Presented to the XXXVII Antarctic Treaty Consultative Meeting Brasilia 2014.

Smith, Jeremy. 2003. '"Stay" a Short Biography'. *Aurora* (ANARE Club Journal) 22(4): 20–22.

Turney, Chris. 2014. 'Antarctic expedition: "This wasn't a tourist trip. It was all about science – and it was worth it"'. *The Guardian*, 4 January 2014.

Turney, Chris. 2014. 'On board the wonderful Australian Icebreaker *Aurora Australis*'. Spirit of Mawson Website, 3 January 2014. http://www.spiritofmawson.com/on-board-the-wonderful-australian-icebreaker-aurora-australis.

Turney, C. 2014. 'This was no Antarctic pleasure cruise'. *Nature* 505: 133

Chapter Ten

AAD and P&O Joint Press Conference, 25 February 2016.

Anon. 2016. 'K-Axis voyage reaches half-way point'. Australian Antarctic Division (News Archive). 17 February 2016.

Anon. 2016. 'Rare krill "super-swarm" a voyage highlight'. Australian Antarctic Division (News Archive), 23 March 2016.

Corporate Communications. 2015. 'Krill "super-swarm" surprises scientists'. *Australian Antarctic Magazine* 30: 8–9. Commonwealth of Australia.

Interview with Andrew Constable, 6 December 2017.

Interview with Brad Collins, 24 November 2017.

Interview with David Thomas, 23 November 2017.

Interview with Doug Hawes, 2 December 2017.

Interview with Evan Peters, 10 November 2017.

Interview with Gerry O'Doherty, 7 December 2017.

Interview with Joe McMenemy, 7 November 2017.

Interview with Lloyd Symons, 7 February 2018.

Interview with Wendy Pawson (nee Morice), 2 December 2017.

Interviews with Andrew Cawthorn, 24 November 2017 and 1 December 2017.

Interviews with Karen Westwood, 31 August 2016 and 19 February 2018.

McMenemy, Joe. 2016. Footage of blizzard from *Aurora Australis* trawl deck, 24 February 2016.

McMenemy, Joe. 2016. Footage of blizzard from *Aurora Australis* helideck, 24 February 2016.

Pyper, Wendy. 2015. 'Spotlight on the K-Axis'. *Australian Antarctic Magazine* 29: 2–3. Commonwealth of Australia.

Symons, Lloyd. Sitrep: Sunday 14 February 2016. Australian Antarctic Division. AAD voyage sitreps: https://secure3.aad.gov.au/public/schedules/sitreps.cfm

Symons, Lloyd. 2016. VL's Report. Department of the Environment and Energy. Document 4, 170812 obtained under FOI.

The Hon. Greg Hunt MP Minister for the Environment. 2016. Media release. 'Australian Government thanks Antarctic community for support'. 12 March 2016.

Chapter Eleven

AAD. 2018. RSV Nuyina Fact sheet.

AAD. 'About the ship'. http://www.antarctica.gov.au/icebreaker/about-the-ship (accessed 14 October 2018).

AAD. 'Australian Antarctic Medal recipients'. http://www.antarctica.gov.au/about-antarctica/australia-in-antarctica/australian-antarctic-medal/recipients (accessed 14 October 2018).

AAD. 'Australian Antarctic Medal'. http://www.antarctica.gov.au/about-antarctica/australia-in-antarctica/australian-antarctic-medal (accessed 14 October 2018).

AAD. 'Icebreaker specifications'. http://www.antarctica.gov.au/icebreaker/about-the-ship/capability (accessed 14 October 2018).

AAD. 'Scientific Capabilities'. http://www.antarctica.gov.au/icebreaker/about-the-ship/scientific-capabilities (accessed 14 October 2018).

Anon. 2017. 'Searching for super-cooled Southern Ocean clouds'. Australian Antarctic Division (News Archive), 29 October 2017.

Anon. 2018. 'Seeding southern clouds'. Australian Antarctic Division (News Archive) 12 December 2018.

Interview with Rob Bryson and Jonathan Reeve, 2 September 2016.

Press, A. 2014. 20 year Australian Antarctic Strategic Plan, 72pp.

Personal communications with Robyn Schofield, 25 February 2019.

THE *AURORA AUSTRALIS'S* AUSTRALIAN ANTARCTIC PROGRAM & OFF-SEASON VOYAGES

Data: Australian Antarctic Data Centre & AAD Shipping Schedule*

NB: with the exception of the first, this table does not include approximately 30 marine science trial voyages, to Port Arthur, Tasmania (usually one per season), unless the voyage had an additional function.

	Season	Voyage	Description	Informal name/description
1	1989/90	V7.1	Trial cruise	First trial cruise up east coast Tasmania
2	1989/90	V7.2	Marine science and ice trials	HIMS- Heard Island Marine Science
3	1990/91	V2	Ice-edge: Casey/Mawson/ Davis changeovers	
4	1990/91	V4	Mawson changeover, PCM (Prince Charles Mountain) in /Davis changeover	
5	1990/91	V6	Marine science, Mawson refuel, Mawson/Davis summer retrieval	AAMBERII- Australian Antarctic Marine Biological Ecosystem Research II
6	1991/92	V1	Macquarie Island summer placement	
7	1991/92	V1.1	Marine science	WOCE-World Ocean Circulation Experiment 1991
8	1991/92	V2	Mawson placement, Davis placement & refuel -ice edge	
9	1991/92	V4	Mawson changeover, PCM placement /Davis changeover & refuel	
10	1991/92	V6	Marine science Heard Island, Mawson/Davis summer retrieval	FISHOG- Fish and Oceanography

---

* On occasion descriptive information was missing from the source data.

	Season	Voyage	Description	Informal name/description
11	1992/93	V1	Mawson/Davis fly-off, Marine science	MONGREL
12	1992/93	V4	Mawson/Davis changeover, Law Base	
13	1992/93	V7	Marine science, Law Base, Mawson/Davis/Casey	KROCK- Krill and Rocks
14	1992/93	V9	Marine science	WOES- Wildlife Oceanography Ecosystem Survey
15	1992/93	V9.1	Marine science	WORSE- Wildlife Oceanography Retry Survey of Ecosystem
16	1993/94	V1	Macquarie Island placement/Marine science	THIRST- Third Heard Island Research Survey Trip
17	1993/94	V2	Mawson/Davis	
18	1993/94	V4	Davis, Law Base placements, Zhongshan place and retrieve CHINARE, Sansom Island fuel depot, Davis/Mawson changeovers	
19	1993/94	V7	Marine science & Mawson/Law Base/ Davis/ Casey changeover, Dumont d'Urville load trawl gear	SHAM (acronym unknown)
20	1994/95	V1	Macquarie Island/Davis placements and Marine Science	BESET-Bain's Expedition Seriously Evading Tasmania
21	1994/95	V2	Casey/Davis changeover, Sansom Island fuel, Law Base retrieve waste, long-range fly-off medivac.	
22	1994/95	V3	Macquarie Island changeover & resupply	
23	1994/95	V4	Marine science and Casey resupply	WOCET-World Ocean Circulation Experiment Transect
24	1994/95	V6	Marine science and Mawson resupply/Davis retrieval	BANGSS-Big ANtarctic Geological and Seismic Survey

	Season	Voyage	Description	Informal name/description
25	1994/95	V7	Casey/Macquarie Island retrieval	
26	1995/96	V1	Oceanography	HiHo HiHo – Heat In, Halide Out—Harmonious Ice and Hydrographic Observations/ ABSTAIN- A Brave Science Trip Amidst Ice at Night
27	1995/96	V2	Macquarie Island/Davis partial resupply, refuel; Marine science seal survey	
28	1995/96	V3	Casey/Mawson/Davis changeover, Bunger Hills placement, Law Base	
29	1995/96	V4	Marine science, Casey refuel	BROKE- Baseline Research on Oceanography, Krill and the Environment
30	1995/96	V6	Davis & Casey retrieval.	
31	1996/97	V1	Marine science, IRB to Macquarie Island	WASTE- WOCE Antarctic Southern Transect Expedition
32	1996/97	V2	Davis resupply, marine science (sea ice and seals)	LIMP- LIMP became the voyage name after the main V16 engine transmission coupling failed and the ship could not use two engines to move through the extraordinary heavy sea ice encountered.
33	1996/97	V3	Macquarie Island changeover & resupply	
34	1996/97	V4	Casey, Mawson, Davis, Macquarie Island changeover, Casey resupply, Zhongshan cargo fly-off, Sansom Island fuel depot, Mirny fuel transfer	
35	1996/97	V5	Mawson resupply, Davis retrieval, marine science	BRAD- Benthic Rocks and Drilling

	Season	Voyage	Description	Informal name/description
36	1996/97	V6	Casey fly-off, marine science, Macquarie Island fly-off	
37	1997/98	V1	Marine science	WANDER- Without Aurora's Normal Displays we Embark Regardless
38	1997/98	V2	Davis resupply, seal survey, Casey/Mawson fly-off	ON-ICE Listed by datacentre as MS but no info available
39	1997/98	V3	Macquarie Island changeover & resupply	
40	1997/98	V4	Casey, Davis, Mawson changeover & Casey resupply, Bunger Hills fuel depot, Sansom Island fuel depot, Macquarie Island retrieval	SEXY – Seal Expedition over Xmas and Yuletide I
41	1997/98	V5	Mawson resupply, Davis summer retrieval	
42	1997/98	V6	Marine science	SNARK- from Lewis Carroll (Subantartctic Oceanography)
43	1997/98	V7	Marine science, Davis/Casey/Macquarie Island summer retrieval	PICCIES- PIC is Polyna Ice Creation but the rest is unknown
44	1998/99	V1	Macquarie Island summer in, marine science polynya study	FIRE and ICE – F** Its a Real Emergency! and I can't email /Engine room fire
45	1998/99	V4	Marine science, Davis resupply, refuel & changeover, Sansom Island fuel depot	SEXY II -Seal Expedition over Xmas and Yuletide II /CPP Failure
46	1998/99	V5	Aim: Mawson refuel, Casey resupply, retrieval	Engine room fire
47	1998/99	V6	Marine science, Mawson refuel & resupply, Casey/Davis/Macquarie Island resupply and retrieval	STAY (acronym unknown)
48	1999/00	V1	Marine science: Polynya study	IDIOTS- In Depth Investigation Of the Seaice

	Season	Voyage	Description	Informal name/description
49	1999/00	V2	Davis resupply, deploy summer expos; Mawson deploy exp.	Diversion to repatriate expeditioner
50	1999/00	V3	Macquarie Island resupply & changeover, Casey fuel and summerers in	
51	1999/00	V4	Seal survey, Davis & Mawson changeover, Sansom Island depot	
52	1999/00	V5	Casey resupply, Macquarie Island retrieval	
53	1999/00	V6	Mawson resupply & refuel, Bunger Hills. Mawson/ Casey/Davis/ Macquarie Island summer retrieval	
54	2000/01	V1	Davis resupply & refuel, LIDAR in, summer in; Mawson in; Heard Island deployment and retrieval	
55	2000/01	V4	Heard Island, Mawson & Davis changeover, Sansom Island depot	
56	2000/01	V6	Marine science, Mawson deployment, Casey assist *Polar Bird*	KACTAS – Krill Availability, Community Trophodynamics and AMISOR Surveys. Polar Bird rescue (breakout)
57	2000/01	V8	Macquarie Island partial resupply, Casey retrieval	
58	2001 off-season		Bass Strait Esso ROV charter	
59	2001 off-season		Malampaya gas platform accommodation charter	
60	2001/02	V2	Macquarie Island and Casey summer deployment.	
61	2001/02	V3	Marine science	CLIVAR – Climate Variability
62	2001/02	V5	Casey resupply, refuel & changeover, Mawson pax transfer	*Polar Bird* rescue (tow & breakout)

	Season	Voyage	Description	Informal name/description
63	2001/02	V7	Marine science, Davis/ Mawson retrievals	LOSS (named after losing a CTD off the Amery)
64	2001/02	V8	Macquarie Island resupply, refuel & changeover	
65	2002 off-season		Subsea spool installation, Bass Strait Allseas and Duke energy	
66	2002 off-season		Drilling platform, Clough Offshore	
67	2002/03	V1	Macquarie Island deployment, marine science	SAZ mooring retrievals and Argo float deployment
68	2002/03	V2	Davis resupply, refuel & changeover; Mawson changeover, Zhongshan pax & stores	
69	2002/03	V4	Marine science AMLR	KAOS (Krill Acoustics Oceanographic Survey) /bunker transfer from *Polar Bird*
70	2002/03	V6	Macquarie Island resupply	
71	2003 off-season		AFMA/Customs subantarctic patrol	
72	2003/04	V1	Marine science, Casey changeover	ARISE- Antarctic Remote Ice Sensing Experiment
73	2003/04	V2	Davis resupply, refuel & changeover; Zhongshan deploy pax & cargo	
74	2003/04	V4	Marine science, Zhongshan ×2, Davis retrieval	HIPPIES – Heard Island Predator Prey Investigation and Ecosystem Study
75	2003/04	V7	Macquarie Island resupply, Casey fly-off	
76	2004 off-season		Customs/AFMA subantarctic patrol	
77	2004 off-season		Yolla platform support. Clough Offshore	
78	2004/05	V1	Ice validation & Marine science; Casey deploy Law Dome pax & changeover	

	Season	Voyage	Description	Informal name/description
79	2004/05	V2	Casey retrieval, Davis changeover, refuel & partial resupply, Mawson changeover	
80	2004/05	V3	Marine science, Davis retrieval	ORCKA- Oceanographic Research CLIVAR- 195, Kerguelen and the Antarctic
81	2004/05	V5	Mawson resupply & refuel, Casey retrieval, Macquarie Island resupply & changeover	
82	2005/06	V1	Casey deploy summer personnel/ Davis resupply & refuel	
83	2005/06	V2	Casey changeover	The *Aurora* carried the Commonwealth Games Queen's Relay Baton to Antarctica
84	2005/06	V3	BROKE West Marine science, Mawson/Davis retrievals	BROKE-West: Baseline Research on Oceanography, Krill and the Environment – West
85	2005/06	V5	Macquarie Island resupply, Casey personnel retrieval	
86	2006 off-season		Accommodation for Challis FPSO shutdown, Northern Territory	
87	2006/07	V1	Casey summer deployment, Mawson changeover & fly-off resupply, Davis refuel & resupply	
88	2006/07	V2	Davis changeover, Casey resupply & changeover. Zhongshan pax deployment.	
89	2006/07	V3	Marine science	SAZ-SENSE – Sub-Antarctic Zone – Sensitivity to Environmental Change

	Season	Voyage	Description	Informal name/description
90	2006/07	V4	Davis and Mawson personnel retrieval. Zhongshan retrieval, ATK to Progress	
91	2006/07	V5	Macquarie Island resupply, refuel & changeover	
92	2007/08	V1	SIPEX Marine science	SIPEX (Sea Ice Physics and Ecosystems eXperiment)
93	2007/08	V2	Casey deploy personnel, Davis resupply, refuel & changeover	
94	2007/08	V3	CEAMARC/CASO Marine science	CEAMARC/CASO (Collaborative East Antarctic Marine Census / Climate of Southern Ocean)
95	2007/08	V4	Casey/Mawson resupply & refuel, Davis personnel retrieval	
96	2007/08	V6	CASO marine science	CASO
97	2008/09	V1	Casey deployment, Davis refuel, resupply & changeover	
98	2008/09	V2	Casey changeover and Davis summer personnel changeover	
99	2008/09	V3	Deploy and retrieve JARE personnel at Syowa Station.	JARE resupply Syowa Station
100	2008/09	V5	Davis personnel retrieval & Macquarie Island resupply	
101	2009/10	VTrials	Marine science trials & Macquarie Island light resupply & refuel	
102	2009/10	V1	Davis changeover, resupply & refuel, Mawson winter/ summer personnel in from Davis	
103	2009/10	V2	Casey resupply & refuel, Davis summer personnel changeover	

	Season	Voyage	Description	Informal name/description
104	2009/10	V3	Mawson resupply, Davis light essential	
105	2009/10	V4	Davis summer retrieval	
106	2009/10	V5	Macquarie Island resupply, refuel and personnel changeover	
107	2009/10	VE1	Pest Eradication Program at Macquarie Island	
108	2010/11	VE2	Retrieve Pest Eradication personnel	
109	2010/11	V1	Davis resupply & changeover, marine science AUV trial	
110	2010/11	V2	Casey resupply & refuel	
111	2010/11	VMS	Marine science SR3 Transect and Mertz Glacier	VMS – Voyage Marine Science
112	2010/11	V3	Mawson changeover, refuel & resupply, Davis light essential cargo	
113	2010/11	V4	Davis & Casey summer personnel retrieval	
114	2010/11	V5	Macquarie Island resupply & changeover	
115	2011 off-season		RAN Charter Hob-JB-Bris-JB-Hob	
116	2011 off-season		RAN Charter Hob-JB-Westernport-Hob	
117	2011/12	VE1	RAN Charter & retrieve MIPEP personnel	*Janas* rescue
118	2011/12	V1	Davis resupply, changeover & refuel	
119	2011/12	V2	Casey resupply, refuel & changeover	
120	2011/12	V3	Commemorative Commonwealth Bay & Mawson's Hut visit, Marine science.	
121	2011/12	V4	Mawson resupply, refuel & changeover	

	Season	Voyage	Description	Informal name/description
122	2011/12	V5	Recover Davis and Casey summer personnel	
123	2011/12	V6	Macquarie Island resupply	
124	2012/13	VMS	Marine science – Sea-Ice Physics & Ecosystem Experiment (SIPEX)	SIPEX II – Sea-Ice Physics & Ecosystem Experiment II
125	2012/13	V1	Davis resupply, changeover	
126	2012/13	V2	Casey resupply, changeover & refuel	
127	2012/13	V3	Mawson resupply, refuel & changeover; Davis heavy resupply, refuel & retrieval	
128	2012/13	V4	Macquarie Island resupply, changeover & refuel	
129	2013/14	V1	Davis resupply, refuel & changeover	
130	2013/14	V2/3	Macquarie Island summer changeover, Casey resupply	*Akademik Shokalskiy* rescue
131	2013/14	V4	Casey retrieval, Davis summer retrieval	
132	2013/14	V6	Mawson resupply, refuel & changeover/via helicopter	Mawson fly-off
133	2014/15	V1	Davis resupply, refuel & changeover	
134	2014/15	V2	Casey resupply, refuel & changeover; Totten marine science	Casey/ Totten voyage
135	2014/15	V3	Mawson resupply, refuel & changeover, Davis summer retrieval	
136	2014/15	V4	Macquarie Island resupply, refuel & changeover	
137	2015/16	V1A	Macquarie Island	
138	2015/16	V1	Davis resupply	
139	2015/16	V2	Casey resupply	
140	2015/16	V3	Marine science, Mawson resupply, Davis summer retrieval	K-Axis voyage

	Season	Voyage	Description	Informal name/description
141	2016/17	V1	Davis resupply, refuel & changeover	
142	2016/17	V2	Marine science, Casey resupply & refuel	Sea ice, polynya and SR3
143	2016/17	V3	Mawson resupply & refuel, Davis summer retrieval	
144	2016/17	V4	Macquarie Island resupply, refuel & changeover	
145	2017/18	V1	Davis resupply, refuel & changeover	
146	2017/18	V2	Casey resupply, refuel	
147	2017/18	V3	Mawson resupply & refuel, Davis summer retrieval	
148	2017/18	V4	Macquarie Island resupply & refuel	
149	2018/19	V1	Davis resupply, refuel & changeover	
150	2018/19	V2	Casey resupply & refuel	
151	2018/19	V3	Mawson resupply, refuel & changeover, Davis summer retrieval	
152	2018/19	V4	Macquarie Island resupply, refuel & changeover	
153	2019/20	V1	Davis resupply*	
154	2019/20	V2	Casey resupply*	
155	2019/20	V3	Mawson resupply, Davis summer retrieval*	

*Correct at time of print. Voyages yet to be conducted and may be subject to change.

INDEX

This is an index to names of people, places, ships and programs discussed in the book. General subjects have not been indexed.